DIVERSITY AND TOLERANCE IN SOCIO-LEGAL CONTEXTS

Diversity and Tolerance in Socio-Legal Contexts

Explorations in the Semiotics of Law

Edited by

ANNE WAGNER

Université du Littoral Côte d'Opale, France

VIJAY K. BHATIA

City University of Hong Kong, China

Routledge
Taylor & Francis Group
LONDON AND NEW YORK

First published 2009 by Ashgate Publishing

2 Park Square, Milton Park, Abingdon, Oxon OX14 4RN
711 Third Avenue, New York, NY 10017, USA

Routledge is an imprint of the Taylor & Francis Group, an informa business

British Library Cataloguing in Publication Data
Diversity and tolerance in socio-legal contexts :
explorations in the semiotics of law
1. Semiotics (Law) 2. Sociological jurisprudence
3. Tolerance 4. Cultural pluralism
I. Wagner, Anne, 1968- II. Bhatia, V. K. (Vijay Kumar),
1942-
340.1'15

Library of Congress Cataloging-in-Publication Data
Wagner, Anne, 1968-
Diversity and tolerance in socio-legal contexts : explorations in the semiotics of law / by Anne Wagner and Vijay K. Bhatia.
p. cm.
Includes bibliographical references and index.
ISBN 978-0-7546-7386-6
1. Semiotics (Law) 2. Law--Language. 3. Law--Philosophy. 4. Semantics (Law) 5. Tolerance. 6. Cultural pluralism. 7. Discourse analysis--Social aspects. I. Bhatia, V. K. (Vijay Kumar), 1942- II. Title.

K213.W32 2008
340'.14--dc22

2008037164

ISBN 13: 978-0-7546-7386-6 (hbk)
ISBN 13: 978-1-138-26767-1 (pbk)

Contents

PART II CASE ANALYSES OF DIVERSITY AND TOLERANCE

List of Illustrations

Table of Cases

Australia

Ben Ward & Ors v The State of Western Australia & Ors (1998) 159 ALR 483
Daniel v State of Western Australia [2000] FCA (26 June 2000)
De Rose v State of South Australia [2002] FCA 1342 (1 November 2002)
De Rose v South Australia [2003] FCAFC 286 (16 December 2003)
Ejai v Commonwealth (1994) (Unreported, SCWA, 18 March 1994, 1774/93
Fejo v Northern Territory of Australia (1998) 195 CLR 96
James on behalf of the Martu People v State of Western Australia [2002] FCA 1208 (27 September 2002)
Mabo v Queensland (No. 2) (1992) 175 CLR 1
Members of the Yorta Yorta Aboriginal Community v The State of Victoria & Ors [1997] 1181 FCA (29 October 1997)
Members of the Yorta Yorta Community v The State of Victoria & Ors [1998] 1606 FCA (18 December 1998)
Milirrpum v Nabalco Pty Ltd (1971) 17 FLR 141
Rubibi Community and Another v Western Australia and Others (2001) 112 FCR 409
Sampi v State of Western Australia (No. 2) [2001] FCA 620 (17 May 2001)

European Court of Human Rights

E.B. v France 2008, application no. 43546/02

US

Board of Education, Levittown Union Free School District et al. v. Nyquist, 459 N.E. 2d 359 (New York State Court of Appeals) (1982)
Brown v. Board of Education of Topeka, Kansas 347 U.S. 483, 74 S.Ct. 686 (1954)
Chaplinsky v. New Hampshire 315 U.S. 568 (1954)
Douglass v. California 372 U.S. 535 (1963)
Dred Scott v. Sanford 19 How. (60 U.S) 393 (1857)
Milliken v. Bradley 418 U.S. 717, 94 S.Ct. 3112 (1974)
Plessy v. Ferguson 163 U.S. 537, 3 S.Ct. 18 (1896)

Plyler v. Doe 457 U.S. 102 S.Ct. (1982)
R.A.V. v. St. Paul, Minnesota 505 U.S. 377 (1992)
Rodriguez v. San Antonio Independent School District 337 F. Supp. 280 – Three-judge panel, Texas (1971)
Rodriguez v. San Antonio Independent School District 411 U.S. 1, 93 S.Ct.1278 (1973)
Saint Francis College v. Al-Khazraji 481. U.S. 604 (1987)
Serrano v. Priest 5Cd 584, p. 5 (*Serrano I* – California Supreme Court) (1971)
Serrano v. Priest 18 Cal.3d 728 (*Serrano II* – California Supreme Court) (1976)
Serrano v. Priest 20 Cal.3d 25 (*Serrano III* – California Supreme Court) (1977)
Shaare Tefila Congregation v. Cobb 481 U.S. 604 (1987)
Swann v. Charlotte-Mecklenberg Board of Education 402 U.S. 1, 91 S.Ct. 1267 (1971)
Williams v. Illinois

Lists of Conventions, Legislation and Rules

Australia

Aboriginal Land Rights (Northern Territory) Act 1976 (Cth)
Australian Law Reform Commission (2005), *Review of the Uniform Evidence Acts*, Discussion Paper 69
Evidence Act 1995 (Cth)
Federal Court Rules 1979, No. 140
Native Title Act 1993 (Cth)

EU legislation

European Convention of Human Rights and Fundamental Freedoms

International conventions

International Covenant on Civil and Political Rights
International Covenant on Economic, Social and Cultural Rights
UNESCO Declaration of Principles of Tolerance
United Nations Charters of 1945
Universal Declaration of Human Rights

The Netherlands

Kamerstukken II [*Parliamentary Documents*], 1985/86, 192 90 (A), 6
Notitie inzake het VN-embargo tegen Irak [*Government Memorandum concerning the UN Embargo against Iraq*], *Kamerstukken* II [*Parliamentary Documents*] 1990/91, 21 664 (25), 9

Notes on Contributors

Vijay K. Bhatia is a Visiting Professor in the Department of English and Communication at the City University of Hong Kong. He is best known for his work *Genre Analysis* on legal genres. He has worked on several research projects, two of which are 'Analyzing Genre-Bending in Corporate Disclosure Documents' and 'International Arbitration Practice: a Discourse Analytical Study', in which he leads research teams from about 20 countries, consisting of specialists from law, arbitration and discourse analysis. His book on *Analysing Genre: Language Use in Professional Settings* (Longman) is widely used by researchers in discourse and genre theory and practice. His more recent book, *Worlds of Written Discourse: a Genre-based View*, develops a multiperspective and multidimensional framework for genre analysis and has been published by Continuum International (2004).

John Brigham is a Professor of Political Science at the University of Massachusetts, Amherst. He has published in the area of constitutional law, social movements and public architecture. His books include *Material Law* (forthcoming, Temple University Press), *States, Citizens and Questions of Significance: Proceedings of the Tenth Roundtable* (1997, co-edited with Roberta Kevelson and Peter Lang) and *The Constitution of Interests: Beyond the Politics of Rights* (1996, New York University Press).

Sophie Cacciaguidi-Fahy is a Lecturer in Law at the National University of Ireland, Galway. Her research interests and publications focus on law and cultural diversity, the semiotics of law, legal language and discourse. Her current research projects involve a comparative analysis of convergence and divergences between minorities and indigenous peoples in international law.

Christopher N. Candlin is Senior Research Professor in the Department of Linguistics at Macquarie University, Sydney. He was the Foundation Executive Director of the Australian Government's National Centre for English Language Teaching & Research from 1987 to 1998, and established the Research Centre in Language in Social Life, also at Macquarie, of which he is currently Associate Director, together with that of the Centre for Translation & Interpreting Research. He has held Professorships at Lancaster (UK), the City University of Hong Kong and the UK's Open University, and currently holds honorary professorships at the Universities of Lancaster, Nottingham and Cardiff in the UK, and at Beijing Foreign Studies University. His current research is in the field of professional communication, particularly in healthcare and law. Among themes in the latter field he has published in the areas of the discourses of arbitration and alternative dispute resolution; he supervises research students in courtroom and community interpreting; and he is a co-investigator of the 'Discourse of International Commercial Arbitration' project centred at the City University of Hong Kong. He is, or has been, a member of the editorial boards of several international journals, including *Applied Linguistics, TEXT & TALK, Health, Risk & Society, Journal of Sociolinguistics, Language Awareness, Journal of English for Specific Purposes* and the journal *Communication in Medicine* (Equinox), and he co-edits (with Srikant Sarangi) the new *Journal of Applied Linguistics* (Equinox). He also edits or co-edits six international book series with Pearson (Longman), Routledge, Palgrave (Macmillan) and Equinox. From 1996 to 2002 he was President of the International Association of Applied Linguistics.

Deborah Cao is an Associate Professor affiliated with the Law School Socio-Legal Research Centre, Griffith University, Australia. She has published in the areas of legal language and legal translation, pragmatics, court interpreting, philosophical, linguistic and semiotic analysis of Chinese law and legal culture, and animal law. She is also a Fellow of the Oxford Centre for Animal Ethics. Her books include *Chinese Law: a Language Perspective* (2004, Ashgate), *Interpretation, Law and the Construction of Meaning* (co-edited with Anne Wagner and Wouter Werner, 2007, Springer), *Translating Law* (2007, Multilingual Matters), and *Animal Law in the West* (2007, China Law Press).

Le Cheng is a PhD researcher at City University of Hong Kong, and an affiliated researcher at the Forensic Linguistics Center, China University of Politics and Law, and is a lecturer and a lawyer in the PRC. He has published journal papers and scholarly chapters in the areas of language and the law, legal translation and semiotics.

Pamela Hobbs is a Lecturer in Communication Studies at the University of California, Los Angeles, where she received a PhD in applied linguistics, and is also an attorney licensed to practice in Michigan, US. Her research interests include legal discourse, medical discourse, political discourse, language and gender, and the evolution of communication.

Frederick P. Lewis is Professor of Political Science at the University of Massachusetts Lowell where he was Department Chair for 12 years. He has a JD from Harvard Law School and a PhD in Political Science from Tufts University. For 2009–10, he has been chosen to serve as President of the New England Political Science Association.

Sarah Marusek is a PhD student at the University of Massachusetts at Amherst (US). She studies the parking space as a site of local politics where identities, rights and types of ownership are contested in everyday places. Currently, she is a Five College Women's Studies Research Center Associate at Mount Holyoke College (US) where she is also a Visiting Instructor in the Politics Department.

Alec McHoul recently retired as Professor in the School of Media Communication & Culture at Murdoch University in Western Australia. Having published widely in the interdisciplinary field of sociology and language studies, he is now dedicated to growing Australian native plants on his semi-rural property and birdwatching. For more details, go to <http://wwwmcc.murdoch.edu.au/~mchoul/>.

William Pencak, Professor of History and Jewish Studies at the Pennsylvania State University, was President of the Semiotic Society of America in 2000–01. He has written *History, Signing In: Studies in History and Semiotics* (1993, Peter Lang), and co-edited *Images in Law* with Anne Wagner (2005, Ashgate). His most recent book, *Jews and Gentiles in Early America: 1654–1800* (University of Michigan Press, 2004), was runner-up for the National Book Award in American Jewish History for that year.

Isabell Petrinic is a journalist and academic, specialising in the field of communication law and media ethics. She has completed a BA in English, philosophy and semiotics, and an MA in professional communication. She currently teaches at the School of Communication Design and Media, University of Western Sydney, Australia, where she is the editor of the student magazine, *Angle*. She is also a senior reporter and sub-editor for Fairfax Media.

King Kui Sin is an Associate Professor at the Department of Chinese, Translation and Linguistics, City University of Hong Kong. His publications and interests are in the areas of language and the law, court interpreting and philosophy of language.

Ira L. Strauber is Professor of Political Science, Grinnell College, Grinnell, Iowa (US), where he teaches constitutional law and politics. His primary areas of scholarship are jurisprudence and the culture and politics of constitutional commentary. His *Neglected Policies: Constitutional Law and Commentary as Civic Education* (2002) received the C. Herman Pritchett Award for the best book on law and politics from the Law and Politics Section of the American Political Science Association. His most recent publication is 'An Indifference Thesis: Constitutional Law and Politics in an Era of "Conservative Domination of the Judiciary"', in *Studies in Law, Politics, and Society* (Austin Sarat (ed.), 2008). He is currently working on a book-length manuscript considering the contemporary US Supreme Court as a potential agent of democratisation.

Tracey Summerfield is a Lecturer in Law at the University of Western Australia and a consultant to the Commonwealth Child Support Agency. Her research interests are in legal theory, law and social justice and child support law.

István H. Szilágyi has been an Associate Professor of Anthropology and Sociology of Law at the Department of Philosophy of Law, Pázmány Péter Catholic University School of Law, Budapest, since 2000. He graduated in 1987 with an MA in law and political science, followed by Doctor Universitatis (1994) in anthropology and sociology of law, and he received his PhD (1998) at the University of Miskolc. He taught sociology and anthropology of law at the University of Miskolc and the University of Debrecen (1989–2000). He has studied and published in the areas of anthropology of law, anthropology of the Hungarian Roma minority, the history of Hungarian legal philosophy, and law and literature.

Hanneke van Schooten is Associate Professor in Constitutional Law and senior researcher at the Centre for Legislative Studies at the Tilburg University, Tilburg, The Netherlands. She has published in the areas of institutional legal theory, legal semiotics and issues of legitimacy and non-state law. Her books include *Semiotics and Legislation* (1999, Deborah Charles Publications) and *International Governance and Law: State Regulation and Non-State Law* (co-edited with Jonathan Verschuuren, forthcoming 2008, Ashgate).

Anne Wagner is Senior Lecturer in Applied Linguistics (Legal Semiotics and Legal Discourse Genre Analyses) at the Université du Littoral Côte d'Opale (France). She is President of the International Roundtable for the Semiotics of Law and runs the <semioticsoflaw.com> website. She is the Editor-in-Chief of the *International Journal for the Semiotics of Law* (<www.springer.com>). She is also a member of the editorial boards of international journals, and edits the *Legal Semiotics Monographs* series for Deborah Charles Publication (<www.legaltheory.demon.co.uk>). She is a member of the international Research Grant Council (RGC), Hong-Kong SAR Competitive Earmarked Research Grant (CERG) funded research project on '*International Commercial Arbitration Practices: a Discourse Analytical Study*', International Collaborator for France (co-responsibility). She has extensively published research papers in the area of law and semiotics, legal discourse, law and culture, and legal translation. Her books include *La Langue de la Common Law* (2002, L'Harmattan), *Contemporary Issues in the Semiotics of Law: Cultural and Symbolic Analyses in a Global Context* (2005, Hart), *Images in Law* (2006, Ashgate), *Legal Language and the Search for Clarity: Practice and Tools* (2006, Peter Lang), *Interpretation, Law and the Construction of Meaning* (2006, Springer) and *Obscurity and Clarity in the Law: Prospects and Challenges* (2008, Ashgate).

Foreword

Sophie Cacciaguidi-Fahy

Major historical and political events mapped the discourse of tolerance, primarily as an ethical concept in the philosophy of law. The rise of nation states reflecting a centralisation of political power, common culture, language and religion, necessary to the construction and identification of the Sovereign, in the sixteenth and seventeenth centuries, tended to manifest itself in intolerant attitudes and behaviours towards those who were perceived as the 'Others'. Yet, many philosophers who wrote on tolerance, such as Bayle, Spinoza and Voltaire, strongly believed that a weak political power would fall prey to religious intolerance and thus argued for political sovereignty as a condition to the expression of religious tolerance. Locke, in his *Letter Concerning Toleration* (1689), appositely conceived the concept of tolerance as a limit to the power of the Sovereign. Today the idea of tolerance, under the influence of contemporary liberalism and legal theoreticians such as Rawls and Dworkin, is conceived as an 'ethical virtue' primarily based on the respect of an individual's fundamental rights and freedoms expressed and protected by political and legal institutions.

Diversity, on the other hand, prompts the idea of plurality: plurality of racial, ethnic, religious and linguistics minority groups. The atrocities of two World Wars, two genocides and the rise of the civil rights movement in the twentieth century have made it clear that the expressions of diversity are in need of special legal protection. Legal and quasi-legal instruments adopted by the international community have stated this in many ways, starting with the adoption of the 1948 Universal Declaration of Human Rights which can be regarded as the touchstone of respect for diversity. Nevertheless, the current climate of insecurity continues to impact on our cultural identities and challenge the acceptance of *l'altérité de l'autre* (the 'Other's otherness').

The release of *Diversity and Tolerance in Socio-Legal Contexts* provides us with a rare occasion to reflect on the concepts of tolerance and diversity and their reception in various legal systems and cultures. The book proposes a systematic analysis of the contribution of socio-legal studies to diversity and tolerance from a semiotic perspective. It not only addresses the many facets of diversity and tolerance from a multicultural standpoint but it also proposes a rigorous and rich interpretation of diversity and tolerance within different legal systems using different methods of analysis.

Indeed, the contributors to this book, by employing methods of inquiry such as semiotics (use of images, symbols, icons, landmarks and rituals) and the analysis of political rhetorical devices and legal language (use of metaphors, metonymies), expose the perceived conceptions of intolerance and the transformative potential of the law as an instrument of cultural and social change. They demonstrate that, in many instances, the law has found itself in the role of the final arbiter where cultural values conflict, providing a remedy often revealing not only the nature of a legal system and its associated culture but also its own limitations. For readers unfamiliar with the use of semiotics in deconstructing the essence of the law and its related impacts, effectiveness and failures, let me direct you to a time and place where signs, symbols, icons and symbolic language took centre stage in the expression of diversity, tolerance and, indeed, intolerance. For many years during the Irish 'troubles' and their slow resolution in the post-Good Friday agreement of the late 1990s, I observed Republican nationalists with their Easter lilies, street murals and tri-colours wage semiotic battles with Loyalist poppies, Orange parades and Union-Jack-painted kerbs. Indeed one of the darkest periods of the 'troubles' would see the largely symbolic right to wear civilian clothes and recognition as political prisoners bring Northern Ireland to the brink of disaster. In the vulnerable and early post-Good Friday period, signs, language and symbols played an important role in reconciliation, tolerance, acceptation of religious diversity and progress: ceasefires became cessations, the RUC (Royal Ulster Constabulary) has become the PSNI (Police Service of Northern Ireland), creating a space for 'terrorists' to become statesmen and 'religious bigots' ministers.

Diversity and Tolerance in Socio-Legal Contexts takes us on an enlightened journey through the ecology of the landscapes that is diversity and tolerance, moving from the frontiers of US constitutional doctrine to the increasingly challenged scholarly confidence in civil rights. Time and time again, we observe through the revealing lenses of semiotics, linguistic and socio-legal analysis the paradoxical juxtaposition that is diversity.

The present book provides a framework for assessing how tolerance and diversity have become an integrated part of developing and interpreting the law. It examines the foundations and expressions of tolerance and diversity in their more modern legal forms: non-discrimination and equality in relation not only to racial and ethnic minorities (Roma, Jews, African/Hispanic Americans and indigenous peoples) but also disability and gender. In doing so, many contributors raise significant arguments relating to the construction of nationalism, group identities and pluralism.

Thirroul, August 2008

Introduction

The International Dual Nature of Law: Tolerance and Diversity

Anne Wagner and Vijay K. Bhatia

> What is Tolerance? – It is the consequence of humanity. We are all formed of frailty and error; let us pardon reciprocally each other's folly – that is the first law of nature (Voltaire, *A Treaty on Tolerance*, 1763).

Religious, cultural and ethnic diversity, together with international, political, and economic integration, bring issues of tolerance and diversity to the forefront; and raise important questions for the semiotic analysis of law. Recent events have shown that tolerance and diversity remain under threat despite the best efforts of the international community, which has attempted, through European and international conventions, treaties and national statutes, to stem the march of intolerance.

This edited volume has invited contributors to reflect on the growing importance of tolerance and diversity in our international community and why attacks upon it have become so prolific. Contributors have chosen to explore semiotic, rhetorical, pragmatic, sociolinguistic, psychological, philosophical and/or visual perspectives on the law, tolerance and diversity.

Mapping diversity and tolerance

Experiencing diversity and tolerance in many countries shows a good map of historical differences and changes in fashion. It involves the rhetorical speculation, or sometimes rhetorical invention, that resembles more 'a doctrine akin to that of the "free finding of law"' (Watson 1985, 86) and can lead to the creation of a new reality. Diversity and tolerance are a dual structure based on unity and fragmentation combining altogether rigidity and fluidity under the legal narrative perspective. Griffiths' idea gives some light when he states that:

> The legal reality of the modern state is not at all that of the tidy, consistent, organized ideal so nicely captured in the common identification of 'law' and 'legal system', but that legal reality is rather an unsystematic collage of inconsistent and overlapping parts (Griffiths 1986, 4).

This dual structure conveys in itself differences/convergences, universalism/individualism, as well as a willingness of opening new avenues for a more coherent international perspective. Indeed, in the context of the free movement of people, concepts of tolerance and diversity have been given significant consideration by international, European and domestic courts within the ambit of the principle of non-discrimination and to respect this cultural ecumene. This idea is also a reference from the UNESCO Declaration of Principles of Tolerance where it states that:

> Tolerance is respect, acceptance and appreciation of the rich diversity of our world's cultures, our forms of expression and ways of being human. It is fostered by knowledge, openness, communication, and freedom of thought, conscience and belief. Tolerance is harmony in difference. It is not only a moral duty, it is also a political and legal requirement. Tolerance, the virtue that makes peace possible, contributes to the replacement of the culture of war by a culture of peace.

Article 27 of the International Covenant on Civil and Political Rights further provides that:

> In those States in which ethnic, religious or linguistic minorities exist, persons belonging to such minorities shall not be denied the right, in community with the other members of their group, to enjoy their own culture, to profess and practice their own religion, or to use their own language.

Article 2(2) of the International Covenant on Economic, Social and Cultural Rights provides that:

> The State Parties to the present Covenant undertake to guarantee that the rights enunciated in the present Covenant shall be exercised without discrimination of any kind as to race, colour, sex, language, religion, political or other opinion, national or social origin, property, birth or other status.

The Council of Europe's European Convention of Human Rights and Fundamental Freedoms (ECHR), which entered into force in 1953, also has a non-discrimination provision in Article 14 stipulating that:

> The enjoyment of the rights and freedoms set forth in this Convention shall be secured without discrimination on any ground such as sex, race, colour, language, religion, political or other opinion, national or social origin, association with a national minority, property, birth or other status.

The European cultural ecumene is difficult to achieve as each member-state has its own individual laws and where breaches with European law are highly visible owing to the numbers of European citizens seeking redress from their own member-state. One of the latest examples is the one of a homosexual couple who were denied adoption by the French State and sought redress before the European Court of Human Rights (*E.B. v. France 2008*, application no. 43546/02).

Legal pluralism is a key issue within the European Union, because 'rather than being ordered by a single legal order, modern societies are ordered by a plurality of legal orders, interrelated and socially distributed in different ways' (Santos 1995, 114).

Nevertheless, 'tolerance and diversity' is not only a European but also an international issue. The basis of many international human rights measures is the United Nations Charter of 1945. Article 1(3) states that one of the purposes of the Charter is:

> To achieve international co-operation in solving international problems of an economic, social, cultural, or humanitarian character, and in promoting and encouraging respect for human rights and for the fundamental freedoms for all without distinction as to race, sex, language or religion.

The Universal Declaration of Human Rights itself refers to the prohibition of discrimination in Article 2 which provides that

> Everyone is entitled to all the rights and freedoms set forth in this Declaration, without distinction of any kind, such as race, colour, sex, language, religion, political or other opinion, national or social origin, property, birth or other status.

Article 27 of the International Covenant on Civil and Political Rights further provides that

> In those States in which ethnic, religious or linguistic minorities exist, persons belonging to such minorities shall not be denied the right, in community with the other members of their group, to enjoy their own culture, to profess and practice their own religion, or to use their own language.

As such exchange processes operate at different levels where the key concepts – diversity/tolerance, unity/fragmentation – cooperate to negotiate and find transitional spaces:

> We live in a time of porous legality or legal porosity, multiple networks of legal orders forcing us to constant transitions and tresspassings. Our legal life is constituted by an intersection of different legal orders, that is, by *interlegality*. Interlegality is the phenomenological counterpart of legal pluralism, and a key concept in a post-modern conception of law (Santos 1995, 473).

The semiotic foundation of diversity and tolerance

Part I of this edited volume addresses the two issues of tolerance and diversity through analyses of the relationship between language of law and its power when drafting, reading, saying and using the law. In response to the relative 'camouflage' of legal narratives (Grossfeld 1990, 47, as cited in Holland and Webb 2003, 108), to the changing power structures, changing societal norms and new faces of injustice, the contributors have tried to show how doctrines are reconsidered, reformulated and partly replaced by more appropriate interpretations and may be secured by video technological means.

Frederick P. Lewis analyses the evolution and development of US constitutional doctrine that reached a peak of activity in the middle of the twentieth century and which can be understood as reflecting and supporting the change in the overall pattern of relationships among politically and culturally significant groupings. This changing pattern, in turn, reflects fundamental alterations in the social and economic context of US life. The development and reinterpretation of traditional concepts of civil liberty to accommodate changing inter-group relations in a modern society has been the principal constitutional business of the US Supreme Court during the last half-century. To continue to preserve tolerance in the face of growing attacks upon it requires that we better understand the workings and requirements of these socio-political-legal arrangements and the nature of their long-run evolution.

Ira L. Strauber addresses the deep uncertainties surrounding the costs and benefits of scholarly confidence in civil rights law and constitutional rights as viable means to remedy acts of intolerance and threats to group identity. The chapter proceeds on the semiotic presumption that the significations of the legal concepts of 'race' and 'ethnicity', as they appear in *Shaare Tefila Congregation*, are, by their very nature, sufficiently indefinite and contestable to give rise to a multiplicity of interpretations by political elites and citizens alike, as they manoeuvre within and around the law in the pursuit of strategic partisan, ideological and policy goals.

Isabell Petrinic critically analyses the court video system as a process of non-verbal communication and the usefulness of video technology as an instrument of mediated semiosis in the courtroom. The communication is non-verbal in so far as inmates see the courtroom through the camera lens and it places the video link technology between the seer and the seen in a position of legal mediation. This chapter also argues that the courtroom of the future should not begin operating as a 'virtual' courtroom with litigants, judges and lawyers only communicating electronically until the communicative properties of the medium are further investigated.

István H. Szilágyi presents the outcomes of two empirical studies concerning the legal position of the Hungarian Roma minority (i.e. the other's otherness). The semiotic perspective is an inherent part of the empirical micro-sociological researches in order to understand the intention of the participants in the social interactions when there is a need to explain the meaning they attribute to the multiple signs and sign-systems used by them in the course of their action. Here, the semiotic analysis helps understand how this meaning is forging and changing in the dynamics of communication through the interplay of different systems of signs or levels of meanings.

Pamela Hobbs identifies the rhetorical strategies by which historical events are organised to create a framework for the presentation of a French national identity that promotes tolerance and diversity and rejects racism and discrimination. It thus demonstrates the role of political discourse in constructing the concept of nation as a system of positively valued inclusion. Yet in many parts of Europe, where changing patterns of immigration over the past several decades have resulted in ethnically diverse populations, the fragility of such mental constructs has become apparent. In such times, government response is critical to the restoration of national unity. Moreover, because national identities are discursively constructed and maintained, the response that is required is rhetorical.

Hanneke van Schooten analyses the meaning of new terminology as being ambiguous and having legal consequences. Since the prohibition of interstate force (the 1945 UN Charter) and in the aftermath of 9/11, remarkable shifts in the concept of war can be distinguished. The terms 'war declaration' and 'war' have fallen into disuse, while warfare continues under different names: 'police actions', 'missions' or 'operations'. The trial against Eric O is a case in point. O, who took part in the Dutch military 'peacekeeping mission' in Iraq, in December 2003 accidentally killed an Iraqi citizen in a dangerous war situation and was prosecuted for murder. The trial concentrated on the question of what rules were applicable: the law of war or the law of peace?

Case analyses of diversity and tolerance

The contributions in Part II address a cluster of closely related aspects concerning the interplay of tolerance and diversity under visual, legislative and interpretative perspectives. The tangible point of articulation remains 'vagueness in normative texts' (Bhatia et al. 2005), a 'set of different legal landscapes' (Vanderlinden 1987), a 'multilevel law' (Tierney 2006), a multileveled maze (Eco 1976, 86) where disaggregation, multiplicity and word fragmentation may pose an odd problem to the legal community (Griffiths 1986). Indeed,

> The meaning of a representation can be nothing but a representation. In fact, it is nothing but the representation itself conceived as stripped of irrelevant clothing. But this clothing never can be completely stripped out, it is only changed for something more diaphanous. So there is an infinite regression here. Finally, the interpretant is nothing but another representation to which the torch of truth is handed along; and as representation, it has its interpretant again (Fish 1980, 492).

John Brigham looks at sovereignty from the perspective of marketing. Barcelona, or BCN, has been marketed as a city of style. The chapter argues that this style and its marketing has branded Catalonia and its capital city. The brand functions much as any other brand to raise the profile of a product. In this case the product is not simply tourism, although it is that, but it is also sovereignty.

Sarah Marusek explores the divide between policy and law in light of the social ramifications of legality which are unaddressed by the stated scope of policy. She examines the impact that the general public has on the everyday governance of the American handicapped parking space against the framework of governance provided by the Americans with Disabilities Act 1990. Eventually she argues that failing to consider the wielding of power by the non-disabled public over the actuality of these particular parking spaces is the intolerant dismissal of a truly constitutive approach to law in which the full spectrum of policy as law must be considered.

Tracey Summerfield and Alec McHoul deal with one aspect of the immense complexities of the legal issues surrounding native title claims in Australia – the use of the visual in establishing claims. They introduce some of the issues that surround a neglected topic: the *culture* of law and its deep differences from the cultures it must deal with when it comes to Indigenous issues. In particular they discuss two kinds of 'evidence' the courts may use to make their determinations; that is, what they call these 'sights' and 'sites'.

William Pencak tackles the issue of race and class before the US Supreme Court in the case of *Rodriguez v. San Antonio Independent School District* that states and districts could not be required to equalise (approximately) funding per pupil as an alternative remedy to racial integration to create better educational opportunities for poor (usually black or Hispanic students). Underlying the majority arguments in this 5–4 decision is the spectre of Communism and the possible equalisation of wealth in the mentality of the judges. Both fears were fuelled by conservative misinterpretations of the contemporaneous movement for reparations to blacks, which in fact were limited demands to aid institutions assisting African Americans rather than a scheme for the overall redistribution of wealth. Because of these fears, even now states are not required to equalise funding for school districts, which has had negative consequences on educational opportunities for the poor and minorities in the US to this day, and reflects that the nation's sense of toleration and appreciation of diversity is severely limited and driven by factors of both race and class, as successful, middle- and upper-class African Americans are increasingly accepted by whites (for example, Barack Obama) while inner city schools continue to deteriorate and jails continue to fill.

Le Cheng and King Kui Sin try to explain from the very start that 'signs [can] move from relations of equilibrium to various stages of dissociation or opposition' (Kevelson 1988d, 167). The sign-relation is then difficult to establish as its determination is based on conceptual thinking; that is, a way of expression and a means of projecting emotion and intuition. Accordingly, words – even the simplest ones – are articulated differently depending on the contextualised definition they convey, since defining a word merely leads to specifying its meaning. Therefore, the question of analysing the concept 'de facto marriage' in Mainland China can be the core issue in legal adjudication.

Deborah Cao examines gender inequality in the legal, cultural and linguistic contexts through a number of recent cases. It is suggested that Chinese women are describable as both subjects and objects in the legal process, with both positive and negative implications for women's rights. The changing status of women in China is conceptualised within the legal system as a hierarchical social order in the male-dominated Chinese culture, with the symbolic as well as actual power of law both empowering Chinese women in the legal process and placing them in an un-winnable position in the social strata.

This collection thus offers a combination of varied perspectives on the analysis, application and exploitation of laws, highlighting the issues of tolerance and diversity in today's society by using a diversity of forms and frameworks within the broader configurations of semiotics, which provide conceptually focused and theoretically sound meeting points. The volume thus illustrates how semiotic resources seek to create and recreate new ideas and interpretations through the employment of a multi-perspectived framework integrating a range of diverse semiotic measures to handle communication, not as a single but a multi-dimensional phenomenon. This is aptly summed up in *Alice's Adventures in Wonderland*:

> 'When I use a word,' Humpty Dumpty said, in a rather scornful tone, 'it just means what I choose it to mean – neither more nor less'. 'The question is,' said Alice, 'whether you can make words mean so many different things' (Carroll 1865, 15).

PART I
The Semiotic Foundation of Diversity and Tolerance

Chapter 1
Tolerance, Pluralism and 'Fighting Faiths': Seeking the Sources of US Constitutional Meaning

Frederick P. Lewis

Constitutional meaning

The formal US Constitution contains words and phrases that are associated with the social arrangements that sustain civil tolerance. It grants 'equal protection of the laws' and 'due process of law' to those whom many may have initially seen as socially unequal. It guarantees 'free exercise of religion' and forbids religious 'establishment'. But these words are broad, vague and extremely general. The meaning of the words, though formally conveyed by the Supreme Court of the United States, has ultimately come from cultural practice; it has arisen from social understandings that have evolved through time as the patterns of inter-group relations have changed.[1]

As a result of both external immigration and internal migrations (not to mention forced importation of slaves as well as the remnants of native settlement) that occurred both prior to and subsequent to the nation's founding, people from many different groups have come to constitute US society. Their experiences upon arrival, their interactions with each other, and with the different political, economic and social conditions they encountered at particular historical moments, have shaped their attitudes and, ultimately, the nature of the preponderant social practice of tolerance.

The overall evolution and development of US constitutional doctrine that reached a peak of activity in the middle of the twentieth century can be understood as reflecting and supporting the change in the overall pattern of relationships among politically and culturally significant groupings. This changing pattern, in turn, reflects fundamental alterations in the social and economic context of US life.[2] The development and reinterpretation of traditional concepts of civil liberty to accommodate changing inter-group relations in a modern society has been the

1 'The sign is part of organized social intercourse and cannot exist, as such, outside it, reverting to a mere physical artifact' (Voloshinov 1973, 21).

2 'The meaning of a sign is not in its relationship to other signs within the language system but rather in the social context of its use' (Chandler 2002, Chapter 1).

principal constitutional business of the US Supreme Court during the last half-century. While this process arguably featured some inconsistencies, and there may be specific decisions that are appropriately subject to criticism, the overall effort was an attempt to take the precepts derived from the dynamic set of cultural practices and social understandings that underlie the Constitution and apply them to new realities.

Pluralism: changing patterns of inter-group relations

The patterns of pluralism in the US have changed over time. To continue to preserve tolerance suggests that we try to understand the workings and requirements of these socio-political-legal arrangements and the nature of their long-run evolution.

From the middle of the nineteenth through the middle of the twentieth century a major change occurred in the pattern of group relationships within the US. The change was the consequence of the decline of the preponderantly rural small-town US and the rise of a modern, cosmopolitan, urban and suburban nation.

The original settlements were composed of people escaping oppression in Europe attracted to the more open North American continent. John Roche (1964, 39, 41) wrote over fifty years ago that the US's early years were not the 'golden age' of freedom that some have claimed and that what diversity existed 'was a consequence not of tolerance and mutual respect ... but of the existence of many communities within the society, each with its own canons of orthodoxy.'

To rephrase this, if an individual made a strenuous effort, he or she could probably find somewhere within the country's expanse a community that shared his or her own particular political, cultural, religious or other views and, once that person joined that community, he or she could help impose its group beliefs on others: 'a microcosm to be intolerant with'. Roche argued that in this older nation, 'while there was no centralized authoritarian state on the European model ... the centralized state is not the only institution capable of oppression; the parish can be as severe in its impact on the individual as the centralized variety' (Roche 1964, 8–9). And 'the US was notoriously the happy hunting ground of what Reisman has acutely termed "vested heresies"' (Roche 1964, 8).

From this point of view, in its early period, the US consisted of a 'number of subcultures living side by side with the geographic expanse of the nation' rather than one integrated national community (Fischer, 1989, 973). David Hackett Fischer has described what he saw as the four principal regional cultures that constituted colonial North America and dominated in particular geographic areas beginning around 1629. The principal four were the Puritan of Massachusetts, the Cavalier of Virginia, the Quaker of the Delaware Valley, and the backcountry people sometimes referred to as the Scots-Irish who settled in the southern highlands of Appalachia. Fischer holds that these cultures and their folkways were derived from particular areas of England (1989, 783–819).[3]

As Hacker (1970, 209) wrote, 'the majority of Americans spent their lives in circumscribed settings which, if not literally feudal, nevertheless forced regimens that tolerated little deviation from established local standards.' In what was primarily an agrarian and decentralised early republic, freedom was essentially conceived of in communal terms. The freedom offered was the right of a group with shared values to acquire control over a piece of territory and its local government.

The institutions and arrangements created at the time the nation was founded were not designed to present a threat to this understanding. The intent, reflected in the structure of the original Constitution, was to protect local communities from the threat of central tyranny but there was little interest in the tyrannical practices that often existed as a practical matter within each subcultural unit.

The diversity of the nation during this early period was largely manifested in geographic terms. If an individual was not comfortable with the values being imposed through the government of a given area, he or she was theoretically free to move on to a place that was more comfortable. Under certain circumstances, the individual might be able to gather together enough other people who shared his or her views and keep moving together until they found a place to establish their own community.

In his writings, Roche (1964, 29–33) argued that this pattern broke down in the twentieth century, and he attributed its demise to urbanisation, industrialisation, and the rise of elites concerned with civil liberties that 'infiltrated' the ever more powerful national government. The result has been to produce a new pattern: a more impersonal society and one characterised by what he described as the 'bureaucratisation' of interpersonal and inter-group conflict.

Of course this type of social change has been discussed for decades. In a sense, Roche's writings add a new aspect to classic works that broadly characterise modern industrial societies as moving from status to contract (Maine 1861) or from *Gemeinschaft* to *Gesellschaft* (Tonnies 1887). At this point, we can now see that the newer pattern has not so much displaced the older as overlaid it. The older pattern still exists and periodically continues to offer vigorous resistance to the newer pattern.

People grouped into a series of geographic subcultures, each one sharing intolerant attitudes and possessing direct majority control of the local legal and political machinery, can impose conformity within their own little community even as each community differs somewhat from the others. But a pattern of

3 Fischer also mentions New Netherlands, which occupied much of the Hudson Valley; the Highland Scots who settled North Carolina's Cape Fear Valley in about 1732; and a culture that developed along the coast of South Carolina, comprised of families from the West Indies, French Huguenots, and some emigrants from tidewater Virginia, with slaves who came from the Congo basin and Angola. He describes these latter groups as developing a unique culture closer to the Caribbean colonies than to the Chesapeake.

pluralism of this kind can best prevail in a rural economy and is further facilitated by the relative isolation of a country significantly shielded from aggressive foreign powers by two large oceans. It is less viable when a large degree of economic and political interdependence is required on a national basis.

Industrial and post-industrial societies require people with skills who move to wherever their skills are needed; they will normally live, work and educate themselves in metropolitan areas. Constant subcultural interpenetration is produced by advanced means of transportation and communication, and it becomes increasingly difficult for a subculture to encompass all its members within a finite geographic area as persons affiliated with one subculture spend large amounts of their time with members of other subcultures in activities to which the subcultural affiliation is irrelevant.

Many of the older subcultures survive but they do not normally combine any longer with either economic activity or significant political control. And newer ones gain social influence. James Davison Hunter wrote about the US that

> [i]t is out of the changing contours and shifting balance of pluralism that the key actors in the contemporary culture war emerge ... After the Second World War, the balance represented in the ... consensus was ... upset. Among the most important contributing factors has been the further expansion of pluralism (Hunter 1991, 67–72).

The US's federal system, and its earlier constitutional doctrine, provided structural support for the older pattern and to some extent it still does. Significant subcultural differences still remain and for many people, their subcultural affiliation and identity remain vitally important. Despite the dominant rhetoric of individual rights, in many respects it is a new pattern of inter-group relations that was created in the twentieth century US and reflected in the doctrinal revolution popularly associated with the Warren Court (but which both preceded it and continued for several years after Chief Justice Warren stepped down). Indeed, despite the increase of conservative influence within the Court, that doctrinal revolution has still continued to some extent in recent years. Robert Horn (1956, vii) pointed out '[t]he truth is that almost all these First Amendment and due process cases of [the twentieth] century deal with the rights of individuals acting as members of organized religious, political and economic associations'.

The frequent inability of many subcultural groups to obtain satisfactory results from state and local governments, which retain the relevant police powers and often use them to reinforce the older pattern of pluralism, has led these groups to seek Supreme Court intervention to secure their equal rights. Operating, in a sense, as the agent of the evolving newer pattern of inter-group relations, the US Supreme Court has frequently, if imperfectly, used the Fourteenth Amendment to the US Constitution as a vehicle to extend basic liberties to these political, racial and cultural minorities during the middle and later decades of the twentieth century and, to some degree still, in the early years of the twenty-first.

Pluralism, individualism and civil peace[4]

The new pluralism in society focuses on function and performance. Peter Drucker (1989, 76) once wrote that

> … both society and polity in developed countries are now full of power centers that are outside of, and separate from, government. It is a pluralism of single-purpose organizations, each concerned with one social task: wealth creation or schooling or health care or forming the values and habits of the young.

Drucker (1989, Chapter 7) saw these developments as part of a long-term trend where social tasks that 150 years ago were done, if at all, within the family (or perhaps, he might have added, by a rather homogenous local community) are now done in and through organised single-purpose institutions. He noted that the pluralism of today's institutions is different from that of the past in that it is based on function rather than power.

It might be more accurate to say that these institutions have legitimate power only within their functional area. Thus, for example, people belonging to different subcultural groups work together in the institutions based upon skills they have that are suitable for the function because individual skill, and not subcultural affiliation, is the relevant consideration. Reciprocally, the power of the social and economic institutions Drucker describes is normally not available to support any particular subcultural group. This weakened subcultural group control and the balance among these institutional forces typically allows individual US identities to be constructed from many sources.

Alan Wolfe (1990) has written that citizens of the US have chosen to be 'modern, not ethnic'. He suggests that we have solved the problem of ethnicity that plagues other nations by transcending it and that groups do not live in peace with each other in the US; individuals do. This is much truth in this though it might be more accurate to say, given that some elements of traditional ethnicity and religion do remain quite powerful, that groups live in peace in the US but that the powerful individualist ethos of US culture, which is responsible for some of the much noted negative aspects of our social, political and economic system, also helps account for our relatively more peaceful inter-group relations. It is also hard not to agree with Wolfe (1990) that the more traditional and classic ethnic arrangements 'have a way of encouraging their people, when not killing each other over roots, to retreat into that special kind of narrowness and superstition that ethnicity alone can legitimate.'

Kevin Phillips (2006, 105) points out that the US has 'a superabundance of denominations and sects compared to Europe, as well as a far higher ratio of

4 Obviously civil peace in the US has not totally prevailed. But except for the Civil War of the 1860s, the struggle for social progress has largely prevailed over incidents and eras of oppression and violence.

churchgoers.' He also claims that Muslims in the US now 'outnumber Presbyterians or Episcopalians' and Los Angeles is the most 'varietal Buddhist city in the world'. Despite the very great religious diversity of the US and the ceremonial religiosity that can often be found in its public sphere, its commitment to church–state separation is arguably more extensive than that of many European countries and that too seems to contribute to peaceful inter-group relations.

The developments that have so changed the US were arguably necessary for the maintenance of political stability. Robert Dahl (1989, 254–60) suggested that in nations where people live their whole lives within a territorial subcultural unit, the potential for explosive conflict between such units is likely to be high.[5]

The new pattern of pluralism, which diminishes the impact of subcultural affiliation upon the political and economic aspects of life, will also have the effect of diminishing the overall importance of subcultural affiliation for some individuals and concomitantly of reducing the potential for inter-group conflict (Wolfe 1990).[6]

Within a territorial subcultural unit, in the short run at least according to Robert Putnam, 'diversity tends to reduce social solidarity and social capital'. The evidence he has accumulated leads him to the conclusion that 'in ethnically diverse neighborhoods residents of all races tend to "hunker down". Trust (even of one's own race) is lower, altruism and community cooperation rarer, friends fewer' (Putnam 2007, 137).

However, over time, he suggests that new forms of social solidarity develop and 'dampen the negative effects of diversity by constructing new, more encompassing identities'. Thus the central challenge for modern, diversifying societies is to create a new, broader sense of 'we' (Putnam 2007, 138–9).

Tolerance, 'fighting faiths' and symbolic reinforcement

Justice Oliver Wendell Holmes wrote famous words that are often cited in defence of libertarian speech approaches:

> [W]hen men have realized that time has upset many fighting faiths, they may come to believe even more than they believe the very foundations of their own

---

5 The implications of some aspects of ethnic demography remain contested. For example, Paul Collier and Anke Hoeffler of Oxford University concluded in 2004 that when an ethnic group makes up more than 45 per cent but less than 90 per cent of a population, the chance of conflict increases. However, James D. Fearon and David D. Laitin of Stanford University concluded in a 2003 study: 'it appears not to be true that a greater degree of ethnic or religious diversity – or indeed any particular cultural demography – by itself makes a country more prone to civil war.' They found that the chance of civil war declined as a country became wealthier regardless of its ethnic makeup. See Bass (2006).

6 This is a review of four books on ethnicity where he characterises these modern cultural arrangements as 'low cost'.

> conduct that the ultimate good desired is better reached by free trade in ideas – that the best test of truth is the power of thought to get itself accepted in the competition of the market, and that truth is the only ground upon which their wishes safely can be carried out. That at any rate is the theory of our Constitution. It is an experiment, as all life is an experiment (*Abrams v. United States*, 250 U.S. 616, 630 (1919)).

This quote tells us to tolerate the expression of ideas that we dislike, recognising that our own strongly held beliefs and ideas may be 'upset' in the long-run search for 'truth'. But to tolerate the expression of such ideas by others means we must also tolerate those who express the ideas, despite their 'otherness'. For different 'fighting faiths' to coexist in a political community, in a geographic place, in conditions of social peace at any given moment in time, those who possess them must all accept arrangements fostering this peaceful coexistence and the building of shared practices even though the logic of their own particular systems of intellectual and moral belief may well lead to rejection of the beliefs and behaviours of others, and possibly of the very idea that we should tolerate them.

We all tolerate people with whom we disagree, those who think differently from us, believe differently, look differently, and who in some ways behave differently. We tolerate them, meaning not only that we do not kill them but that we work with them, do business with them,[7] socialise with them, live next door to them and occasionally marry them. These arrangements, which derive from conclusions reached both consciously and unconsciously about everyday experience, frequently coexist with intellectual or moral-based beliefs we may have that reject, implicitly or explicitly, the beliefs and behaviours of these other people we tolerate, and indeed, frequently also logically reject the notion that we should tolerate them. Thus tolerance is really less a matter of logic than it is an empirical position – one that emerges primarily from practical conclusions we reach, both consciously and unconsciously, about everyday social experience over long periods of time.

Indeed, in *The Tolerant Society*, Lee Bollinger (1986) argued that traditional functionalist rationales for free speech that suggest truth will emerge from the clash of ideas while each of us gains satisfaction from self-expression are naïve; and he is equally uncomfortable with defining free speech's primary function as a check on a government that cannot be trusted. Instead he holds that the US 'tolerates extremist speech because coming to terms with it teaches each of us tolerance and self-control'.[8] Bollinger concludes that this tolerance benefits democratic

---

7 Voltaire (1961), who was himself often intolerant, attributed the tolerance he found in England to the practice there of market capitalism. No doubt the mutual profit that a good trade exchange can provide is an important practical factor in this process but it is not the only one. For a more contemporary discussion, see Friedman (2005).

8 Bollinger, who is now President of Columbia University, was recently involved in a much publicised invitation to and confrontation with Iranian President Mahmoud

society by 'symbolically reinforcing our need to resist the ever-present tendency to intolerance' (Lewis 1998).

Tolerance and experience

The cultural practice that largely sustains tolerance in the US – and has implications for sustaining tolerance elsewhere – also forms the basis of US constitutional understanding. Since in the US it is the Supreme Court that polices this process, which the Constitution and its evolving doctrine reflect, to be successful it must avoid an overly theoretical, formalistic approach to adjudication. It must do so even where that requires individual justices to ignore the dictates of their own religion or value system. The ultra-conservative critique of US constitutional adjudication fails to appreciate this and has not encouraged people to understand that constitutional values must reflect and encourage the tolerance that most US citizens claim to support. Constitutional interpretation needs to reflect what is now a long-term, but still developing, cultural practice that sustains pluralism and tolerance in the US.

It is no secret that, in the US, all this is under significant attack and the influence of ultra-conservative Christianity upon the policies of the national government has reached a peak in recent years.[9] Of course, the prior growth in influence of secular thought in US society and politics in the twentieth century, which strengthened the development of meaningful constitutional doctrine of church–state separation, was likely facilitated by the strong antipathy which many leaders of the most conservative elements of Protestantism, Catholicism and Judaism felt toward each other's religions. Ironically, the subsequent increase in the political strength of the religious right in the US occurred in large part because many in these groups and their leaders have come to accept each other on a pragmatic level despite their continued adherence to basically antithetical religious doctrines. Experience over time has led them to make practical alliances against what they tend to see as a more threatening common enemy of liberalism and secular humanism.[10] In the US many conservatives have also vigorously insisted that constitutional adjudication

---

Ahmadinejad, who tested Bollinger's theories about tolerance with his comments about the Holocaust and his assertion that there were no gay people in Iran.

9 Notably, Kevin Phillips titled his recent highly critical book on contemporary US politics, *American Theocracy*. And the replacement of Justice Sandra Day O'Connor on the Supreme Court by Justice Samuel Alito has moved outcomes from closely contested doctrinal struggles in a more conservative direction.

10 Former Massachusetts Governor Mitt Romney is a member of the Church of Latter Day Saints, more commonly known as the Mormons. In his unsuccessful quest for the Republican Party nomination for President of the US, he attempted to overcome Evangelical Protestant opposition to many of the doctrines and practices of the Mormon religion by stressing shared social conservative values and the common 'threat' all religion allegedly faced from unbelief and secularism.

must be constrained by adherence to the precise original intent of those who drafted the words of the document long ago. They criticise, even sometimes ridicule, those who describe the Constitution as a living document that evolves to fit changing circumstances.

But the US Constitution is 'living' and its interpretive doctrine adjusts and alters because the cultural practice that constitutes and underlies it (and always has done so) continues to both persist and evolve. That cultural practice and the rough 'understandings' that surround it make demands upon new groups that rise to social, economic and political influence in the US while simultaneously accommodating somewhat to their needs and demands.

I believe that the underlying dynamic of the long-term process and practice described here retains much of its vigour. Highly imperfect as this process is, and despite the many other grave difficulties the US and its society faces, there is some reason to believe that the process continues to function.

Chapter 2
'When the Law Speaks': Acts of Intolerance, Threats to Group-Identity, and Confidence in Law and Rights

Ira L. Strauber

Introduction

This chapter[1] addresses some of the (deep) uncertainties related to costs and benefits of having confidence in civil rights law and constitutional rights as a means to remedy acts of intolerance and threats to group-identity. The focal point for this analysis is the 1987 US Supreme Court case of *Shaare Tefila Congregation v. Cobb* (and, to the extent relevant, its companion decision upon which it depends, *Saint Francis College v. Al-Khasraji*).[2] When decided, *Shaare Tefila Congregation* and *Saint Francis College* were considered significant case-law because the decisions held that Jews and Arabs (respectively) were eligible, despite their contemporary status as part of the Caucasian race, to seek redress under nineteenth-century Federal civil rights provisions prohibiting racial discrimination. Since 1987, the cases can be located in law review essays on race and ethnicity, primarily because (as to be explained in due course) they can be interpreted as (if not altogether untroubled) examples of how the law can speak in terms of the favoured social construction approach to race and ethnicity rather than a generally disfavoured essentialist or scientific approach to them. Hence, *Shaare Tefila Congregation* is the chosen focal point for this chapter because of its seminal place in civil rights law and the academy. It is also the focal point because it is robust enough to

---

1 The original momentum for the ideas behind this chapter came from a panel on *Saint Francis College et al. v Majid Ghaidan Al Khazraji* and *Shaare Tefila Congregation v. William Cobb et al.* for 'The Afro-Semitic Experience Program', 9 April 2005, and a panel, 'The Resurgence of Anti-Semitism in the West', for The Center of the Humanities, 5–7 April 2006. Both events were at Grinnell College, Iowa. The groundwork for this chapter was constructed in my oral remarks, 'When the Law Speaks: US Constitutional Law, Acts of Intolerance, and Threats to Self-Identity', prepared for the 5th International Roundtable for the Semiotics of Law, Université du Littoral Côte d'Opale (France), 17–20 May 2006. I would like to thank my research assistant, Whitney Knopf, for her assiduous attention to detail, her inexhaustible patience, and her sense of humour in the preparation of this chapter.

2 *Shaare Tefila Congregation v. Cobb*, 481 U.S. 615; *Saint Francis College v. Al-Khazraji*, 481 U.S. 604.

provide insights into understanding present-day uncertainties about the law as a remedy for purported acts of intolerance and threats to group-identity.

This chapter proceeds on the semiotic presumption that the significations and gestures of the legal concepts of 'race' and 'ethnicity', as they appear in *Shaare Tefila Congregation*, are, by their very nature, 'complex signals' (McCann 1999, 76) that are sufficiently 'open-textured', 'inherently ambiguous, indeterminate, and contestable' (McCann 1999, 79) to allow for 'multiple constructions and contestation over time by differently situated legal actors' (McCann 1999, 79). The semiotic complexity of these legal concepts thus gives rise to possibilities, by legal and political elites and citizens alike, to manoeuvre within and around the law's significations in the pursuit of strategic partisan, ideological, and policy goals (McCann 1999, 79). But, of course, these are only strategic opportunities, and opportunities are no guarantee of success.

For one, the complexity of these signals notwithstanding, there is what Stanley Fish referred to as the process of 'efficacious formalism' to be taken into account: the legal process has its own internal dynamics, such that when the law incorporates manoeuvres, and allows for change, it does so only to the extent that both are compatible with deciding the case at hand in terms that are consistent with maintaining the law's overall consistency and coherence (Fish 1994, 152–6). Moreover, political institutions, processes, and the political culture generally, are obviously also efficacious constraints on manoeuvres and change. These exogenous factors all tend to coalesce with the law's own efficaciousness so that, arguably, whatever advantages the law's variation and contestability provide tend, by and large, to accrue to the reproduction of the existing political and social order (McCann 1999, 79). Consequently, semiotic analysis as pursued here is attentive to the unwelcome, unintended and unanticipated consequences that disappoint opportunities for those who have some confidence the law might speak on their behalf.

In this chapter, analysis of *Shaare Tefila Congregation* thus coincides with a crucial disquiet about the law: whether there ought to be confidence in the law when it comes to a group's legal aspirations to use the law for counteracting acts of intolerance and threats to their group-identity. The roots of this disquiet are to be associated primarily with the Critical Legal Studies movement[3] as it evolved

---

3 The Critical Legal Studies Movement originated in law schools in the 1970s. Politically, its participants were critics of the likes of the Vietnam War, US racial politics and the unequal distribution of wealth in the polity. Legally, its participants attacked all dominant forms of jurisprudence as internally inconsistent and incoherent, based as they were on an indefensible distinction between law and politics and a failure to appreciate the indeterminacy of all legal concepts. As the literature of Critical Legal Studies evolved it encompassed a range of ideological justifications for these attacks (for example, neo-Marxism, socialism, feminism, race theories, deconstruction and forms of anarchism and nihilism). Arguably, many of these justifications have become incorporated into 'conventional' thinking about law and politics, particularly in political science (where

out of ideological convictions that the efficacious formalism and the constraints of institutions, processes and political culture justify deep scepticism about strategic opportunities and dialogue with the law for the sake of social change. But today this disquiet goes beyond ideology because it has received some considerable measure of credible support from social scientific studies[4] that find that courts and law tend to be weak instruments of social change, especially for marginalised groups and minorities, unless exogenous forces happen to strongly coalesce in their favour (something which appears to be too rarely the case).

However, disquiet about when the law speaks does not necessarily mandate thoroughgoing pessimism, to say nothing of cynicism. An alternative opens up if commentary adopts a pragmatic working hypothesis that law and politics are more unpredictable than ideology ever makes them out to be, and that social scientific findings depend not on blanket generalisations but a case-by-case and contextual approach to analysis. Specifically, this working hypothesis is the equivalent of an ever-cautious weather eye on the law's efficaciousness and exogenous factors: it directs attention to (a presumed) intrinsic uncertainty about how those factors play themselves in response to strategic efforts to manipulate the systemic resistance of law, courts, and political institutions to social change.

This hypothesis is inspired by what is now a generally agreed upon classic (1987) essay in Delgado and Stefancic's *Critical Race Theory* by Patricia Williams, 'Alchemical Notes: Reconstructing Ideals from Deconstructed Rights' (Williams 1987). In effect, what I take away from this essay is the lesson that, however deservedly and deeply the law disappointments, aspirations for the law should not be rejected as a desirable means toward social change too readily. It is experience and the practicalities of mounting material or symbolic challenges to discrimination, intolerance and the legal status quo that should be the test of whether or not confidence in the law is justified. The trick, and it is a trick, is to use the law and courts, rather than be used by them. If this trick can be pulled off, then the limits of law and courts can be appropriately expanded to make room for reconstructed and transformative conceptions of rights that are compatible with group-identity and liberating 'marker[s] of … citizenship, …participation, [and] … relation[s] with others' (Williams 1987, 88).

The working hypothesis of this chapter is designed to analyse this trick in relation to the semiotic complexity of the law's significations and to practical politics. Accordingly, semiotic complexity and exogenous factors suggest that this trick will be complicated by the fact that groups are likely to be disagree internally about what counts as appropriately expanded conceptions of rights, when and how much confidence to have in those conceptions, and whether it is prudent to depend on using the law against itself and the power of the state to recognise the

often, as here, its analytic insights about law and politics are, for better or worse, adapted and qualified rather than taken whole cloth.

4 Perhaps the master work here is Gerald N. Rosenberg's *The Hollow Hope: Can Court Bring About Social Change* (1991).

legitimacy of putatively reconstructed and transformative markers. Thus, what will count as 'reconstructed and transformative conceptions of rights compatible with group-identity' (Williams 1987, 88) is likely to be contestable, and disagreements will follow about what should count as material or symbolic gains and losses and whether or not the law and courts have responded with silence, antagonism or support (Bamforth 1997; Roithmayr 2001). In sum, disconcerting as it might be from the perspective of ideology, principle or policy preferences, the working hypothesis is compatible with finding complexity, uncertainty and contestability around every corner when it comes to confidence in the law, and therefore dashes expectations for direct and comforting answers to questions about confidence in the law.

With all this by way of introduction, the chapter is structured as follows. The first section characterises events preceding Supreme Court adjudication of *Shaare Tefila Congregation v. Cobb* and aspects of its litigation politics subsequent to those events. The second section summarises the Court's understanding of civil rights law and constitutional rights regarding 'race and ethnicity' in the case, and, from the perspective of the working hypothesis, characterises facets of the mixed semiotic and political messages of the Court's adjudication. It is these messages which constitute grounds for some considerable disquiet about confidence in the law. The third section provides a small-scale case study of consequences of *Shaare Tefila Congregation*'s mixed messages as they relate to aspirations for legal remedies for acts intolerance and group-identity traduced. The concluding section fleshes out the tacit implications of the working hypothesis as a pragmatic approach to the semiotic analysis that has informed the chapter as a whole.

Acts of intolerance group-identity traduced

'On November 2, 1982, the outside walls of the synagogue of the Shaare Tefila Congregation in Silver Spring, Maryland, were sprayed with red and black paint and with large anti-Semitic slogans, phrases, and symbols.'[5] Eight men, one with a Nazi tattoo and another with a Ku Klux Klan burning cross tattoo, were drinking in a drug store parking lot across from the synagogue, and defaced the walls of the drug store with Nazi and Ku Klux Klan slogans (Cohen 1988, 96).[6] One of the men suggested that the group go over to the synagogue and spray-paint it. The eight then spray-painted Klan symbols, a burning cross, and the words 'Dead Jew', 'In, Take a Shower Jew', and an eagle over a swastika with the garbled spelling of the word *Totenkopfverbände* (the 'death head' units of Nazi concentration camp guards) on the walls of the building (Cohen 1988, 96).

5 *Shaare Tefila Congregation v. Cobb*, 481 U.S. 615, at 616.

6 Alcohol was involved in this incident, and, for some, its role poses a question about whether the acts involved were 'anti-Semitic'. Of course, what should count as an anti-Semitic act is often contestable.

The synagogue interpreted the spray-painting as a graphic statement of Nazi ideology. The synagogue's initial response was to pursue the conventional path of pressing criminal charges against the men.[7] After the trial, though, the synagogue filed a Federal civil proceeding against the men asserting a violation under three sections of the Civil Rights Act of 1866 (originally promulgated to protect the rights of blacks) and a set of post-Civil War sections of the US Code (¶ 1981, 2, & 5) prohibiting racially discriminatory violations of property rights. Apparently, the primary goal of the suit was to raise the profile of the incident beyond that of property damage to attacks on Jews as a (religious) group.

Both the Federal District trial court and the Fourth Circuit Court of Appeals rejected the suit. The lower courts held that Jews were not a racially distinct group (as conceded by the synagogue), and that it was irrelevant that the perpetrators perceived Jews as a racially distinct group (as evidenced by their Nazi and Ku Klux Klan tattoos and the graphics on the synagogue). Consequently, the synagogue, and therefore Jews, were denied a cause of action under those statutory provisions originally designed to provide relief for newly freed slaves from public and private discrimination, and later held applicable to non-black and white ethnic groups.

The prospect of further appellate adjudication triggered significant differences of opinions between the synagogue litigation team (the Jewish Advocacy Center) and some prominent, older, and more traditional, major national organisations about advocating Jewish group identity in 'racial' terms for the sake of a remedy for threats against them. Illustrative was the Anti-Defamation League, a major Jewish organisation dedicated to protecting Jewish interests, which initially opposed litigation for fear of elevating the visibility of threats to Jews and because of concerns that a legal link between Jews and a race-based remedy would only underline hoary anti-Semitic racialism and undermine contemporary Jewish efforts to be seen as a fully integrated group in American society (Cohen 1988). (The ADL eventually changed its position and participated in the Supreme Court case.)

Other national Jewish organisations deemed further litigation too uncertain and dangerous, even beyond any negatives associated with linking Jews and 'race' or sensibilities about integration, because of concerns that the attendant publicity surrounding an appeal might trigger the hazard of '... stirring up additional hatred by over blowing the actual episode' or because it might encourage 'the nuts' to commit more anti-Semitic acts (Cohen 1988, 98).[8] These differences of opinion about judicial politics among national organisations that are highly experienced, efficacious and well-financed advocates for a Jewish population that enjoys comparative social and economic security[9] is something that ought not be passed

7 The paragraphs that follow depend on a single source – Cohen 1988.

8 It cannot be discounted that organisational tensions are involved here, along with considerations about whether the financial costs of litigation outweighed its benefits.

9 There are, to the best of my knowledge, no data on the poverty rate among Jews in the US. Anecdotal reports suggest an average figure for Jews, but then distinctions have

over. It is apparent from these differences that relative Jewish social and economic security is insufficient to insulate some Jewish organisations from fears that pursuing legal redress for perceived injuries is risky business.

With these differences, these organisations can be said to mirror the ambivalence of the Jewish community as a whole about its social status in the US. Over the last decade, surveys of the American Jewish community appear to confirm this sense of insecurity. A growing, and today overwhelming, majority of Jews believe that anti-Semitism in the US is a somewhat or very serious problem,[10] and currently a majority of Jews believe that over the coming years anti-Semitism will be a problem here and abroad.[11] Yet, and if the past is an indicator, a majority of Jews do not report having themselves been victims of anti-Semitism; less religious Jews (more likely living in non-Jewish communities), better educated Jews (seeking professional advancement in environments without a strong Jewish presence), and older Jews (not being the beneficiaries of contemporary culture) are those more likely to report having been victims of anti-Semitic incidents.

One way of understanding these differences about anti-Semitism among Jews is to frame them in terms of 'intersectionality', a concept that connotes group-identity as an amalgam of simultaneously reinforcing and cross-cutting self-perceptions, commitments and values.[12] In the context of contemporary Jews, these differences are to be seen as symptomatic of the relative indeterminacy of contemporary (Jewish) group-identity: that is, by and large, even if Jews are socially and economically secure, 'group-identity' is differentiated internally along religious, demographic and other lines.[13] Therefore, from the perspective of intersectionality, it is not surprising that individual Jews vary in the extent of their respective anxieties and fears about their social security and fears over acts of intolerance and threats to their group-identity.

Understanding variation in fears and anxieties about anti-Semitism is further complicated on the ground of social facts. In 2006, there was a 12 per cent decline

---

to be drawn on the basis of age or ethnicity (perhaps recent Russian immigrants inflate the poverty rate). Social security is also elusive because distinctions are to be drawn between its 'objective' and 'subjective' measures.

10 This datum is from the most recent source I could find, Samuel C. Heilman's *Portrait of American Jews: the Last Half of the 20th Century* (1995, 105–23). Heilman reports that one scholar has suggests 'anti-Semitism is a core element of modern Jewish identity'. He also indicates that there is variation here, particularly in relation to age and proximity to Jewish–Black antagonisms (Heilman 1995, 123).

11 AJC 2006 Annual Survey of American Jewish Opinion, available at <http://www.ajc.org/site/c.ijITI2PHKoG/b.851561/apps/nl/content2>. Last accessed 31 December 2007.

12 See Minow 1997, 38–40 for the basis of this characterisation.

13 To illustrate, variation in Jewish group identity is to be expected because: (1) there are four main denominations of Judaism distinguished by dissimilar (even antagonistic) religious beliefs, practices and conceptions of Jewish law; (2) from a social scientific perspective, social attitudes and beliefs are known to vary along the lines of such things as age, gender, regional differences and political beliefs.

in reported anti-Semitic incidents (the greater number being harassment, threats and assaults rather than vandalism), and this represented the second decline in two years. But it is also the case that anti-Semitic incidents have risen sharply from 1986 to 1995, and have waxed and waned from 2001 to 2004; the number of incidents is still significantly greater than at any point before 1990).[14] Furthermore, there is general agreement that there has been a 'resurgence of anti-Semitic incidents at American colleges and universities ...' (Marcus 2007, 837), and there has been a significant increase in anti-Semitic incidents in Germany, Austria and the Scandinavian countries recently (Barkat 2007). Events such as these tend to unsettle some, but not all, in the American Jewish community. In sum, there is ample room for understanding variation in Jewish perceptions about when and how it confronts threats to their (variously self-characterised) group-identity.

Nonetheless, those who favoured litigation saw litigation politics as an opportunity for aggressive and intense group-identity politics.

> The desire for federal jurisdiction also bared a deep emotional need. To the post-Holocaust generation of Jews, vandalism of a synagogue ... was a hate crime whose perpetrators linked it directly to Nazi teachings. ... [O]utrage on the part of American Jews stemmed not from fear but from anger; communal pride demanded that anti-Semitism and not mere vandalism be punished, preferably in a *federal* forum (Cohen 1988, 99).

As the attorneys for Shaare Tefila argued:

> Unlike a criminal prosecution for trespass ... under state law..., a federal civil rights action tells the perpetrators that it is the racist character of the acts – and the resulting injury to individual dignity – that society deplores, not just damage to property. The symbolic gesture of the federal government's denunciation of anti-Semitism seemed all-important. One member of the Executive Committee of the American Jewish Congress argued: 'After having lived through Hitler it was unthinkable that we would stay out of the case'[15] (Cohen 1988, 99).

These sentiments reflect a version of group-identity with roots in existential and historical victimhood and an intense sense of dignity traduced. To use the law to associate anti-Semitism with race discrimination and not just 'Jew hatred' thus signifies a desire for social-psychological and symbolic (might one dare say semiotic) solace by repairing injury to Jews with a signal that *their* Federal government, in contrast to the Nazi regime, protects Jews. As fate, even irony, would have it, the remedy Jewish petitioners sought became inextricably connected

14 Anti-Defamation League's 2006 annual 'Audit of Anti-Semitic Incidents', at <http://www.adl.org/main_Anti_Semitism_Domestic/Audit_2006.htm>. Last accessed 31 December 2007.

15 Internal citations omitted.

to litigation brought by an Arab-American citizen seeking repair and solace from his government. Born in Iraq, Professor Majid Al-Khasraji alleged discrimination in his tenure dispute with Saint Francis College (Pa.) and sought relief under the Civil Rights Act of 1964 and the statutory provisions involved in *Shaare Tefila Congregation*. Professor Al-Khasraji claimed that, as an Arab-American, he was guaranteed the complete and identical benefit of all laws enjoyed by white citizens. But the District Court dismissed his suit, primarily because it found that statutory relief did not reach claims of discrimination of 'white' persons like Al-Khasraji, even if such persons were of a specific national origin or religion (Prochaska 1987). On appeal, the Fourth Circuit Court of Appeals reversed the District Court, holding that Arab-Americans were persons of a genetically or physiognomically identifiable group of persons and therefore were among those citizens that Congress intended to protect by providing for relief from discrimination.

Saint Francis College appealed the Fourth Circuit decision to the Supreme Court, and the Court ordered sequential oral arguments in *Shaare Tefila Congregation* and *Saint Francis College*. Subsequently, Jewish and Arab-American groups filed *amicus* briefs on each other's behalf. For anti-litigation groups that feared exciting embers of anti-Semitism, this turn of events was decidedly awkward, and potentially unwelcome, to the extent that it might reinforce anti-Semitic thinking about Jews as a genetically or physiognomically identifiable group, which, in turn could undermine Jewish group-identity as an assimilated group. Nonetheless, some pro-litigation forces in the Jewish community actually welcomed linking Jews with the concept of racially identifiable legal traits because such a link resonated with constituting a new stage in Jewish identity politics.

For these forces and those who agreed with them, relative Jewish security in the polity, lessons learned from the experience of post-World War II European Jews who were overly dependent on their social and economic security and cultural assimilation, and concerns about the disintegration of the mid-twentieth century alliance between Jews and left-liberals all suggested that it was time to rethink strategies for protecting Jewish group-identity. Even so, joint Jewish and Arab-American litigation involving race-based categories as a new page in the Jewish identity politics was a big step beyond the Jewish group-identity as an (albeit diverse) religious group, and opponents of activism were understandably alarmed by the threat of the law speaking in terms that constitute Jews as 'a people' of identifiable traits (Cohen 1988, 98).

Arguably, the litigation strategy that Shaare Tefila Congregation settled upon appears to reflect that alarm and its potential social costs: most specifically, by contending that the *perpetrators'* racial motivation is sufficient to trigger statutory relief, rather than 'race' as an identifiable trait of alleged victims (thereby eliding arguments over whether Jews were a 'race'). The implication of this strategy was to simultaneously contend that what counts as 'racial' discrimination in terms of statutory relief should include the victim's conception of his/her 'race' (hence the appeal for Civil Rights protection), and that it encompass the status of an alleged victim, as a member of a group that perpetrators have generally or historically perceived to be a 'racial' group.

In addition, the litigation strategy proposed that, to the extent that 'race' as an identifiable trait was pertinent, the concept of 'race' should not be limited to twentieth-century scientific conceptions of it, thereby eliding the argument that if Jews were not a 'race' in scientific terms then perpetrators of anti-Semitic acts could not be accused of reflecting racial animus toward Jews. The litigation strategy also had to confront Congressional intent behind nineteenth-century provisions relating to relief from discrimination. Here the litigation contention was that, in providing for legal remedies, Congress sought to reach more than merely 'racial' discrimination *per se*, thereby eliding the argument whether 'white' Jews could seek statutory relief. To substantiate this contention, the argument was that the concept of 'race', as found in the foundational nineteenth-century statutes, included 'ethnic' or 'ancestral' groups (like Jews and Arabs), and, therefore, in terms of Congressional intent, remedies for 'racial' and 'ethnic' discrimination overlapped (Cohen 1988, 97).

Clearly this bobbing and weaving in and around significations of 'race' and 'ethnicity', and in and around a victim and perpetrator perspective on discriminatory acts, was meant to maximise litigation success as well as to minimise anticipated costs associated with linking Jewish group-identity to 'race'. Even so, and perhaps even more so than with litigation strategies as usual, Jewish organisations delivered themselves into the hands of the judiciary's discretion to constitute Jews in terms of legally identifiable traits with all of its anticipated and potentially unwelcome consequences.

Legal remedies for 'a people' of legally identifiable traits

The Supreme Court's response to this strategy in *Shaare Tefila Congregation* was as knotty as the differences surrounding Jewish group-identity and disagreements about the potential benefits and dangers of judicial politics. Writing for the Court, Justice White categorically dismissed the claim that the perpetrators' racial motivation was sufficient to trigger a charge of racial discrimination. Nevertheless, *Shaare Tefila Congregation* reversed the lower court finding that the synagogue lacked grounds for a cause of action under the provisions of the nineteenth-century racial discrimination provisions. As a result, the Court confirmed most, but not all, of the synagogue's remaining litigation strategy. Citing his opinion in *Saint Francis College*, Justice White confirmed that neither contemporary scientific understandings of 'race', nor its everyday conventional understandings, were signifiers of the meaning of 'race' for the purpose of statutory interpretation of provisions providing remedies for discrimination.[16] White concluded that the legally controlling significations of 'race' and who is or is not a member of the 'white'

16 *Saint Francis College v. Al-Khazraji*, 481 U.S. 604, at 613.

race were to be drawn from the original meaning and history of the nineteenth-century civil rights code[17] as he constructed them in *Saint Francis College*.

In *Saint Francis College*, White turned to mid-nineteenth-century dictionaries to specify that, for the purposes of statutory interpretation, 'race' meant 'descendants from a parent[al] ... stock', 'the lineage of a family', 'descendants of a common ancestor', '... a family, tribe, people or nation.'[18] He elaborated by holding that, although twentieth-century dictionaries refer to 'race' by terms such as 'Caucasian, Mongolian, and Negro', it was those nineteenth-century meanings of 'race' that were controlling (that is, a nineteenth-century encyclopaedia narrowly 'described race in terms of ethnic groups', and others 'divided the Arabs into a number of subsidiary races', and 'represented the Hebrews as of the Semitic race', or 'referred to Arabs, Jews' and some white ethnic groups 'as separate races').[19] To further substantiate this historical instantiation of 'race', the Court cited the historical record of the debates over the nineteenth-century Civil Rights and Voting Acts[20] to show that Scandinavians, Chinese, Latinos, Spaniards, Jews, Anglo-Saxons, Blacks and others were referred to as distinct 'races'.[21] Accordingly, the Court said it had little difficulty concluding that Congressional statutory provisions relating to discrimination do reach more than 'racial' discrimination *per se* (in terms of skin colour) because 'Congress intended also to protect from discrimination identifiable classes of persons who are subjected to intentional discrimination solely because of their ancestry or ethnic characteristics.'[22]

By this reasoning the Court fashioned its legal nexus between a nineteenth-century conception of 'race' and present-day Jews as a protected class. In doing so, it also potentially signified what some Jews feared, even for the purposes of civil rights enforcement: legal identification as members of a separate, distinct, or 'different race'. In this respect, whatever its benefits on the policy side of things, this signification also resonates with that deep, virtually primeval, fear of how antagonistic 'others' or (even) governments can situate Jews as a racial group. As such, and apart from Jewish concerns, this nexus serves as a semiotic marker for that always-present, and potentially troublesome, risk that all identity politics confronts upon entering the legal arena: losing (some degree of) cultural

17 By virtue of this move, the Court tacitly rejects the claim that what counts as 'racial' discrimination should include the victim's conception of his/her 'race'. But it tacitly accepts the claim that the victim is a member of a protected group if generally or historically that person has been perceived to be a member of a 'racial' group by non-racists (in this instance, members of Congress in the nineteenth century).

18 *Saint Francis College v. Al-Khazraji*, 481 U.S. 604, at 610, 611, 611, 611 respectively.

19 *Saint Francis College v. Al-Khazraji*, 481 U.S. 604, at 612.

20 The Civil Rights Acts of 1866 and the Voting Rights Act of 1870 are treated as foundational for understanding the sweep of the statutory provisions at issue.

21 *Saint Francis College v. Al-Khazraji*, 481 U.S. 604, at 612.

22 *Saint Francis College v. Al-Khazraji*, 481 U.S. 604, at 613.

control over the shape and status of their group-identity, even if the law speaks on their behalf.[23]

To return to risks to Jewish group-identity, it has been widely commented upon that in the context of Jewish existential and historical victimhood, linking American Jewish group-identity and a nineteenth-century legislative history and statutory intent is a potential double quandary. On the plus side, the nexus is beneficial because it is compatible with the litigants' objection to twentieth-century scientific conceptions of 'race' as a criterion for constituting the category of 'racial' animus. However, on the minus side, this nexus confirms the Fourth Circuit's finding in *Saint Francis College* that persons of genetically or physiognomically identifiable traits are among those citizens that Congress intended to protect by providing for relief from discrimination.[24] The minus side potentially outweighs the plus to the extent it indicates that a Court that endorses the criteria of genetic and physiognomic traits gestures in the direction of scientific figurations of 'race' (Lopez 1994, 17), and, in doing so, manifests the Court's apparent incapacity to reject those 'biologically tainted racial beliefs' (Lopez 1994, 17) that make some Jews so very anxious.

On the plus side, coming down primarily on the side of legislative history and statutory intent rather than scientific categories of 'race' and 'ethnicity' signifies that 'race' and 'ethnicity' are primarily political constructions, established via legislative choices made in specifiable historical circumstances in relation to debates about social fact considerations. This could be interpreted as signifying endorsement for treating 'race' and 'ethnicity' as a social construction ('race' discrimination based on a perpetrator's intent and perceptions), thereby providing reasons for seeing its gesture toward scientific constructions of 'race' and 'ethnicity' that fix them in 'nature' or 'biology' as, on balance, at least undermined if not false and pernicious.

Yet, on the minus side, the otherwise welcome gesture toward the social construction of 'race' (if that is what it is) is a limited one, narrowed, as it were, by the Court's nineteenth-century historicism. There is a broad (or let us call it a generous) social construction of race (favoured in identity politics) which carries with it the idea that 'race' and 'ethnicity' are characterised by persistent temporal variations making 'race' and 'ethnicity' fluid and dynamic ways of thinking about group-identity. Advocates of the social construction of race favour this broad view because it is compatible with intersectionality, and with the identity politics of groups choosing appropriate constructions of race based on their sense of appropriate political strategies and tactics. But when the Court speaks (favourably) as it does in this case, its social constructionism actually fixes or 'essentialises' (inappropriately reduces to a single form) 'race' and 'ethnicity' in terms of

23 'When governmental power is mobilized to invest group categories with significance and to assign individuals to those categories, the use of identity groupings can injure as easily as it can help' (Minow 1996, 672).

24 *Saint Francis College v. Al-Khazraji*, 481 U.S. 604, at 613.

nineteenth-century politics, and that officially narrows 'race' and 'ethnicity' much as any scientific conception that depends upon 'nature' or 'biology'. The minus side outweighs the plus side when the Court's historical essentialism, legitimising a past-oriented construction of 'racial' animus, frustrates the present-day litigation strategy to have the law acknowledge a civil rights remedy based on the *perpetrators'* perception of Jews in 'racial' terms.

By way of recapitulation, the quandary here is that, notwithstanding a policy victory, the law of legally identifiable traits in *Shaare Tefila Congregation* is constituted by complex signals that simultaneously provide opportunities for political and legal strategies for legal remedies that simultaneously open up litigants to unintended, unanticipated and unwelcome consequences. The quandary of when the Court and law speak in this way is evidence of the law's decidedly mixed messages, and disquiet about the law. With this in mind, it is time to turn to a case study which demonstrates some of the potential implications of the quandary when the law today speaks about acts of intolerance and threats to group identity.

Disquiet about law: a case study

As a prelude to the case study, consider what was indicated earlier – that today, for a variety of reasons,[25] colleges and universities have become sites of perceived anti-Semitic incidents. A matter of significant concern to the Jewish community, one legal issue that has arisen out of these incidents is whether Title VI of the Civil Rights Act of 1964, prohibiting discrimination on the basis of race, colour or national origin in institutions receiving funding from the Federal government, prohibits acts of anti-Semitic harassment of students and/or faculty on a campus. (The potential penalty for institutions that are found to be in violation of Title VI is the loss of Federal funds.) However, and despite *Shaare Tefila Congregation*'s nexus between Jews, race and the Civil Rights Act of 1866, the US Department of Education's Office for Civil Rights (OCR), until 2004, held that Jews were not a distinct 'race' or 'ethnic' group in relation to Title VI (based on contemporary social scientific and conventional understandings of Jews). Then, in 2004, the OCR reversed its holding, in part following *Shaare Tefila Congregation*, indicating that anti-Semitic harassment did indeed fall under the prohibitions of the 1964 Act (Marcus 2007, 85).[26]

To be sure, there are credible arguments on either side as to whether Title VI should be interpreted to include Jews (or, more generally, religious groups) under the umbrella of its protection. But these do not concern us here. Regardless of them, the point is that on the surface the pre-2004 holding appears to be a straightforward reason for disquiet about the law's efficaciousness as an instrument

25 *See* Marcus 2007, 842–850.

26 Marcus 2007, 859. Arguably, the intent of Congress was to exclude religious discrimination from Title VI protections (Marcus 2007, 858).

of social change: first, from a policy perspective the pre-2004 holding conflicts with the Shaare Tefila Congregation's litigation strategy to include Jews under the umbrella of anti-discrimination statutes. Second, and at a deeper and even more troublesome level, there appears to be good reason for disquiet because the pre-2004 holding is arguably legally and conceptually consistent with *Shaare Tefila Congregation*'s social constructionism. It can be understood as legally consistent with social constructionism because, at the time Title VI became law, Jews were not considered a distinct 'race' or 'ethnic' group, either on a social scientific basis or on conventional terms. And it can be understood to be conceptually consistent with social constructionism at the level to which constructions of 'race' and 'ethnicity' are expected to vary over time and context. In relation to Jews and anti-discrimination law, that the definitions of 'race' and 'ethnicity' in the 1866 Civil Rights Act are different from the pre-2004 reading of Title VI law also reveals how 'social constructionism' can yield welcome policy results in one context and unwelcome results in another context. This is not only evidence of how the complex signals that constitute the law can turn against advocates. At least in instances such as this, it appears that irony is an appropriate companion of disquiet about the law and confidence in it. It is also worth noting that the post-2004 OCR holding, which is (apparently) a policy success, confirming Shaare Tefila Congregation's litigation strategy, is also an indicator of the limits of the law's efficaciousness, since this policy victory (if that is what it is) that satisfies legal aspirations for social change depends upon a political exogenous factor (the OCR) rather than the law itself. (More will be made of the use of the parenthetic 'apparently' shortly).

Irony also reveals itself in the interplay between the Shaare Tefila Congregation's holding and the exogenous role of the OCR as a political institution because the post-2004 holding actually does nothing to settle the legal and conceptual issues identified above. In fact, in 2006 the US Commission on Civil Rights requested that Congress settle the issue whether Title VI should protect Jews from anti-Semitic harassment (Marcus 2007, 862). Of course, the move from the judiciary to a bureaucracy and then to Congress only amplifies the role of exogenous factors, and thereupon the extent to which Jewish interests are dependent on the state in ways over which they have (comparatively or relatively) less control, and thereupon are that much more vulnerable to the vicissitudes of party, partisan, Congressional, Presidential and electoral politics.

Vulnerability to the vicissitudes of politics is also to be associated with the question of the extent to which the post-2004 holding might be only an *apparent* policy victory for Jewish concerns about acts of intolerance and threats to their self-identity. Consider the implications of a location shift in purported anti-Semitic incidents, from synagogues to college or university campuses. The aspect of this shift that I want to highlight is how it complicates implications of Jewish intersectionality and confidence in the law. You will recall the premise that, by and large, Jews are socially and economically secure in the polity. I want to argue that, even so, and taking into account variation in anxieties and fears about the harms of acts of intolerance and threats to group-identity, it is reasonable to contend that the potential negative consequences of any association between Jewishness and race in the context of seeking legal relief from discrimination are more likely to be tangible on campus than synagogues. The use of the term 'tangible' is meant to convey the difference between psychologically significant fears and anxieties (as in the synagogue context) and fears and anxieties related to social conditions and others' behaviour. In contrast to the synagogue context, the comparative intimacy of a campus situates Jews so that they are potentially in regular contact, as purported 'victims', with their purported 'victimisers' and others who might react in unintended, unanticipated or unwelcome ways to Jews seeking legal relief from 'racial' discrimination. In turn, this context makes political vicissitudes more immediate and that has a correspondingly more direct impact on the consequences of having confidence in the law.

To understand why this might be, consider the following (perhaps overly dramatic but nonetheless plausible) hypothetical situation. Imagine a campus where a group of domestic and international students (including those from the Middle East) request and receive permission to hold another of what have been a number of rallies protesting against Israeli policies in the occupied territories of the West Bank and Gaza as well as what is referred to as American complicity in the oppression of the Palestinian people. Banners and signs in the past have included references to 'Zionism as Racism', 'Fascism' and 'Militarism.' The campus has also experienced noisy and aggressively pro-Israel, pro-Zionist and pro-American rallies as well. This time around, the rally was prompted by especially intense series of cross-retaliatory violence in the West Bank and Gaza. For this rally, students cover the cement floor of the campus central plaza (routinely used for student gatherings, political and otherwise) with red and black chalked graffiti. The graffiti include their standard political fare, but this time there are a few more aggressive scripts, including a swastika imposed on the Israeli flag, caricatures of persons with big noses and German World War II military helmets, and here and there the phrase appears 'A Curse on the Jew' and 'Death to the Jew Oppressor'.[27]

As this rally progresses, a speaker becomes energised and protests that American policy in the Middle East is part of broader policy driven largely by a capitalist coalition that includes a domestic and international Jewish political, media and financial hegemony (remember, this is a campus). As the rally draws

---

27 Here I play off an incident in Sweden, in 2006, where the Chancellor of Justice, Goran Lambertz, ended an investigation to determine whether anti-Semitic tapes sold in the Great Mosque in Stockholm violated Sweden's laws prohibiting 'incitement against an ethnic group'. Lambertz concluded that the expression 'Jihad is called for, to kill the Jews, whereby suicide bombers – celebrated as martyrs – are the most effective weapon' is not a crime in Sweden because the expression is made in the context of the conflict in the Middle East. In the spirit of full disclosure: Goran Lambertz is a family friend and we have twice had extended discussions about this issue that included a comparison of Swedish and US law and politics related to free speech and expression.

on its own energy, the concluding speaker, a domestic student, asserts that there can be no middle ground in a conflict over oppression, makes references to Nazi Germany and Darfur, and asserts that Jews are the economic and political agents of harms perpetrated against Islamic peoples and people of colour and faith in the Third World generally. The speaker's remarks end with the demand for the end of Israel as 'colonial state', either by non-violent or, if necessary, violent means, and burns an Israeli flag before a cheering crowd to the chant of 'Palestinian Death Requires Jewish Death'.

A few days after the rally, Jewish organisations on campus submit a petition to the president of the institution. It is signed by a constellation of students similar in composition to those at the rally, calling on the president to punish the organisers of the rally and its speakers. The text of the petition asserts that the rally created a hostile environment for learning and teaching on campus, that Jewish students feel that their self-identity as students and Jews has been traduced, and that the administration was responsible for allowing an environment where 'racist', 'fascist' and 'Islamic terrorist' individuals have created a 'clear and present danger' to others on campus. The petition further asserts that the administration was responsible for stopping the rally when it spun 'out of control', and that, in not doing so, was now responsible for a 'radically hostile environment' for, in particular, Jewish students on campus. The petition concludes by putting the administration on notice that the Jewish student organisations intend to file a Title VI grievance (remember this is a campus) to the effect that administration must discipline rally organisers and participants, establish 'racial awareness' training on campus, and provide counselling for student and faculty 'victims of alleged racial harassment'.

The administration's response is to acknowledge the need for a voluntary programme of 'racial awareness' on campus and for counselling students and faculty who perceive themselves to be victims (for whatever reasons) of racial, ethnic, gender and sexual (but not religious) discrimination on campus. But the administration is adamant that rally participants were engaged in protected political speech and symbolic expression on campus, regardless of whatever unfortunate excesses might have occurred. It also states that, on advice of university counsel and the trustees of the institution, the administration is prepared to challenge a Title VI grievance both on the basis of academic freedom and because it believes that the pre-2004 holding was rightly decided and that Jews are not, in fact, a protected group as intended by Title VI regulations. All of this – the rally, the petition and threat of a Title VI grievance, and the counter-response – has the potential to create a scenario wherein aspirations to use the law actually instigate a 'lose:lose' environment for those with confidence in the law as a political and social remedy.

Even if the 'racial awareness' programme and counselling are viewed as collective benefits for students and faculty generally, the risk to be considered in this scenario is that the very threat of a Title VI grievance (whether or not there is a finding against the institution) could be viewed as a collective cost by students and faculty generally. The logic here is that a Title VI grievance, in and of itself, could trigger the complaint of 'playing the race card', which is to say, the accusation that 'race' has been insinuated into a political controversy in order to undeservedly exploit its emotional cache and thereby underscore the illegitimacy of opponents' points of view (in general, the political voices of those who oppose Israeli and American policies and, more specifically, the voices of minorities and the marginalised on campus such as Middle Eastern students). And, whether or not there is a finding against the institution, a Title VI grievance could well be viewed by a majority on campus as an attempt to exploit the law and enjoin the power of the government to limit freedom of speech and expression on campus.

In this campus scenario, in contrast to the plausibly more sympathetic context of using the law to protect a house of worship, a Title VI grievance risks the unsympathetic response that the advocates of a Title VI grievance exploit the law to have it speak for their own political purposes in a way which is altogether at odds with the basic principles and values of both anti-discrimination law and an institution of higher learning the advocates claim to be their home. Specifically, accusations of playing the race card and attempting to trump freedom of speech and expression on campus are certainly compatible with the perhaps conventional legal view that chalked phrases like 'A Curse on the Jew', the words at the rally, and the chant 'Palestinian Death Requires Jewish Death' are not, in and of themselves, fighting words'[28] – that is, they do not cross the line of protected speech and expression because the words are not personally abusive in the sense of being likely to provoke violent retaliatory actions (particularly if no violence against Jews has been associated with the rally). And, even if the words and actions at the rally do appear to fall into the category of protected speech and expression, what of the social fact that there are those who felt threatened or intimidated by words and action that were arguably obnoxious, offensive or even hurtful in relation to group-identity? Even so, assertions about a 'radically hostile environment' are plausibly counter-balanced by the constitutional doctrine that, on balance, the greater harm arises when the governmental force regulates the content and viewpoints of citizens.[29] And for those inclined to look at the petition as playing the race card, exploiting the law, and enjoining power of the government to limit speech and expression, the pre-2004 OCR holding and the post-2004 continuing uncertainty about Jews, 'race', *Shaare Tefila Congregation* and Title VI give all the more reason to side with the administration.

---

28 The doctrine of fighting words is that the government can punish the expression of specific words if, as a matter of everyday knowledge, those words are sufficiently abusive to provoke an ordinary citizen to a violent response. See *Chaplinsky v. New Hampshire*, 315 U.S. 568 (1954).

29 The doctrine here, in effect, is that what constitutes fighting words cannot be determined solely on the basis of the content of speech and expression motivated by ideology or racial animus. See *R.A.V. v. Saint Paul, Minnesota*, 505 U.S. 377 (1992).

Under circumstances like these, because of its lose:lose dynamics, there is a more than ample basis for disquiet about the law. On the one hand, it is a loss if a Title VI grievance is unsuccessful: political and ideological conflict being what it is, and, appropriately or not, failure to get the law to speak on the behalf of a Title VI grievance reinforces the accusation that the race card was being played. It is also a loss because an unsuccessful claim gives some vindication to the contention of political expediency and that grievance advocates were willing to manipulate law and sacrifice the good of the institution for their own political ends. Disquiet about comes into play here twice: the law and exogenous factors disappoint aspirations for a legal remedy for purported discrimination, and the very use of the law has immediate unintended and unwelcome (if not necessarily unanticipated) consequences.

On the other hand, it is a loss if the grievance is successful because politics and ideology being what they are, the law having spoken on behalf of grievance advocates is not likely to change opponents' minds about the race card being played, or about good uses of the law or the good of the institution. Ironically, disquiet about the law comes into play here because a policy success risks the same losses associated with a policy failure. Under these circumstances, at least in the short term, the law disappoints as an agent of social change because it risks aggravating anti-Jewish and perhaps anti-Semitic sentiments (for example, accusations about the race card and sacrificing the good of the institution to Jewish interests). To the extent this loss:loss could be anticipated, Jewish confidence in the law (and by extrapolation, minority confidence in the law generally?) runs the risk of marginalisation and forces Jews (or by extrapolation, a minority group) to confront the dilemma of acting on their sense of 'Jewishness' (or group identity) in terms of 'racial' and 'ethnic' markers of citizenship on the one hand and sustaining assimilation in academic life (or by extrapolation, an intimate community) on the other hand. Note that this dilemma appears to confirm the concerns of those Jewish organisations, which originally opposed a litigation strategy to reconstruct and transform civil rights law to include protection of Jews as a 'race' for fear of its consequences.

Even apart from lose:lose situations, the path to social change is almost certainly marked by (sometimes significant) short-term material and symbolic costs. How then to evaluate the gap between what might be short-term losses attributable to semiotic indeterminacy and exogenous factors and longer-term confidence in the law? This question brings to a head the complexities and uncertainties that this chapter's analysis of semiotic indeterminacy and exogenous factors has characterised. As foreshadowed in the introduction, the answer to the question about maintaining confidence in the law is embedded in complexities and uncertainties, and they should dash any response in the form of blanket generalisations.

Conclusion

Perhaps unintended, unanticipated and unwelcome consequences that follow in the wake of semiotic variability and the impact of exogenous factors are more or less inevitable phenomena. Presumably, as the previous case study is meant to illustrate, those consequences can be expected to be especially significant for minority and marginalised groups, regardless of whether they are more or less vulnerable in social, economic and/or political terms. Consequently, the point of this chapter is to suggest that commentary about semiotic variability, exogenous factors and confidence in the law in relation to minority and marginalised groups should be presumed to require revision, qualification and, to some degree, even invalidation. This would be semiotic commentary with a pragmatic sensibility.

Apropos of what has gone on in this chapter, semiotic commentary with a pragmatic sensibility presumes that the implications of significations of 'race' or 'ethnicity' (or 'gender' and others like them) raise puzzling and confusing questions about the benefits and costs of confidence in the law. Primarily this is because, by its very nature, the law as an assembly of complex symbols and exogenous factors makes what count as costs and benefits of using the law a matter of dispute. Thus, there is no way around the conclusion that answers to questions about confidence in the law will have multiple and competing answers. Of course, a pragmatic sensibility requires that the previous sentence be subject to revision, qualification and, to some degree, invalidation based on specific case-by-case analysis. That is to say, what we have found at work in the implications of *Shaare Tefila Congregation* might be different in degree or kind from what might be found in other circumstances and in relation to other groups and their use of the law.

Even so, pragmatism's attention to unanticipated, unintended and unwelcome consequences suggests that confidence in the law will be justified *despite* positive policy implications not because of them, but rather because those positive implications are almost always off set by uncertain costs and consequences. What this uncertainty has meant for concepts like 'race' and 'ethnicity' in this chapter, for example, is that legal aspirations are not likely to be achieved on anything close to their intended goals (Strauber 2003, 511). Consequently, and this is both essential and disconcerting, a pragmatic approach to semiotics blocks appeals to any moral or ideological high ground when arguing about confidence in the law.

The lack of a high ground does not mean that there is no room for moral or ideological principles in semiotic analysis of the law. What it does mean is that principles should not carry any more weight than (indeterminate) cost and benefit considerations allow. Here again is the theme of revision, qualification and, in some instances, invalidation. In semiotic analysis, the efficaciousness of legal principles, as is the case with confidence in the law, can never be much more than the expression of a provisional claim that is mindful of uncertainties associated with law's significations. If this implication is too stringent for some scholars then an alternative implication of pragmatism (with its lack of a high ground) that does not elide the uncertainties of the law's significations is to make conclusive claims about confidence in the law, but only as rhetorical 'improvisations'.[30] Such claims identify themselves as improvisational by specific acknowledgment that they are ultimately dependent on a scholar's policy predilections and ideology, and that semiotic analysis can just as well justify competing claims.

If this implication is too accommodating then a third implication of pragmatism (with its lack of a high ground) is that semiotic commentary, by its very nature, cannot help but put a scholar in a quandary between the inclination to be provisional or to be conclusory. In this quandary the only recourse for semiotic analysis is to imbue itself with self-avowed 'contradiction, irony, alienation, [and] despair' (Kennedy 1997, 346)[31] in order to try to dislocate closure about being either provisional or conclusory (Kennedy 1997, 339–64). What I have tried to do in this chapter is to indicate that an ever-cautious weather eye about the law's significations can be pragmatic in all three of its implications.

30 This alternative implication of pragmatism is extrapolated from Stanley Fish's discussion of a pragmatic approach to multiculturalism (Fish 1999, 63–5).

31 In this sentence I have appropriated Kennedy's words about the implications of his 'leftist and a modernist-postmodernist point of view' (Kennedy 1997, 1) for my own purposes.

Chapter 3
Mediated Semiosis in the Courtroom: Non-Verbal Communicators and the Usefulness of Audio Video Technology as a Tool by which to Oversee Justice

Isabell Petrinic

Introduction: video link technology as legal mediation

The often-repeated allegations of 'verballing', or the fabricating of evidence by police, led to the introduction of the Police and Criminal Evidence Act (PACE) 1984 in England, which placed as a matter of legal requirement the onus on police, whenever possible, to make a contemporaneous audio or video recording of verbal evidence (Coulthard 2004, 19). In Australia, the High Court decision *McKinney and Judge v the Queen* (1991) similarly recognised the dangers of 'verballing' by police by establishing as a general rule of application that trial judges must warn juries of the dangers of convicting on the basis of a disputed confession, unless the making of it can be corroborated by video and/or audio tape (Bronitt 2002, 65), serving to emphasise the important role video technology now plays in the recording of confessional evidence. As was pointed out by Dawson J in *McKinney v the Queen* (1991), a fair trial is one that is fair to both sides. The adage 'Justice can be seen to be done' can, however, best be exemplified in the use of (audio-visual) video link technology in today's courtrooms (Lienert 1992, preface).

Video-linked courts are courts connected to another room inside a prison, from which the inmate 'appears' in a court matter without physically leaving the correctional centre. The court video system, as a cultural apparatus of the state,[1]

1 The New South Wales Government of Australia provides custodial and community-based correctional services to its public via the Department of Community Services. The New South Wales Government Department of Corrective Services, along with six other agencies, has now implemented operational videoconferencing studios across the state. The primary aim of these studios is to facilitate the hearing of mentions, inmates' bail applications and other nominated court matters without the use of external escorts. Since the implementation of videoconferencing within the justice agencies in 2001, the Legal Aid Commission (an independent statutory body established under the Legal Aid Commission Act 1979) along with its public defenders has used videoconferencing to take instructions

uses an instrument of mediation to administer justice. A camera in the room transmits in 'real time' sound-images of inmates to a television monitor inside the courtroom, placing the technology 'between the seer and the seen in a position of mediation' (Ihde 1990, 73) in so far as the inmate sees the courtroom 'through' the camera lens, putting him or her at once in the courtroom and on the other side of the media (the optics). The ambition of the legal semiotic enterprise therefore would be 'to be a text in and on jurisprudence' (Rush 1990, 123).

It is through the study of semiotics that one comes to see how, from the standpoint of those on the other side of the television screen, the sound-image of the inmate can come to 'stand for' the actual inmate, even as it becomes an extension of his or human body; albeit an impersonal and estranged one. It is by such means that the judge or magistrate, the prosecutor and defence lawyer, are able to question the inmate and observe his or her feedback in a range of semiotic systems (tone of voice, expression, behaviour, etc.). Face-to-face confrontation has, as it were, been supplanted by instant interface. One could even say that audio-visual technology has now begun to reproduce the actual movement of bodies by such means displaying, in Peircean[2] terms, a 'genuine relation' between the 'sign' (significantly, the 'representamen' (and not necessarily physical) form of the inmate) and the object (the actual inmate). To borrow a line from Peirce (1931 in Chandler 2002) this relation does not depend purely on the 'interpreting mind' (Chandler 2002, 41). The majority of people in Western cultures have an affinity with the logonomic rules of a television as a text and thus will understand without prompting that the sound-image on the courtroom monitor 'is' in fact the accused. They will, in their role as interpretant, connect the sign and its object through a careful study of the cues 'on the box', such as, among others, the inmate's non-verbal behaviour.

Semioticians are familiar with the subject of non-verbal communication in the context of proxemics (the immediate closeness to the body). It is the intention of this chapter to critically analyse how meanings are made and how reality is represented in the courtroom via this computer-mediated interpersonal tool of communication commonly referred to as a 'prison video link' in NSW[3] and in

---

from their clients in New South Wales correctional centres. The technology is also used in special circumstances in place of family visits.

2 The two dominant models of what constitutes a sign are those of the Swiss linguist Ferdinand de Saussure and the American philosopher Charles Sanders Peirce (Chandler 2002, 17). In his book, *Semiotics – the Basics*, Chandler (2002) explains Peirce's three modes of signs: symbolic, iconic and indexical. Indexical signs, to which I am here referring, 'direct the attention to their objects by blind compulsion' (Peirce 1931, 58, 2.306, in Chandler 2002, 37).

3 New South Wales (abbreviated as NSW) is Australia's most populous state, located in the far east of the country, north of Victoria and south of Queensland. The estimated population of NSW at the end of June 2007 from Australian Demographic Statistics was 6.89 million people. There were a total of 27,244 prisoners (sentenced and un-sentenced) in Australian jails on the night of 30 June 2007, when the national prisoner census was

other parts of the world. As part of this social enquiry, I will also critically analyse the court video system as a process of non-verbal communication and the value of video technology as a tool through which to administer justice.

Few would argue with the genuine benefits afforded to society by this semiotic system which transmits images or signs of human beings from prisons into courtrooms, where their (non-verbal) performance may be judged by, thus far, litigants, judges and lawyers. Academic studies argue that because the inmate is not required to remove his or her body from the correctional facility at which he or she has been placed in order to appear before the court, the practical advantages of the prison video link technology have consequently included savings in transportation and personnel costs, reduction in security problems[4] and in waiting times for both the courts and those in custody, less interruption to inmate education and rehabilitation programmes, and reduced risk of contraband introduction to correctional centres (Archbold 2005; Gibson 2006; Hatzistergos 2005; Sharp 2004; Quock 1998; Vertigan 2005). This is not, however, a cost–benefit analysis, nor is it an attempt to undermine public confidence in the Australian justice system.

The right for anyone charged with a criminal offence to defend himself or herself in person or through legal assistance of his or her choosing is covered in article 14 of the International Covenant on Civil and Political Rights and article 6 of the European Convention for the Protection of Human Rights and Fundamental Freedoms, which are aimed at guaranteeing fair and public hearings by independent tribunals in both civil and criminal cases. At the same time, the requirement to appear in person is satisfied by an appearance by video link (Evidence (Audio

---

conducted, which represented a rise of 4 per cent, or 163 prisoners, from 30 June 2006 and an increase of 23 per cent from 30 June 1997 (137 prisoners). Based on current figures there is an imprisonment rate of 195.4 prisoners per 100,000 adult population in NSW, compared to 169.4 Australia-wide (Australian Bureau of Statistics website, 2008).

4 Each day staff in NSW court complexes are punched, kicked, bitten and spat on, according to *Daily Telegraph* reporters Martin Wallace and Kelvin Bissett in 'Courting Violence: 67 Prison Officers Hurt by Criminals' (*Daily Telegraph* 2004). Citing figures from the Australian Bureau of Statistics, the authors reported that 67 prison officers were assaulted by prison inmates within court buildings in 2002. One of the injured officers had to undergo an AIDS test. Fifteen prison officers required treatment to head wounds and a further 14 suffered bodily injuries. Another five were bitten, seven received injuries after being pushed, one was hurt by a thrown object and another suffered a back injury. Wallace and Bissett stated that most injuries were meted out by desperate prisoners trying to escape before being sentenced. In an address to the NSW Legislative Council on 6 May 2004, Bob Debus observed that in 2003 the NSW Government 'took steps to ensure that sheriff's officers are trained and equipped with capsicum spray, a significant deterrent for anybody who is bent on disrupting court proceedings or, for instance, menacing a victim in court' (Debus 2004). In theory, use of the prison video link obviates the need for this practice altogether.

and Audio Visual Links) Act 1998 (NSW) s 3A).[5] The court may also order the attendance of the detainee if it is satisfied that it is in the interests of justice for the accused detainee to appear physically before the court (Evidence (Audio and Audio Visual Links) Act 1998 (NSW) s 5BA (4)), showing at once the two modes of appearance by the accused that are, according to Nancy (1993), 'the same (not identical) in their difference' (Nancy 1993, 40). As duly noted by Wallace (2001), 'the issue is not the technology, but rather, how we use it' (Nancy 1993, 10), which leads one to question whether more familiarity with the technology will lead to a greater, although perhaps different, access to justice.

Chief Magistrate Sue Kluss observed in Practice Note 5/2007 that whilst audio-visual appearances have been in operation now for some time in NSW there has been no evaluation of the current scheme, particularly from the perspective of prisoners and confidence in the impact of technology on justice generally. The findings from a Law and Justice Foundation of NSW roundtable conducted with community and non-government organisations on 16 October 2002 revealed that most research into prisoners' legal needs is undertaken by the NSW Government Department of Corrective Services, and is mainly statistically based. Round-table participants reported that there is very little independent qualitative-based research into prisoners' needs, as there is very little opportunity for independent researchers to gain access to current prisoners within the NSW prison system. Contributors also reported that research into the legal needs of people who face multiple disadvantages is lacking. In addition, academic inquiries indicate that there has been very little research in Australia and overseas up till now that has explored how non-verbal cues influence the courts. Some of the research undertaken has however looked at how judges, attorneys and witnesses convey messages non-verbally (Blanck and Rosenthal 1992; Knapp and Hall 2002), the behavioural cues to lying (Ekman et al. 1999; Vrij and Semin 1996), and the face and body cues in the judgement of emotions (Ekman and Freisen 1967 and 1971).

Despite the growing usage of video technology in Australian courtrooms and even though scholars have long recognised that most non-verbal cues are not transmitted effectively via videoconferencing (Billinghurst and Kato 2002), there has been no research undertaken into the non-verbal cues conveyed over the video by inmates in court matters (Sharp 2004). Given the lack of research, I will maintain throughout this chapter that the courtroom of the future should not begin operating as a 'virtual' courtroom with litigants, judges and lawyers only communicating

5 The NSW Government introduced laws to parliament on 7 December 2007 to amend the Evidence (Audio and Visual Links) Act 1988. Pre-empting the new law, the NSW Attorney General John Hatzistergos remarked via a media release on the LawLink NSW website on 13 November 2007 that the Evidence (Audio and Audio Visual Links) Amendment Act 2007 No. 75 would presume in favour of using the audio-visual link for procedural matters, bail hearings, sentencing hearings and committals and that this would apply to adults and juveniles alike. Formerly, this law has only applied resolutely where adults were concerned.

electronically until the communicative properties of the medium are further investigated, thereby ensuring the equity of the system that is, for the purposes of this discussion, presently used in NSW, as well as in overseas, courtrooms. As this chapter will illustrate, audio-visual technology in its present form cannot guarantee the same access to the judicial system as a face-to-face appearance. That is not to say, however, that therein this different (virtual) performance there does not lay equal or matching justice.

The legal framework: the NSW justice model

In 1992, Lienert compared the use of videoconferencing facilities in courts and prisons in Canada, the US and the UK, crediting the successful introduction of video recording of police interviews in Western Australia[6] as a precursor to the use of video link technology in Australian courtrooms. Lienert (1992) observed that in order to determine the veracity of confessional statements made to police in Western Australia, a select committee consisting of members of the judiciary, the crown counsel, law society, Department of Correctional Services and police, and chaired by a supreme court judge, compared the number of guilty pleas and allegations made against police when video tapes were admitted into evidence in place of hand- or type-written interviews (Lienert 1992, 6). The result from this trial, which was conducted in 1987, showed a 50 per cent rise in guilty pleas and almost no allegations being made against police where video interviews were used, whilst convictions in the Perth Superior Court, which deals with trials by jury, rose from 60 per cent where videotapes were not used, compared to 93 per cent where videotaped interviews were used (Lienert 1992, 6), showing the importance of opening court procedures up to visual assessment.

A decade later, the NSW Government Department of Corrective Services trialled a real-time transmission that used radio beam technology from 1997 to 1998 before utilising the video technology in December 2001 for bail applications for remandees at the Metropolitan Reception and Remand Centre (MRRC), which is one of three correctional facilities that make up the Silverwater Correctional Complex at Silverwater in NSW. The video system has since been implemented at all maximum security remand and reception centres in NSW in partnership with the NSW Attorney General's Department, the NSW Police Force, Legal Aid, Community Relations, Public Prosecutions, Juvenile Courts and Juvenile Justice. Videoconferencing studios have been installed in NSW in regional correctional centres at Goulburn, Cessnock, Bathurst and Grafton, and in metropolitan correctional centres at Long Bay, Silverwater, Mulawa, Parklea and the MRCC (Sharp 2004). The Annexure to the Chief Magistrate's (Local Court NSW) Practice Note 5 of 2007 lists the regional local courts with audio-visual facilities

6 Western Australia is Australia's largest state in area, covering the western third of the mainland, and is bordered by South Australia and the Northern Territory.

in NSW as being located in Albury, Bathurst, Armidale, Bourke, Broken Hill, Campbelltown, Coffs Harbour, Dubbo, Gosford, Goulburn, Grafton, Griffith, Lismore, Moree, Newcastle, Orange, Port Macquarie, Tamworth, Wagga Wagga, Walgett, Wentworth, Wollongong and Woy Woy. Metropolitan courts with audio-visual facilities in NSW are shown to be at Bankstown, Blacktown, Burwood, Central, Liverpool, Mount Druitt, Parramatta, Penrith and Sutherland, according to the Annexure.[7]

Today, corrective services employ video technology in NSW for bail applications for remandees, court matters such as mentions and stand-over matters, and for regional serious offender review hearings and assessments of revoked periodic detention.[8] Since implementing the technology on 24 February 2004, the NSW Parole Board has conducted all of its custody matters via videoconferencing. Other states, such as Tasmania, have expanded its use to include civil hearings, arraignments and civil and criminal trials, following the model of overseas jurisdictions. Wallace (2001) notes that in Victoria, on at least one occasion, videoconferencing technology has been used to bring a substitute magistrate 'online' to a country court to overcome difficulties caused by the unanticipated absence of a resident magistrate, leading her to pose the question: 'If the judicial officer can participate in that way, why not the jury?' (Wallace 2001, 7–8). Turning for one moment to issues of access, fairness and social justice, even the introduction of the Evidence (Audio and Audio Visual Links) Amendment Bill 2007 has not removed the need for an inmate to make his or her first appearance before the court in person, suggesting, for the time being at least, that the courts and counsel are still only comfortable with using the technology for parts of the trial process even if, according to Wallace (2001, 7), 'its use to date does not seem to have given rise to any great objection'.

---

7 Interestingly, anecdotal information suggests that inmates housed in NSW prisons that so far have not had video conferencing booths installed are being driven to other prisons so that they may 'appear' in court via video link. In separate personal communications Vertigan (2005) and Gibson (2006) made reference to NSW inmates housed at Parramatta prison in O'Connell Street, North Parramatta, being driven 7.6 kilometres (roughly 15 minutes travelling by car) by prison personnel to Silverwater Correctional Centre (which is the nearest correctional centre with a videoconferencing studio) to 'appear' in court via video link, even though there is a court about five minutes' drive from the prison at 1–3 George Street, Parramatta, where they could make an in-person (physical) appearance instead. Neither Vertigan nor Gibson could explain why this practice persisted although both felt it defied logic, when there was a court house nearby to which the inmates could be driven and in consequence minimise interruption to the prisoner's routine. The new changes to the Audio and Audio Visual Links Act do not deal with this anomaly.

8 As at 28 December 2007, the NSW Attorney General's Department had installed 166 audio-visual link (AVL) systems in courtrooms, correctional facilities and other justice agencies sites across NSW (LawLink website 2007). Furthermore, the NSW Government had allocated an extra $A2.9 million in its 2007/08 budget to continue to expand and improve its AVL network to courts, Legal Aid and correctional facilities in rural and regional areas.

Video links are also employed by the prison system to enable women, who, according to the 2006 National Prisoner Census, currently account for 7 per cent of the total Australian prison population, to maintain relationships with their children. However, there have been obstacles to its successful implementation. Sharp stated that the initial programme was

> … received well but we had to build the cold relationship between people again, tackling it via video. That was one of the big issues, whether the family would be able to adopt the technology to re-establish the relationships they once had … A lot of people in gaol have a concern [the video link] might replace their personal visits, which it certainly does not. Others are concerned about whether it's going to be taped, which we don't do, either (in Mudie 2007).

Despite the challenges that have arisen from the use of the system, among which are cost and some of the distractions associated with variable picture quality and set-up (Gibson 2006; Sharp 2004; Vertigan 2005; Wallace 2001), the number of inmates who have appeared in court via video link in NSW has more than quadrupled in the period 2002 to 2007, from 6,000 appearances in 2002 to 26,000 in 2007, with bail applications accounting for 80 per cent of all use (Hatzistergos in NSW Legislative Hansard 2005, 14398, and LawLink website 2007).[9] In an address to the NSW Legislative Council[10] on 2 March 2005 the then State[11] Justice Minister, John Hatzistergos,[12] argued that a reduced number of prisoner movements to and from correctional facilities during the 2003 calendar year had, as a consequence, led to the number of escapes from NSW jails having fallen to a record low for that period, with just 22 from a possible 8,400 prisoners absconding from correctional facilities and, for the second straight year, there were no escapes from either a maximum or medium security jail in NSW, which in turn has influenced the general sense of safety felt by people in the community.

---

9 In an address to the NSW Legislative Council on 2 March 2005, the then NSW Justice Minister, John Hatzistergos, described the main benefits of the prison video link technology, which cost $A4.1 million to implement across NSW. He cited figures released on 14 February 2005 which showed during the 2004 calendar year that 15,400 inmates had appeared in court via video link, 'reducing the number of external movements by more than 30,000 inmates, which represented an increase from 10,700 in 2003 and 6,400 in 2002 and an estimated cost avoidance of more than $A3 million each year by obviation of the need to transport inmates from correctional facilities to court' (Hatzistergos, NSW Legislative Hansard, 2005, 14398).

10 The NSW Legislative Council is the Upper House (state Senate) of the Parliament of NSW.

11 The State to which is referred is NSW.

12 John Hatzistergos was appointed the NSW Minister for Justice and the NSW Attorney General on 2 April 2007 (accurate as at 9 March 2008). He also served two years, four months and nine days as the NSW Minister for Justice from 2 April 2003 to 10 August 2005.

Australian media reports have shown that prisoners are not only at risk of escaping from correctional facilities; they have also been known to abscond from actual courtrooms. Writing for Fairfax Digital on 21 June 2005, journalist Les Kennedy described how on 30 May 2005 Steven Eatts

> … stunned guards, sheriffs and police prosecutors by climbing to the top of the two-metre, glass paneled, roofless defendant dock. He then did a balancing act, walking along its rim before jumping two metres across to the top of an ornate door leading to the vestibule. From there the alleged burglar hoisted himself 1.5 metres onto a window ledge, opened the skylight and bolted across the roof to freedom, all in 60 seconds.[13]

Three weeks after escaping from the Central Local Court[14] the 25-year-old defendant from Glebe was before the same court, this time on a big screen via an audio-visual link from Silverwater Prison, demonstrating the extent to which the text (in this case, the binary codes of virtual technology) has manufactured 'the conditions in which any distinction between the "real" and the "simulation" is confounded' (Graham 2002, 192).

Nigel Vertigan, a senior advocate with Legal Aid NSW, observed that courts would only agree to an in-person (physical) appearance if the inmate were somehow disadvantaged by a (virtual) appearance via the prison video link (Vertigan 2005). In this circumstance, the courts clearly felt Eatts would not be adversely affected by not appearing in court in the flesh. This is despite Peter Sharp, the videoconferencing coordinator for the NSW Department of Corrective Services and the person responsible for the implementation of this technology in NSW courtrooms, having described a lack of research into the communicative properties of the prison video link, both in its verbal and non-verbal forms (Sharp 2004). He stated that the communicative properties of the medium in its current form would, due to cost, remain un-researched so long as the agencies using the medium did not make formal representations for the technology to be improved which, up till then, they had not (Sharp 2004).

Of course, judges and lawyers and other agencies utilising the technology may not even be aware that a problem exists, or how to address it. However, there is a growing body of agencies who are dissatisfied with the status quo. For example, the Chief Magistrate of the Local Court of NSW, Judge D. Price, informs us that the Penrith/Mt Druitt Domestic Violence Scheme is among those of the belief that the disadvantages of the technology outweigh the benefits, although these

---

13 In a personal communication, 1 June 2005, Nigel Vertigan, a trial advocate within the NSW legal system, queried the ability of correctives service officers working within the court system to chase an 'agile youth' who was attempting to flee from a courtroom. Vertigan stated that most of the corrective services officers who are appointed to work in the court system are 'older' and/or 'nearing retirement'.

14 Central Local Court is situated in NSW, Australia.

perceived disadvantages were not expounded (Price 2003). The need for vigilance has also more recently been documented by Legal Aid NSW, which, in its 2007 annual report, highlighted as a challenge for its Criminal Law Division the need

> … to ensure the increased use of audio visual facilities is balanced against the requirements of a fair and open justice system where accused persons and witnesses can effectively engage in the justice process and the needs of clients to be able to adequately communicate with their lawyer and the court are met (Price 2003, 43).

Howell and Buxton (2002, 272) define this type of visually mediated interaction as 'a process of facilitating interaction between people, either remotely or locally, using visual cues which are often similar to those used in conventional, everyday interaction with people'.

In their study of connectionist techniques for visually mediated interaction to be used in videoconferencing, the authors distinguish between verbal and non-verbal usage, which, for the purposes of my discussion, I have also done.

Communicating in the courtroom: defining non-verbal communication

Generally, when people refer to non-verbal behaviour they talk about the signals to which meaning will be attributed, not the process of producing meaning. This may include the environmental structures and conditions within which communication takes place, the physical characteristics of the communicators themselves, and the various behaviours manifested by the communicators (Knapp and Hall 2002). Professor Albert Mehrabian, known for his pioneering work in the field of non-verbal communications since the 1960s, observed how feeling is transmitted in messages. He found that as much as 93 per cent of emotional meaning is transmitted non-verbally (Mehrabian and Ferris 1967). Mehrabian's research further indicated that in face-to-face interaction, the total affective (or emotional) meaning may be sent as follows:

- 38 per cent of the emotional meaning of the message is paralinguistic (the way that words are spoken);
- 55 per cent of the emotional meaning of the message is expressed via facial expression; and
- 7 per cent of the emotional meaning of the message is expressed verbally.

In contrast, Birdwhistell (1970) takes as a more conservative estimate that nearly two-thirds of the meaning in any social situation is derived from non-verbal cues. Therefore, if we accept the premise that our ability in non-verbal communication is important and that some people are more effective in non-verbal communication than others (Rosenthal et al. 1978) and if there is evidence to suggest that judges' attitudes and non-verbal cues may influence the outcome of a trial (Blanck and Rosenthal 1992), then we can also legitimately ask whether an inmate's attitudes and non-verbal cues can likewise influence a trial outcome.

Knapp and Hall (2002, 24) describe attorneys and witnesses who have been videotaped in pre-trial practice sessions to determine whether they are conveying non-verbally any messages they want to avoid. When a technique is videotaped and then 'broken down to frame-by-frame analysis in order to find the most efficient form of communication, it is clear that a technology has been employed to perfect a technique' (Ihde 1993, 47). Ihde (1993, 48) would argue that the technique, in this case, 'is clearly technologically implicated, although it itself is not a technology'. Accordingly, an appearance via the prison video link would likewise be technologically implicated.

Krampen (1997, 90), drawing on Pross (1972), points out that for mediated semiosis to work, 'the sender or both sender and receiver need to introduce some kind of equipment in between them in order to communicate successfully'. In the case of the prison video link, all the participants in the court proceedings need equipment, as is shown in Figure 3.1. Chandler (2002, 3) points out that 'the more frequently and fluently a medium is used, the more "transparent" or "invisible" to its users it tends to become'. Litigants, judges, and lawyers in today's courtrooms have become more and more practised at the use of this technology. However, an inmate, even forgetting that he or she is a repeat offender, would have very little, to no, experience with the technology.

Significantly, academic research indicates that not all inmates are given clear instructions on how to use this technology either (Archbold 2005; Gibson 2006; Sharp 2004). This is despite scholars having recognised that nearly two-thirds of the meaning in any social situation is derived from non-verbal cues (Birdwhistell 1970). Speaking from a prisoner's standpoint, former prison inmate Chris Nursanlo[15] suggested that the prison link procedure was so inherently complex and prison personnel so inadequately trained that this must necessarily impact on the proper use of the video technology by inmates. In a personal communication on 14 October 2004 he stated that when he 'appeared' via audio-visual link to the NSW Supreme Court, he did not have legal representation and that the prison personnel did not provide him with adequate practice directions for the use of the technology. However, this is not to say that these practice directions are not available. Guidelines and practice directions, in some cases quite detailed, can be accessed via the Internet[16] though one possible concern was that prisoners

15 Chris Nursanlo was sentenced to 12 months in Cessnock Prison (in NSW) in October 2002 for driving while disqualified, negligent driving, stating false name and resisting arrest. He 'appeared' to the Supreme Court in Sydney, NSW, for an appeal of bail.

16 See, for example, the Supreme Court of New South Wales 'Protocols & Procedures for Video & Audio Link' (issued in October 2001) at <http://www.cso.nsw.gov.au/lawlink/supreme_court/ll_sc.nsf/pages/SCO_video_link/>, 12 March 2008; the Supreme Court

who were more computer-literate would be advantaged over those who were not. Lawyers and prison guards confirmed that the level of direction was indeed in many cases dependent on the goodwill of the prison personnel, leading to disparities in access. Wallace (2001, 12) argued that disparities in access, combined with a lack of common operating protocols, can 'result in a situation where the technology can be used as a weapon, rather than a tool'.

Of course, sign systems are sets of potential meanings, the output of which is the actual choices, what people say or do. However, the actual meanings made are limited by two important conditions, those of access and of context, and not everyone has access to the same educational opportunities, for instance. Notably, in Northern Australia, which includes the top end of the Northern Territory, Darwin and its environs, a large proportion of clients who will be required to communicate via videoconferencing will likely be those facing language and culture barriers, as the Yilli Rreung Regional Council stated in its submission to the Senate Legal and Constitutional Reference Committee Inquiry into Legal Aid and Access to Justice in 2003. The report from the Yilli Rreung Regional Council highlighted the council's concern at a shift from face-to-face delivery for, in its own words, 'economic reasons'. 'While they [the clients] may have physical access to justice, this will not necessarily translate to a real understanding of the legal advice, representation and process being undertaken,' the report claimed (Yilli Rreung Regional Council 2003, 4). As contended by Jackson, 'the reader of the legal text cannot understand that text without a pre-existing body of knowledge' (in Rush 1990, 124).

The logonomic rules coming out of the court video system are specific to that environment. However, in this set of circumstances we have a 'modified body that becomes a commodified body' (Staiano-Ross 2005, 73). It is saleable because the technology that communicates the literal body is purchased by the hour,[17] and this meaningful unit is necessarily made different when, according to Pederson (2005), 'we translate a person's physical movement to positive signs in language'.

---

of Tasmania 'Video Conferencing Guidelines' at <http://www.supremecourt.tas.gov.au/about_us/courtroom_technology/video_conferencing_guidelines/>, 12 March 2008; and the Magistrates' Court Victoria Practice Direction No. 10 of 2004 'Video Conferencing Guidelines' at <http://www.magistratescourt.vic.gov.au/CA256902000FE154/Lookup/Chief_Magistrates_Directions/$file/pd1004.pdf/>, 12 March 2008.

17 See, for example, the Federal Court of Australia 'Charging For Use of Videoconferencing' Press Release (1 February 2005), which states that, from 1 February 2005, transmission costs for a video link would cost between $A9 per completed 15 minutes for 128 kilobytes (KB) per second @ $A36 per hour to $A28 per completed 15 minutes for 384 kbps (the standard speed for videoconferencing) @ $A112 per hour. All charges are inclusive of GST. Charges may also apply for other costs incurred by the court, for example for a cancelled video link or for video links undertaken outside normal business hours.

Embodying the technology

The praxis is non-verbal communication in so far as inmates see the courtroom through the camera lens and it places video link technology in a position of legal mediation. As stated by Ihde (1990, 73), 'the technology is actually between the seer [the inmate] and the seen [the courtroom] … but the referent of the seeing [the judiciary], towards which sight is directed, is "on the other side" of the optics', creating a series of removes that take us further from the truth whilst purporting to bring us closer to it.

Ihde (1990, 73) observes that if the technology, in this case the camera lens, is transparent enough, 'then it becomes possible to embody the technology'; however, therein lies the problem because, as previously acknowledged, 'embodying must be learned' (Ihde 1990, 73) and in the case of the video link the appearance is often a first-time experience of the technology for the inmate. In Nursanlo's case, for example, he described feeling alien to his own person the first time he appeared via the prison video link, as if he was 'only an image on a television screen' which could 'easily be dismissed' (Nursanlo 2004). 'All you have to do is turn away from the screen,' Nursanlo remarked. He said that the prison video link made it very difficult to 'represent yourself properly'. He went so far as to say that it 'was hard to appear sympathetic' and that 'even the solicitor looks different', highlighting, in strong visual terms, the degree to which he believed his courtroom appearance had been 'made different by the technology' (Ihde 1990, 75) and showing, in no unequal measure, the importance, to him, of justice being seen to be done. Thus, it is fair to say that the literal body is not communicated in the courtroom. On the contrary, the image has gained sway over the object to create a de-realisation of the accused, and in subsequence 'identity is reconstituted as pure data or information – as text' (Graham 2002, 187) and a new symbolic of presence is produced.

In the same way, Vertigan accepts as true that the accused has been 'de-humanised' by the technology, 'reduced to a two-dimensional image' (Vertigan 2005). He observes: 'They [the inmates] are even more de-humanised than if you have to deal with them in person … it's a weird experience trying to cross-examine a television screen.'

Vertigan proceeds to speak to the heart of his complaint, of instances when he has observed his defendant's body from a distance and not always recognised the man or woman on the screen staring back at him. To coin an expression of Virilio, it was as if he were experiencing 'the growing confusion between "ocular reality" and its instantaneous, mediated representation' (Virilio 1993, 73). 'How do you get the jury to empathise with my victim if he or she is an image on a screen?' Vertigan asks. 'All you have is this disembodied voice.'

My point in citing Vertigan in depth is to focus on my analysis such that it can be seen how the inmate is transformed via the video link into 'a walking signifier' (Martinez 1993 in Staiano-Ross 2005, 66). The Tasmania Department of Justice similarly recognises how legal discourse denies 'person' a presence in the courts. On its website, in a section entitled 'Video Link/Court Attendance', the court states that 'If your client is to physically appear in court, a "body" warrant will need to be obtained from the court before the prisoner/detainee will be released under custodial supervision' (Tasmania Department of Justice website 2007).

To cite Staiano-Ross (2005, 57) in 'Losing Myself: Body as Icon/Body as Object(s)', 'Our bodies can never be fully under our control, for each body narrates a social and biological history of humankind and possesses the capacity to generate utterly unique signs'. Staiano-Ross (2005, 58) made the further observation that 'When the body lacks iconicity, when it has lost its power to represent other bodies, and when it contains the possibility of producing never before seen signs, it is at its most dangerous.'

So, suitably, I will now focus on the House of Lords decision in Polanski v Condé Nast Publications Limited (2005), to illustrate the extent to which 'identity in a cyberworld is fluid and negotiable' (Graham 2002, 191) and how technology can be used to enable a claimant to avoid the consequences of his or her criminal action.

To cite Burke (in Pederson 2005, 184), 'Humans are both a cause and an effect of the sign system in which they signify'. Burke's definition treats humans as sign makers, users and misusers. The latter way of thinking is reaffirmed by Lord Nicholls of Birkenhead who, when speaking to the House of Lords *Polanski v Condé Nast Publications Limited* decision, stated, 'There is no question of this libel action as being an *abuse* of the process of the court'. Pederson shows how Burke's definition of humans also reveals them as designers. In accordance with this view, Mr Polanski, the claimant, comes 'closest to a conception of self as performative, where the electronic domain is the stage and where relationships and selves can be "enhanced, augmented, changed, or erased"' (Springer 1996, 132 in Graham 2002, 191).

Treating the video link as a rhetorical text 'helps us understand how interfaces can be both manipulative and transformative' (Pederson 2005, 183). Mr Polanski is, perhaps significantly, a film director with a long list of credits to his name which include, among others, an Oscar for Best Director (for *The Pianist* in 2002) and a Life Achievement Award at the European Film Awards in 2006. To borrow from Ihde, one could argue that he comes closest to taking technologies into his experiencing in such a way that the camera lens becomes 'part of the way I ordinarily experience my surroundings; they "withdraw" and are barely noticed, if at all. I have then actively embodied the technics of vision' (Ihde 1990, 73), through which Mr Polanski has erased his 'self' and in so doing has made his body 'non-iconic' in so far as it no longer stands as a representation of all bodies past and present, not in the UK at least, for as Lord Carswell states in his judgment, 'No libel has ever yet been sought in this country [the UK] in the claimant's absence'.

The non-iconic body

In Polanski v Condé Nast Publications Limited (2005) the crucial question was whether Roman Polanski, who is a fugitive from US justice, should be allowed to present his evidence orally to an English court in (libel) defamation proceedings properly brought by him in England, without being physically present in the court room.[18] The High Court's feeling that the general policy of the courts should be to discourage litigants from escaping the normal processes of the law rather than to facilitate this reveals the modernist occupation with the authenticity of the subject.

The Polanski case alters traditional legal relations to the extent that his lawyers found a way to protect his physical body from extradition even as his virtual body was permitted to enter into an English courtroom, by means of a video link, to present its oral evidence. One can see from this example that the sign of his body was swapped for an assurance from the courts that his physical self would not be removed without his permission to the US, even as his virtual self was made manifest by others and at their discretion. In a sense Mr Polanski contrived to structure or design what Pederson would call 'an alternative physical reality … a here and now that is not here and now' (Pederson 2005, 190–191). Here is a world in which 'truth and reality are indistinguishable from illusion or simulation' (Graham 2002, 191), where ownership of the body can be contested even when litigants are escaping the normal processes of the law.

On the other hand, Lord Nicholls of Birkenhead (Westlaw Australia website 2006) maintained that the use of the audio-visual link would not assist the 'fugitive's [Mr Polanski's] evasion of justice', rather it would 'enable him to present his evidence orally to an English court in proceedings properly brought by him here, without being physically present in the court room' (Westlaw Australia website 2006).

Lord Nicholls (Westlaw Australia website 2006) added that

> A direction that Mr Polanski's evidence may be given by means of video conferencing, or VCR in short, would not prejudice Condé Nast [the respondents] to any significant extent. If anything, as Simon Brown LJ observed, any prejudice would more likely be suffered by Mr Polanski, by reason of the lessoned impact of his evidence and celebrity status on the jury.

18 As noted in the Westlaw Download Summary Report (Westlaw 2006) the appellant was suing the respondent for libel in the English courts. In 1977 he pleaded guilty before a Californian court to a charge of unlawful sexual intercourse with a girl aged 13 years. He fled the US before he was sentenced, and returned to France. As a French citizen he cannot be extradited from France. However, if he visited the UK he would be at risk of being extradited to the US. He therefore sought to give evidence in his libel proceedings from France by means of a video link pursuant to Civil Procedure Rule 32.3. The High Court granted his request. On appeal the Court of Appeal discharged the High Court's order holding that the general policy of the courts should be to discourage litigants from escaping the normal processes of the law rather than to facilitate this. The appellant appealed. The order allowing the appellant to give evidence by means of a video link was restored by the House of Lords.

Lord Slynn of Hadley (Westlaw Australia website 2006) likewise observed that 'If indeed there is any disadvantage it may be to the person asking for video link evidence and it is not established that the respondents would be adversely affected by the use of video link evidence.' Lord Slynn maintained that the only effect of refusing the order would be to deny Mr Polanski access to justice. This is because the principle which guarantees access to justice does not distinguish between different types of claims, nor does it distinguish between different classes of litigants. In this present situation, the law does seem however to make a distinction between the visual manifestation of a man or woman and his or her physical (re)presentation.

The law is a meditative system of signs and in the case of Polanski v Condé Nast Publications Limited the appellant was enabled, quite literally, to leave his body elsewhere, to have it edited, cropped out of the (court) frame. In this context, an 'appearance' via audio-visual link is clearly not the same as an in-person court appearance for if it were Mr Polanski would not pursue this option, as it would not be an option for the reason that to 'appear' would be to step inside an English courtroom and risk having his body snatched, except here no such risk exists because he has learnt to 'be' with the technology that others in his situation have struggled to understand.

This idea of 'being-with-technology' goes back to Aristotle who considered the goal of *techne* as being to create what nature finds it impossible to achieve (Guattari 1993), and in nature it is not possible to be in a here and now that is not here and now. Hence, *techne* sets itself up between nature and humanity as a creative mediation (Guattari 1993, 13) in much the same way as a video link sets itself up between the seer and the seen as a legal mediation. As an example, in 2004, in a case in Sandpoint, Idaho, in the US, Jason Charles Miller was brought before the courts on suspicion of manslaughter and his initial court hearing was conducted telephonically because the video link connecting the jail and the courthouse was not working, reported news editor Keith Kinnaird of the *Bonner County Daily Online*. Kinnaird wrote that 'Miller's defense attorney, Doug Phelps, was unable to attend the hearing and planned to take part via telephone, but the line was being used to conduct the court hearing', thus illustrating how the (failure of) technology has impacted on the administration of justice. Being-with-audio-visual-technology had a positive outcome for Mr Polanski, however, although who is to say what the courts would have ordered if he had been their prisoner seeking an 'indulgence from the court'?[19]

19 In his judgment Lord Nicholls of Birkenhead stated that 'Mr Polanski has said he will not come to this country [England] to give oral evidence at the trial of his libel action. Instead, he has sought a pre-trial direction that he may be allowed to give his evidence from France by means of a video link .... Eady J gave this direction on 9 October 2003. The judge said the reason underlying the application was unattractive, but this did not justify depriving Mr Polanski of his chance to have his case heard at a trial.'

Of concern is an acknowledgment by the NSW Parliament's Legislation Review Committee that the right of an accused person to be tried in his or her presence may be affected by the Evidence (Audio and Audio Visual Links) Amendment Bill 2007. In its summary of conclusions in the Legislation Review Digest (No. 7 of 2007) the committee noted 'Appearing by video link may alienate an accused detainee from the court proceedings and affect the interaction between the accused detainee and his or her legal practitioner' (Section A), raising some of the issues that can develop out of being-with-audio-visual-technology.

Being-with-technology

Ihde's *Technics and Praxis* (1979) began with observations on the ways in which science and philosophy are related to technology and praxis. Ihde (1993, 112) argued that 'such human-technology relations exemplify ways in which humans – with technology or instruments in a mediating position – experience an environment or world in a new or technological way.'

It is in much the same way that an inmate, through the use of video technology, learns to experience the legal setting in a new or technological way, without leaving the prison.

Ihde (1993) defined an object as having counted as a technology when a human was able to use, design, make or modify a material aspect of the object to fit a given praxis, or use. The non-neutral, transformative power of humans enhanced by technologies is an essential feature of human-technology relations (Ihde 1993, 51). Nancy (1993, 40) describes technology as not a means, 'but a mode of execution, manifestation, and effectuation in general'. She observed how it is 'precisely that mode of performance that distinguishes itself from the natural mode as its double and its rival in perfection' (Nancy 1993, 40), further demonstrating how making oneself manifest in person or through the camera lens are two modes of performance that are 'the same (not identical) in their difference' (Nancy 1993, 40). These two modes of communication continuously refer to each other in a double relation called, since Plato and Aristotle, 'mimesis'. Nancy (1993, 41) suggests that the one does not 'copy' the other, rather it 'plays itself out twice' to the degree that the inmate 'appears' twice, both in the courtroom and in the videoconferencing studio. Virilio (1993, 4) calls this 'Teletopia', meaning 'to be here and elsewhere at the same time'.

With the revolution of instantaneous transmissions, such as the video link, we are witnessing the beginnings of a type of general arrival in which everything arrives so quickly that departure becomes unnecessary (Virilio 1993, 8). The inmate in this case is at once in the courtroom and in the prison. His or her message is derived by non-verbal communication in so far as the inmate sees the courtroom through the camera lens, which places the video link technology in a position of legal mediation. This system 'induces a sense of a more fluid identity: one effectively "performs" a persona which may be very different from one's own embodied "real" self' (Graham 2002, 189). The formal signs or representations of physical presence are thus re-written and representations of criminals are challenged to the degree that cultural meanings normally associated with courtrooms are disrupted.

Protocol for the use of video courtrooms: how the inmate 'appears'

Prison conference studios in NSW are connected to remote courtrooms via a worldwide digital communications network, called the Integrated Services Digital Network, with a bandwidth[20] requirement of 512 kilobytes (KB) per second, where 1 megabit per second (Mpbs) equals 1,000 Kpbs, which, according to Sharp (2004), creates a real-time transmission, or continuous presence. Thus, in an ideal world, this would make the inmate 'appear' as he or she would in person, as if he or she were in the same room with the litigants, judges and lawyers. Obviously the near-real experience will improve with higher available bandwidths.[21] The inmate, meantime, 'appears' only as a head and shoulders and, as a consequence, is literally disembodied from his or her self during court proceedings.

The operating studio is a 3.5 square metre room within the correctional centre which can potentially positively affect the non-verbal messages received by the courtroom. Research suggests that in a seating arrangement where physical closeness is limited, increased eye contact can signal immediacy and increase psychological closeness (Richmond and McCroskey 1995, 209), which has positive outcomes for an inmate who in this case is in close proximity to the screen and whose eye behaviour can therefore be seen, which, according to Hickson et al. (2004), is all-important in a court of law. Certainly, one frequently cited problem with older videoconferencing models was the disconnection between the image on the screen and the camera set up to the side. In the prison setting, corrective services place a camera on the end of a boom that lets it rest in the middle of the screen, which allows the inmate to look at the screen and the camera at the same time. Thus when the inmate and those in the courtroom use it, eyes can come much closer to gazing into each other.

This view can be compared with that of Ed Wachowicz, senior specialist in multimedia applications for Verizon, who has previously criticised current videoconferencing models because they do not create a lot of eye contact (in

---

20 The data rate that an Internet connection can support usually is referred to its bandwidth.

21 ZDNet Australia (online) reported on 16 January 2008 that the University of Melbourne, Australia, had discovered a way to transmit data at 'speeds of over 1000Mbps, 250 times faster than the fastest broadband connections offered in Australian capital cities'. University of Melbourne's Dean of Engineering Professor Iven Mareels told ZDNet Australia that 'It's like having a direct line, but a virtual one' (ZDNet Australia 2008). He observed that the data transmission speed would make discussions and sharing information 'as intimate' as if researchers from across the globe were 'in the same room'.

McGee, 2003). Wachowicz raises the implications for non-verbal communication that have arisen from the creation of the Teleporter, an apparent 3-D display by Dallas, TX-Based Teleportec, which creates the perception of the physical presence of a virtual person with the same aspect ratio and line of sight as a physically appearing person (Wachowicz in McGee 2003). Wachowicz asserts that when you see the Teleporter, 'It isn't a television. It's a person sitting in front of you. So we're selling the experience, and although the person isn't literally three-dimensional, you absolutely get the feeling that the person is in the room' (in McGee 2003). Could this be the way of the future? Tentative research findings are promising.

In an independent study (Wagner in McGee 2003) a live salesperson was measured against a two-dimensional videoconferencing system and a Teleporter. When physically present, the salesperson sold 92 per cent of the time as opposed to 50 per cent when using the traditional videoconferencing system, as compared to when using the Teleporter where there was also a 92 per cent selling rate, which could be a valid reason to consider its use in the courtroom where, according to Fontaine and Kiger (1978 in Hickson et al. 2004, 408), 'the first few minutes the person is seen are the most crucial'.

Besides spatial arrangement, the available evidence suggests that colour is also associated with people's moods (Burgoon et al. 1996; Hickson et al. 2004; Ketcham 1958; Knapp and Hall 2002; Mehrabian 1976; Richmond and McCroskey 1995), which means the colour of the videoconferencing studio interior, in this case blue, could potentially positively affect those watching the screen from the courtroom. This positive effect may also be felt by the inmate. Mehrabian and Ferris (1967) believed that the most pleasant hues are, in order, blue, green, purple, red and yellow. The colour blue denotes calmness, dependability, dignity, truth, tranquillity and acceptance (Ketcham 1958) so in the context of its use in the videoconferencing studio, it may be assumed that all positive non-verbal messages will be communicated to the message receivers inside the courtroom and that these positive messages will also be received by the prisoner inside the painted room. On the other hand, one empirical study into the effect pink holding cells had on prisoner behaviour failed to turn up any long-term affects due to the colour, which was originally believed to reduce an inmate's violent behaviour. A number of environmental design researchers have also expressed scepticism as to the effect of colour on the message receiver (Pellegrini et al. 1978, in Burgoon et al. 1996, 114).

The actual message is transmitted via three cameras in the videoconferencing booth, placing the technology 'between the seer and the seen, in a position of mediation' (Ihde 1990, 73) in so far as the inmate sees the courtroom 'through' the camera lens, putting him at once in the courtroom, where his or her head and shoulders are seen, and on the 'other side' of the optics. The cameras in the room are positioned such that looking at the image on the screen will transmit as looking at the person being addressed at the far end. Sharp (2004) described each of the cameras as having 'a special purpose'. He said camera A allowed the magistrate only to observe the accused during judicial proceedings, camera B allowed corrective services only to observe the accused, while the fixed camera transmitted a remote image to the entire courtroom (see Figure 3.1). The magistrate's bench has set up on it a 14-inch (36-cm) television monitor, only viewed by the magistrate, with an in-built camera that can be zoomed out to see the entire video studio to 'ensure the inmate is not being intimidated' (Sharp 2004). Even if the video and audio unit is not activated at the remote end, witnesses should assume that they will be visible to the court at all times while in the videoconferencing room.

Sharp said that the inmate sits alone in the studio faced towards a split screen, as shown in Figure 3.1.

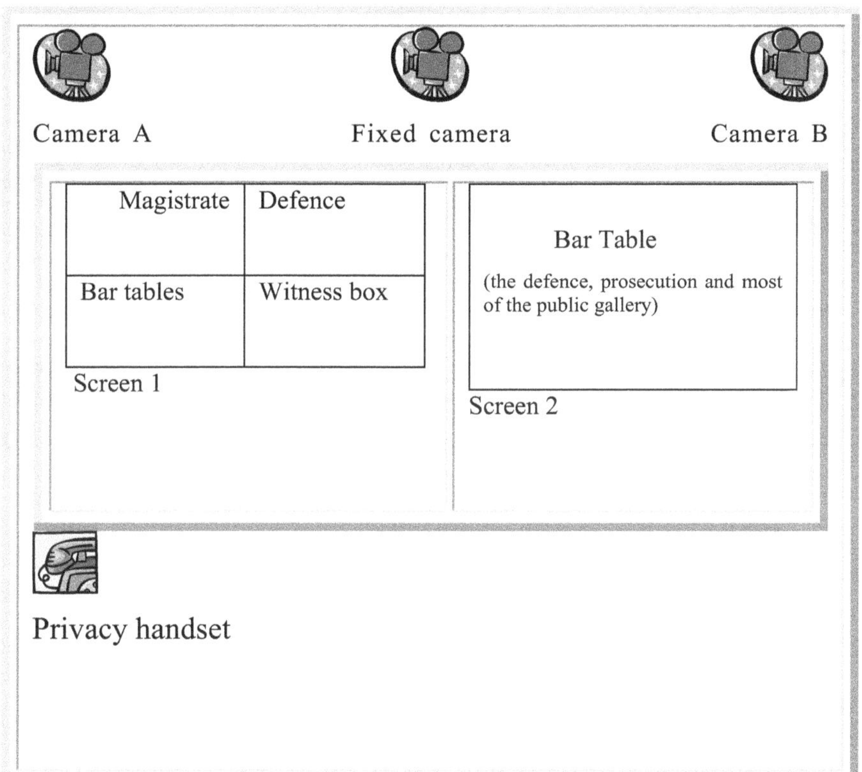

From left to right: What the accused sees from inside the video conferencing studio (not to scale)[1]

Figure 3.1 Australian prison video link – the accused's view

The screen to the inmate's left is divided into four parts and shows in real-time separate shots of the magistrate, the defence, both bar tables (in a single frame) and the witness box. The second screen, to the inmate's right, shows, in a single frame, both bar tables and most of the public gallery. The studio also contains a secure telephone line, which can be used by the inmate to speak confidentially with his or her legal representative. When this happens, the audio relay in the studio is muted, which means that the inmate can no longer be heard by the people in the courtroom or those in the room from which the inmate is being observed by the Department of Corrective Services.[22]

Despite the court's assurances, lawyers maintain that many of their clients are not convinced these conversations are secure and, in circumstances where they have believed their conversation is likely to be listened to,[23] have refrained altogether from interrupting proceedings to direct questions to their legal representative (Archbold 2005; Sharp 2004; Vertigan 2005). Archbold (2005) worried that prisoners who refused counsel might potentially damage the outcome of their case. He said that many a case 'hinged on just one question'. Having recognised some of the shortcomings of the present system, Chief Magistrate Kluss remarked that 'funding for additional conferences for … communicating with persons unable to use, or distrusting of technology will have to be sought on a "case by case" basis from legal aid' (in Practice Note 5/2007).

Perceived privacy issue: surveillance

Under Commonwealth law it is an offence to intercept, or in other words to listen to or record, a conversation passing over a telecommunication system without the knowledge of the person making the communication, as outlined in s 7 of the Telecommunication (Interception) Act 1979 (Pearson 2004, 316–317). Regardless,

22 See, for example, the Magistrates' Court Victoria Practice Direction No. 10 of 2004 'Video Conferencing Guidelines' at <http://www.magistratescourt.vic.gov.au/CA256902000FE154/Lookup/Chief_Magistrates_Directions/$file/pd1004.pdf/> as at 12 March 2008, which states that 'Where the prison is the remote point and any person other than the accused and his legal representative are present in the room that person should leave the room during confidential discussions unless the good order and security of the correctional facility is threatened' (p. 7).

23 According to the Parliament of NSW website (2007), in an address given to the General Purpose Standing Committee No. 3 on 22 September 2005, the then Minister for Justice, the Hon. Tony Kelly, made reference to the Arunta telephone system used by the Department of Juvenile Justice which he described as 'a computer-based telephone system that enables detainees to make approved pre-programmed external telephone calls without the need for a staff member to supervise the call' (p. 6). The system, which was introduced when the Drug Intelligence Unit became operational in January 2003, allows for the recording and monitoring of all detainee calls at all eight juvenile correctional centres, and is primarily aimed at determining whether detainees have access to, and use of, contraband, as well as addressing other security threats affecting juvenile justice centres. However, it is conceivable inmates may perceive other telephones in the correctional centre, including other correctional centres, as being tapped, as well.

Archbold,[24] a criminal defence lawyer with Marsdens Law Group at Parramatta in NSW, argued that defendants, especially repeat offenders, had been taught to only discuss their situation in person, 'never over the phone', 'in case' they were overheard. Archbold argued that there was no express guarantee the conversation was not being recorded and confided that he himself felt 'reluctant' to address his client over the secure phone line during proceedings 'because if I pick up the phone and speak out loud, I've just given my line of questioning away' (Archbold 2005). This argument was supported by Toutant (2005) in the US who found that the attorney–client relationship suffered when a defendant was unable to speak face to face with his or her lawyer.

Toutant reported that, 'They [defence lawyers] say problems occur during videoconferencing hearings when the prosecution unexpectedly raises damaging information about their client.' In his 2005 study, entitled 'Beaming in the Defendant (Problems Occur during Videoconferencing Hearings)', Toutant quoted Bergen County Deputy Public Defender Louis Acevedo who said that 'If the client was in court, we'd say, "One minute, judge." [At a video hearing] we have no way of immediately having a confidential conversation about the issue that was raised' (Toutant 2005). Although he did not have legal representation during his videoconferencing hearing, Nursanlo (2004) said that he also chose not to ask questions during his appearance because 'You don't want to make a distraction to the magistrate or do anything to tick him off [as] his decision is what matters'. Acevedo (in Toutant 2005) wants judges trained in how to put defendants at ease when they face the camera and to ensure that defendants 'feel like their matter, for that minute or two, is being given the attention it deserves'. In other words, he is asking for judges to 'behave towards this virtual image the same as they would to a real person in their space [by] attempting to make eye contact with the remote [prisoner] and using the same gaze cues for turn taking common in face-to-face conversations' (Billinghurst and Kato 2002, 81).

Lawyers argue that the private telephone creates difficulties for interpreter services as well, due to the mute function on the secure phone line. Some have maintained that interpreter services are unable to hear discussions between the defendant and his or her legal representative when conversations are muted during proceedings (Archbold 2005; Sharp 2004; Vertigan 2005). Archbold recommended introducing real-stream interpreters into the courtroom who operate from a call centre to obviate this problem.

In contrast, the Community Relations Commission, a governmental agency providing interpreters for the court system in NSW, have described no reported deficiencies in the prison video link system (Duncan 2005), and until such time as they do, the system would remain unchanged according to Sharp (2004). Interestingly, three years later in an article published in the metropolitan newspaper

24 Before working as a criminal defence lawyer, Benjamin Archbold worked as a policeman and later as a detective in Victoria, Australia, and therefore has a unique perspective on the way the criminal justice system operates in Australia.

The Sydney Morning Herald (Mudie, 2007), Sharp conceded that the NSW Attorney General's Department would consider other options 'such as high-tech webcams to tackle problems arising from a lack of video conferencing facilities in remote areas'. Problems arising from the secure phone line were not mentioned in this article.

Sharp has in the past noted some of the technical problems that can arise from a poor transmission signal. In 2004 he argued that the weather could interfere with the video signal, for example, 'thereby decreasing the overall frame rate of the image and as a consequence distorting the quality of the image and the speed with which it is delivered', which in turn may affect the way an inmate sounds, with sounds being yet another aspect of non-verbal communication. Hickson et al. (2004, 407) followed a different line of reasoning when they noted that 'Most in the legal profession attach little credibility to the notion that non-verbal communication has a significant impact on judgements in court.' Those in the legal profession believe that the verbal aspect of the communication process has a greater impact (Conley and O'Barr 1990).

The rationale behind those in the legal profession discounting the importance of body language is that the record of the case is verbal (Hickson et al. 2004, 407). In contrast, academics such as Fontaine and Kiger (1978, in Hickson et al. 2004, 408) and legal representatives such as Archbold (2005) stress that non-verbal communication, in particular how one 'appears', is all-important. For example, they state that the client should not 'appear to be' a prisoner.[25] Hickson et al. (2004, 408) take this one step further by suggesting that an accused criminal should be dressed in a manner that is 'inconsistent with the crime', showing the extent to which environmental factors can distort how a situation may appear even in so far as the camera system itself can be seen to distort reality.

Physical appearance

Raiscott (1985, in Hickson et al. 2004, 408) observes that the first few minutes the person is seen are the most crucial. Given then that your appearance is part of your non-verbal behaviour (Huns 2003) it can be seen as significant that no inmate has asked to appear in plain clothes since video conferencing was introduced to the NSW courtrooms (Sharp 2004). Archbold (2005) described how much effort it took to dress the part: 'You have your clothes searched. You get out of your greens[26] and into your clothes. You "appear". You're searched and then backwards, all for a two- to three-minute appearance … they [the inmates] hate it.' Archbold argued that prisoners should not appear via videoconferencing at all because 'in

25 In a personal communication on 1 June 2005, Vertigan stated that it was not uncommon for prisoners to appear in court in handcuffs. He said that this could 'make them appear menacing and dangerous', which could be prejudicial to the trial outcome.

26 Inmates' uniforms are commonly referred to as 'greens' in NSW.

person is everything in court ... the best way to tell if a person is telling the truth is to have them in the room with me, to touch, feel ... see if they sweat' (*ibid.*). Archbold was of the opinion that an inmate was more 'accountable' in person. This view is supported by Section 3.9 of Report 101 (2003), a study undertaken by the NSW Law Reform Commission into the legal processes of trying a person charged with a sexual offence and the current limitations on cross-examination generally, which states that cross-examination promotes the reliability of the trial by testing the witness's evidence. Accordingly, there is an assumption that face-to-face confrontation is likely to elicit truthful testimony and will enhance the accuracy of fact-finding.

This is to be contrasted with Eastwood and Patton (2002, 4–5) who argue that the purpose of cross-examination has

> ... very little if anything to do with accuracy or truth. Rather, the purpose of cross-examination is more a process of manipulating the witness through suggestive questioning, avoiding unfavourable disclosures and obtaining jury sympathy. Cross-examination techniques are specifically designed to damage the effectiveness of the testimony and mute the voice of the complainant.

If this is taken as true, it shows the inmate as not being adversely affected by the use of prison video technology. Writing in 1999, Ekman et al. concluded from a study into three professional groups with special interest or skill in deception that there is evidence that some professional lie catchers are highly accurate, and that behavioural clues to lying are detectable in real time. The study, entitled 'A Few Can Catch a Liar', also postulated that most people cannot tell from demeanour when others are lying.

Conclusion

Given the prison video link is regulated by a government office which will encourage the use of technological advances in the conduct of civil and criminal litigation where there can be significant savings as to both time and cost (Sharp 2004), it would be appropriate to establish an independent monitor, and to publish, in accessible places, the issues arising from the process of 'non-verbal communication' in the courtroom as a consequence of human-technological mediation.

Notably, there is a lack of existing research into this new communication medium for the courtroom, particularly in NSW where corrective services is yet to receive input from some agencies, such as Community Relations, as to the effectiveness of its praxis as non-verbal communication (Sharp 2004). Further research should therefore also explore the extent to which the terms of reference encourage a greater level of participation by people who face multiple non-verbal communication barriers, such as people from a culturally and/or linguistically diverse background, and those with intellectual disability and mental illness. The efficacy of secure videoconferencing for assessing medical problems would be a most useful measure against which to compare the legal videoconferencing model, in so far as both can be used to assess a person through a camera lens.

That said, the courtroom of the future should not begin operating as a 'virtual' courtroom with litigants, judges and lawyers only communicating electronically, until the communicative properties of the medium are further investigated. By such means we may more reasonably ensure that the 'walking signifier' is on the same 'page' as that other class of body still making its corporeal appearance before the court.

There is no disputing that the NSW justice system has joined the computer age, but without a reliable understanding of the effects of visual technologies, both on the jury and trial process itself, the benefits and risks of emerging technologies cannot be readily and accurately evaluated. We are not at that point where courts and lawyers use artificial intelligence to resolve disputes (Rose 1998) but that is not to say we are far off, given the necessary technology is already available. Time may soon run out for in-depth research into the communicative properties of the prison video link. By 2009 the NSW Police Force, Public Prosecutions and the NSW Government Department of Corrective Services will be able to log into a $A48 million groundbreaking computer system that will include live procedural hearings on the Internet on matters such as bail and court appearances for prisoners,[27] illustrating yet another way in which a prisoner's access to the judicial system will be made different from an in-person appearance. It is not the prisoner's literal body that will be communicated in this courtroom. Rather, physical bodies 'reconstituted as pure data or information – as text' (Graham 2002, 187) will be able to be pulled up at the touch of a button to produce a new symbolic of presence, one in which the prisoner is 'the same (not identical) in their difference' (Nancy 1993, 40). If prisoners have not learnt the praxis thus far, they will now need to learn a new way of 'seeing' justice to be done.

27 According to a press release, 'Online Court Hearings Save Time and Money', issued on 3 February 2008 on the LawLink New South Wales website, the new computer system will enable prosecutors and defence lawyers to log into a bulletin board, where they will type their arguments. The JusticeLink will alert the judge to his or her post by email and he or she will be able to log in to the system to make determinations in real time. By February 2009, the computer system is expected to be operating in every criminal and civil court in NSW, including 160 local courts. 'JusticeLink is the first multi-jurisdictional court computer system in the world,' NSW Attorney General John Hatzistergos noted. He further remarked that 'while the time-honoured traditions of our legal system will remain intact, JusticeLink will streamline the process, saving millions of dollars in costs and countless hours spent in the courtroom.'

Chapter 4
The Roma Way[1]

István H. Szilágyi

Two research studies

Over the past several years, I have had the opportunity to take part in two empirical research studies which, at first glance, seemed to have dealt with rather different questions. In reality, however, in addition to some theoretical and methodological considerations, they are only connected by their common subject of research. The term 'subject of research' is quite a good example of the artificial and inhuman character of scientific language alienated from life, reflecting the negative attitude of Hungarian society toward the Romas to a certain degree. Nevertheless, I think that it is more correct to refer to the subjects of these studies as the *protagonists* rather than subjects, and in particular to the fact that the majority of Hungarian society regards these men/women as Gypsies.

Regarding theoretical and methodological considerations, the two studies share the intellectual background of the concepts that took shape in the fields of cultural and legal anthropology in the 1980s and 1990s. Moreover, the outcomes of the studies, as it often occurs (Kevelson, 1988a, 23; 1988b), invite also semiotic analysis. The semiotic perspective is an inherent part of the empirical microsociological researches in order to understand the intention of the participants in the social interactions when we have to explain the meaning they attribute to the multiple signs and sign-systems used by them in the course of their action. The semiotic investigations are needed in a more abstract or a higher level too in this kind of study when we seek to find the meaning of the observed interactions from the perspective of the society as a whole – and not from that of an individual participant – what maybe even remains out of consideration of the participants themselves. Here the semiotic analysis helps understand how this meaning is being forged and changed in the dynamics of communication through the interplay of different systems of signs or levels of meanings.

The two researches presented below shed a light on how the Hungarian law which formally – that is, on its semantic level – meets the standards of the Rule of Law becomes a means of rejection and stigmatisation (criminalisation) in the social practice contributing to the segregation of Gypsy minority. Here the concept of segregation – if we want to put this sociological category in semiotic terms –

1 An earlier version of this chapter appeared in 2005; see Szilágyi (2005). In the English translation Emese Gál and Andrea Fenyődi helped me.

can be defined as the breakdown of the communication between the majority and the minority.

The 'Gypsy trial'

Chronologically, the first research study was carried out between 1997 and 1999 at a local court (of first instance) in Borsod-Abaúj-Zemplén county (in the northwestern region of Hungary).[2] Originally, the study was designed to examine the question of whether or not the Romas have certain cultural patterns which might influence their relationship to the law. The question was inspired by the contradiction between the findings formulated in the Hungarian criminological literature concerning the so-called 'Gypsy crime' and those of contemporary legal anthropology and comparative law. According to the former, the 'Gypsy crime', namely the fact that the Romas are over-represented among the perpetrators of certain types of crime, is basically a *sociological problem*, rooted in the poverty and lack of education of the Hungarian Roma minority, because the non-Roma population, characterised by the same 'hard facts', has the same criminality rate (Tauber 1986; Tauber, Vigh and Madácsi 1988; Pózcik 1997). The anthropological and comparative approach, on the other hand, emphasises the importance of the *Roma culture* in the Romas' relation to the law (Weyrauch and Bell 1993; Grönfors 1997). The researchers adapted this latter perspective, which influenced both the choice of setting and method of research.

According to the first conception, the research study would have been conducted at a court of first instance, investigating the court proceedings in civil law cases and applying the method of participating observation. The researchers would have compared the records of cases in which either the plaintiffs or the defendants were Romas with those of a non-Roma control group, aiming to draw conclusions on the Roma cultural patterns. The supposition behind this first conception was that the eventual distorting effect of prejudice against the Romas – which is prevalent among the Hungarian majority and even appears in the affairs of the police and other state organs (Szilágyi and Loss 2002) – on the court would be the least present in civil law cases, in which the initiative of the procedural acts would have belonged to the parties.

However, the errors of this conception became obvious towards the end of the first year of the study. First it turned out, as others had already made the observation (Egyed 1996), that there was practically a negligible number of Roma clients appearing in civil law cases; that is to say, the Romas are heavily under-represented in civil law cases. Secondly, the researchers had to face the realisation that their efforts to exclude the effects of discriminative prejudice are futile and mistaken. They concluded that they must take into account the *entire* process of interaction that takes place in the courtroom, as well as expand the

2 For the final report of the research see Szilágyi and Loss (2002).

scope of the research to include criminal cases. The value judgements, prejudices and attitudes of non-Roma participants will necessarily be present in the totality of the interaction in the courtroom proceedings, alongside the patterns of Roma culture – if these exist at all – that influence the behaviour of Roma parties, mostly defendants in criminal cases. This conclusion led to the re-formulation of the basic question of the research study and to the introduction of the concept of 'Gypsy trial' which exhibits different features from those trials with non-Roma parties (defendants).

At the same time, the researchers opted to keep the method of participating observation, as it appeared to be more effective in the study of courtroom communication than the questionnaire method – the latter is not so much descriptive, but conveys the opinion of the actors. The development of the system of criteria to be applied in the observation, the training of 'field workers' (third-year law students and students of cultural and visual anthropology at Miskolc University in 1997–98) and their introduction to the court had all been accomplished by the end of the first year. In the next year and a half they collected information for about fifty case studies of court proceedings. They tried to make 'thick descriptions' (Geertz 1973) and accurately record the behaviour of the persons involved in the proceedings – their appearance, clothes, gestures, linguistic abilities, emotional depth, etc.

An important requirement when using the method of participating observation is for the observer 'to fade' into the background and not disturb the 'normal' course of events. This is, of course, the ideal case of this methodological requirement, since, under real-world circumstances, the presence of the observer always influences the observed events to some extent. Our case was not an exception either, particularly during the first part of the study. Several observers (especially female law students) noted that their presence influenced the judges' behaviour, who tried to 'do their best' and gave more detailed reasoning for their measures and decisions, thereby helping and educating the future (female) colleagues. Later, however, as the judges gradually got accustomed to the presence of observers, this effect diminished. The judges still remained helpful, and many of them allowed the observers to be present in the courtroom before the proceedings, during sentencing and after the proceedings were closed.

The scene

Courts play a significant role in every legal system which relies on the 'rule of law', even if this is somewhat different in importance in the common law and in the Continental systems. In the literature of the contemporary legal sociology, however, it is a widely accepted position that the weight of the courts cannot be attributed to their manifest function, which is their role in individual conflict resolution, but rather to their particular symbolic and ideological functions. The essence of this lies in that courts, as critical organs of justice administration, embody and represent the unity of the law, and thereby the unity of society. The court must present and specify the legal principles, which might otherwise express somewhat contradictory social values and ideas (such as freedom, equality, solidarity and the like) in coherent unity. In addition, the system of independent courts functions as an autonomous branch of power, which limits and, at the same time, legitimises the legislative and executive powers. That is why the 'impartial', 'unbiased' sentences can exercise such great influence upon public opinion and the system of social values.

Nevertheless, fulfilling this symbolical and ideological function becomes rather difficult at times when society is divided into isolated social groups to such a degree that it poses the threat of social disintegration. Such a situation could easily become more aggravated if the communication between the isolated social groups is burdened with discriminative prejudices.

The difficult situation described above has arisen in the present-day Hungary in the so-called 'Roma-dense' counties, between the majority and the Roma minority. Borsod-Abaúj-Zemplén is one of these counties where the percentage of the Roma population is the highest, and the public opinion is pervaded by discriminative prejudice against the Romas – as shown, for example, by a sociological examination of the police officers' mindset (Csepeli, Örkény and Székely 1997). The courts and the judicature are burdened with a grave responsibility, as under these conditions the situation can worsen further if any overt or hidden discrimination occurs in their work.

The aim of the research study, however, was not to assess discrimination in the work of the courts, but to clarify the question as to whether or not there are any differences between the proceedings where the parties are Romas and those involving non-Romas. If such differences actually occur, these can arise not only from the discriminative prejudices of the non-Roma persons partaking in the proceedings, but, to some extent, also from the patterns of the behaviour of the Romas.

It is not so easy to discover the unique characteristics of a 'Gypsy trial'. At first glance there are no striking differences between the 'Gypsy trial' and the 'normal procedure', in which all parties belong to the non-Roma majority. For this reason, as a first step, we should consider the common elements of these valuable case studies.

The Romas

A recurrent fundamental problem of sociological inquiries is the definition of an ethnic or national minority group: how can it be determined whether a person belongs to this group? This is a particularly difficult task in case of the Romas, who live in a number of receiving countries and are divided into segmented groups. They speak different languages and have various ways of life. The most conspicuous feature of the Hungarian Roma population is its sociological and cultural heteronomy. At one end of the scale there are the Romungros, 'musicians', whose mother tongue is Hungarian and who are more or less assimilated into the Hungarian majority, the colour of their skin being the only sign of their origin. One of the groups on the other end of the scale are the Vlach Gypsy [*oláhcigány*] groups which have preserved their traditional family system, language and traditions (Stewart 1987). The majority of the Hungarian Roma population, constituting about 5 per cent of the Hungarian population at the time this research study was conducted, live between these two extremes. The main characteristic they share is their disadvantaged social position comprising nearly all sociologically measurable 'hard facts', from their state of health to education, from income to housing (Havas and Kemény 1995).

Researchers know that the only *politically correct* way of deciding a person's identity is by 'self-determination'. Under certain circumstances, however, this method will prove sociologically useless, especially in a case that can be described as discriminative.[3] Researchers found that in a situation largely defined by the value judgements of the majority, such as in court proceedings, the best solution is to entrust the observers with the determination of the actors' identities.

In the cases described in the study – with the exception of two[4] – the Romas appeared in court as defendants or witnesses in criminal cases. Most of these criminal cases involved theft, robbery and disturbance of the peace; there were no cases of rape or homicide. These facts are in line with the criminological findings showing the Romas as over-represented in the previous types of crime, their criminality being considerably lower in homicide and attempted homicide as compared to that of the non-Roma population (Huszár 1998, 158–9).

The physical appearance and clothing of the Romas does not differ significantly from that of non-Romas living under similar social conditions. The difference may be grasped in their preference for the highly 'fashionable' cuts of suit, for bright colours, and in the inferior quality of the material of their clothes. Nonetheless, the overall impression – enhanced by a slight untidiness by majority standards (dirty nails, greasy hair, less than spick-and-span clean clothes, and so on) – is fairly characteristic, and it can make a person's Roma origin unambiguous, even if this would be impossible to determine otherwise from her/his physical anthropological features. The Romas try to do their best to 'dress properly' for the occasion, although they may often not know the nature of that; that is, whether the court proceedings are similar to a funeral, a mass or a wedding. It happened only by exception that an elderly Roma woman came before the court in slippers and in strikingly untidy clothes.[5]

---

3 László Huszár's inquiries (Huszár 1998, 148–65) are eye-opening in this respect: he compared the percentage of Romas among the Hungarian prisoner population based on 'self-determination' with that estimated by prison wardens, and he found an extreme difference of 62 per cent (between 13 and 75 per cent).

4 One was a claim for damages in which both the plaintiff and the defendant were Roma. The other was a criminal case arisen from an old and aggravated conflict between two families that culminated in a mass brawl. In this latter case the defendants, witnesses and victims were all Roma.

5 'Untidy Gypsy woman, violet dress, tousled hair, scanty teeth. She has a bandage on the left hand, which is black from the dirt,' wrote an observer.

The Romas generally speak politely and respectfully when addressing the members of the court, and they try to answer the judges' questions to the best of their ability. However, their communication with the court is frequently troubled, as they do not always understand the legal terminology (such as 'accomplice'), and often are not familiar with the meaning of foreign words (such as 'insult'). Sometimes even common expressions have to be translated by the judge (for instance, 'marital status' which is often interpreted by the Romas as a question referring to the number of their children). These phenomena are obviously connected with the Romas' lack of education, and sometimes with the local dialect they speak.

Obviously, beyond the participant's psychological character, this basic scenario is influenced by two factors. One is the prison culture in the case of the repeat offenders, and the other being the case when a greater number of Roma who know each other well are present in the courtroom. The prison culture has a contradictory effect on the Romas' behaviour. On the one hand, it can substantially diminish the disadvantages in communication, the affected Romas being capable of understanding the meaning of certain legal terminology that might even be incomprehensible to the lay non-Roma people. On the other hand, the prison culture reduces these Romas' respect for the court.

It has been observed a number of times that the Romas' behaviour changed when there were at least ten of them present in the courtroom. In such a case, the questioned person speaks not only to the judge, but also to his kinsmen, which can understandably lighten the otherwise sullen atmosphere of the proceedings.[6] Moreover, the judge needed all his strength to maintain the authority of the court in one case that involved a 'payoff' between two Roma families.

The court authorities were apparently aware of this 'critical mass effect', and the violet-uniformed guards at the reception not only checked the ones entering with metal detectors, but they also inquired about the purpose of their visit and politely advised those to leave who have not been summoned to the court. (It is an entirely separate question how this practice could be reconciled with the principle of publicity of court proceedings.) This is why the researchers observed others than those summoned in the courtroom (relatives or acquaintances) in fewer instances than expected. In turn, however, they could see various sizes of Roma groups loitering in front of the court building quite regularly.

6 'When the ten defendants entered the courtroom, they were taken aback by the crowd. Numerous witnesses were already present. They are tough, laid-back and they are enjoying the circus. They are guffawing, chewing. The judge is constantly threatening to control the troublemakers: "There is no need to defend being at large!" The situation is hardening, because the judge ordered in the room some people among those, who are waiting before the building of the court, and haven't been let in yet.'

Judges, assessors, prosecutors and lawyers

In most of the observed cases the judges (women and men of approximately equal number) belonged to the younger generation, being in their thirties and forties. Regarding the judges' outward appearance, the robe represents authority and commands respect. As an elderly Roma woman noted: 'I got really frightened by the robes. I thought they were priests.'

In these cases the judges played a dominant role in conducting the proceedings. The prosecutors or lawyers – not to mention the assessors – did not ask questions directly of the defendants or witnesses. The proceedings were correct from a strictly procedural point of view, and the negative bias – if any – was manifested only in hidden form. For example, in an ambiguous phrase probably intended to be humorous), the judge made the remark to the legal representative (father) of a juvenile defendant accused of theft: 'I also tell my son that you must study even if you want to be a bum, because if you don't go to school you're finished these days!' In another hearing it was noted, that the judge continuously used such foreign words that the witness apparently could not understand, such as: 'Have you suffered some kind of atrocity?' (Silence.) 'Have you been insulted?' (After an awkward silence.) 'Have you been beaten up?'

The judges more openly voice their dislike toward the Romas before or after the proceedings when they converse with the assessors. For instance, the judge began setting forth the case to the assessors with the sentence: 'These Gypsies, they will lie up a storm for me!'

The assessors in the observed cases were members of the older generation, usually in their sixties. Near-perfect passivity during the hearings describes them the best. They tried to distinguish themselves from the dead decor of the courtroom with half-suppressed yawns, officious air and repeated nodding. Their respectable age and appearance, however, unquestionably enhances the authority of the court.

In most cases the public prosecutors, women and men approximately of equal number, similar to the judges, belonged to the younger generation. They were not too active during the hearings, and the observers did not notice any manifestations of discrimination, but no positive interest either. They handled the cases as simple and routine. They were on good terms with the judges and they usually compared their standpoints in the given case with the judges' in a few-minute discussion before or after the hearing. It only happened once that the prosecutor rushed to the judge's aid, because the latter had some difficulty keeping the defendant detained. 'I shall move for imprisonment either way, then you can maintain the detention,' said the (female) prosecutor. 'And I shall find something for the second order,' from the (female) judge acknowledged the favour.

In the observed cases the lawyers, regardless of their age and gender, shared the common characteristic of almost revolting disinterest and unpreparedness. It often visibly irritated them that they had to spend their time at the hearings, so they walked in and out, or let lawyers-in-practice sit in for them, who were obviously incapable of handling the defence (or to make any personal contact with their clients whatsoever) because of their young age and lack of experience. What seemed to be of highest importance for these lawyers was to minimise the energy spent on the case, which is why they did not even make most basic motions to the benefit of their clients – a fact striking even to a third-year law student. Under such circumstances it is understandable, that the Romas trust the judges' benevolence more than their counsels, who sometimes lack the minimum knowledge of the case they are representing before the court. This observation supports the findings of László Huszár's sociological inquiry showing that 42 per cent of the imprisoned Romas were discontented with their lawyers (Huszár 1998, 159).

Apathy dominates the relations between the non-Romas who come before the court as witnesses or often as victims and the Romas, at least in the courtroom.[7] This lack of emotions, however, is primarily due to the respect-demanding atmosphere of the hearings.

The relations among the Romas themselves are quite different. Be they a member of the family, a friend, a lover or just an acquaintance, the attached emotions are more important than the outcome of the procedure, or legal rationality in general. The father, being a witness for his daughter, angrily calls her stupid before the court.[8] An accused man prefers to bear witness against his lover just so that she also goes to the prison while he is there, thereby not being able to leave him.

Ritualised jurisdiction

The most obvious characteristic of the observed proceedings was their *speediness*. If the necessary persons appeared before the court, then everything went like clockwork. This is so in part because of the above-described passivity of the assessors, prosecutors and lawyers, and in part because the judges do their best also. They try to resolve all contradictions or uncertainties in the evidence under the banner of 'free deliberation of the evidence'. It is ignored if the defendant changes the confession he made during the pre-trial process, as long as he does not confess every crime included in the bill of indictment or only one victim out of ten recognises him as the offender.

The communication in the courtroom basically becomes limited to the conversation between the judge and defendant, dominated by the judge, due to his right to ask questions. This is why the character of this communication depends largely on the judge's personality. There are some judges who try to 'take it easy', especially in the case of 'bad boys', others adhere to a more formal and reserved style, while some of them make paternalistic or maternalistic gestures toward

7 An observer entered into conversation with the victim of a case (a young woman, around 35, owner of two inns in a village; the accused had burgled one of them) who was not too angry with the boys, although she made a remark that she would line up and shoot all such men.

8 'My daughter has any illness but idiocy!'

the younger defendants, but the style of communication will also depend on the defendant's reactions.

Nevertheless, the researchers found that these formal characteristics of the 'Gypsy trial' are not enough to grasp the essence of the phenomenon. The presence or absence of all these elements does not even touch the heart of the matter. What then is the essence of such a trial?

If we were to answer this in short, then we could say that the 'Gypsy trial' is not a trial but a *rite*. The rite is a formalised sequence of acts that has no inherent meaning.[9] More closely, in the terms of the 'Gypsy trial' this statement means that *there is no legal dispute running* in the formal structure of the court proceedings.[10]

It is clear to the Romas, regardless of how uneducated they may be, that they had already lost the trial when they were born Gypsy. What can a Roma expect from the *gadjos*' court when he can only count on his family, clan and other kinsmen? What can a Roma do if he is born in a clan specialised in pickpocketing? Not much beyond the fact that he tries not to get caught. What can a Roma do if he is born into such a poor family that he has to steal in order not to starve to death?[11]

The proceedings are not of too much importance from the judge's point of view either, since he could mete out punishment without a hearing, basing the sentence merely on the bill of indictment – the defendant's lawyer would not appeal against it anyway. The judge knows that his sentence will be presumably useless, for the sentenced will never be able to get out of the criminal way of life or subculture, because of his lack of education and poverty. Neither can the injured parties expect compensation for their damages from the sentence.

The assessors could not care less.

The court proceedings are utterly unimportant to the prosecutor as well, since the judge will accept everything written in the bill of indictment and he has already discussed his proposal for punishment with the judge before the hearing anyway. On the other hand, he agrees with the judge that the imposed punishment could not

---

9 On the meaninglessness of the rites see Winn (1991), Schreiner (1996). Classical works on the general role of rites in the process of conflict resolution: see Gluckman (1965), Moore and Myerhoff (1977).

10 The phenomenon of ritualisation can be conceptualised from a semiotic point of view both on the basis of the Peircean and the Greimassian approach – see Jackson (1995, 140–141). According to the former, ritualisation can be described as an interplay between the verbal and non-verbal sign systems (Kevelson 1988c, 4), in which the non-verbal sign system deprives the verbal signs of meaning. In our case, the arising new sign – the 'Gypsy trial' – functions as a symbol of the majority's judgement in the communication between the majority and minority, of which the primary meaning is: 'Whatever you say, we shall convict you'. In the Greimassian theory, ritualisation can be explained as the 'narrativisation of the pragmatics', in which the 'story of the trial' entirely prevails over the 'story in the trial' (Jackson, 1995, 160–161, 166–7).

11 In one of the cases the Romas stole some potatoes. They were so hungry that they ate some of them raw on the spot.

elicit any deterrent or educative effect on the future behaviour of the sentenced. The only question remains: how long must the offender be 'withdrawn from circulation' in order to protect society, but the judge could decide this on his or her own.

On a final note, the defendant's lawyer would be grateful indeed if he did not have to waste his valuable time on such petty cases.

If we tried to characterise the 'Gypsy trial' with just one word, then it would be 'terrible'. As a witness, how terrifying it could be! Here is an excerpt from an observer's (a third-year law student) note:

> The essence of the case: 5 accused, stole aluminium scrap worth 4200 HUF (!) [ca. 20 Euro]. Only two of the accused were present, there were no witnesses or lawyers. The two defendants were a Gypsy couple, but those most beaten down kind, with the emptiest eyes. They have completed four elementary grades – they have surely forgotten even how to read by now; three children, the fourth on the way. They have no skills, no job, nothing. This was the first time I felt the total defencelessness in the courtroom. The case didn't degenerate only thanks to the judge, who didn't sharpen the situation, but most wonderfully tried to help them with as much tolerance as she could muster. The whole thing was very formal, but really. Disgusting. Automatic questions, automatic answers, the formal language had to be translated continuously for the defendants. Awful to see. The judge runs out to arrange something in relation with the case, but the silence she left behind was horrifying. This is unbearable. And most of the cases are just like this. Is it really worth it? There's even tension between the assessors. Some sort of rivalry. Who observes better ... This tension is unbearable. Not a peep. Nothing. Silence-king. Nihil.

The researchers found that those peculiar patterns of the Roma behaviour (appearance, speech culture, emotional behaviour, etc.) exhibited during the course of the formal analysis of the 'Gypsy trial' are, in fact, only of secondary importance as compared to the sociological conditions which determine their chances in life and the effect of discriminative prejudice against them. That is, the presence of these behavioural patterns could only further the development of a 'Gypsy trial' but not necessarily create it. This means, on the one hand, that not every case involving Romas turns into a 'Gypsy trial', and, on the other hand, the trial of non-Roma persons can, in fact, turn into a 'Gypsy trial' as well.

The fact that rite has no inherent meaning does not preclude it serving some kind of social function. According to the researchers, this function in case of the 'Gypsy trial' becomes the *maintenance of the system of mutual prejudices* between the majority and the Roma minority, in a way that it becomes contributive to the segregation of the latter.

The conclusion drawn by the researchers on practical grounds is that if we want to eliminate the 'Gypsy trial', and if we intend to avoid the courts involuntarily becoming an institutional means of strengthening segregation and discrimination, then we should attempt to (re)make real legal disputes out of these cases, instead of preserving them as empty, meaningless rites. The general conditions for these efforts lie primarily in the wider world of social interactions and politics, which does not mean that lawyers themselves could not contribute in the law's empire. For instance, they could serve this goal by helping Romas get access to the law by means of offering free legal advice services, or by reforming the absolutely counterproductive assessory system.[12]

Between the two worlds

The second research study was based on a half-year's fieldwork which began in the autumn of 2000. The protagonists of this study were the members of a scavenging Roma family, who lived in an industrial city in northeastern Hungary.[13] The immediate objective of the research study was not a legal anthropological one – even if it involved interesting legal aspects, as we shall see it later – but to study the way of life of three members of the family: Old Tóni, Mari and Feri. The theoretical background for this had three major components. One was the fact that the researchers relied on the classical sociological tradition when defining the concept of lifestyle, in accordance to which they divided this family's life into different dimensions and aspects: living environment, subsistence, relations to work, state of health, patterns of hygiene and alcohol consumption. When analysing the relationship between this micro-environment and the broader social setting, with special regard to the police and other state institutions, the researchers made use of the concepts and findings of legal anthropology, in particular those concerning semi-autonomous social fields.[14] Last, the researchers relied on the recent literature born from the anthropological study of traditional Roma communities discussing issues of livelihood, identity and marginality (Stewart 1987; Prónai 1995). Participating observation played a decisive role in collecting data in this research study also, performed by two highly skilled anthropologists with accuracy measuring up to classical standards, and even included common pubbing and participation in scavenging.

The family lived outside official city limits, on a 'no-man's land', delimited by the last houses of the city (the 'garage-line'), the railroad tracks, an industrial access road and a private riding-school. Old Tóni had a tent covered by nylon strips, while the young couple lived in a more stable shack. Sometimes other 'homeless' people appeared around their places, on the other side of the railroad tracks, seeking shelter in these huts or in abandoned military bunkers for various periods of time. Old Tóni and his folk were the 'hard core', though. Their place

12 The institution of the 'public lawyer' happened to be introduced recently.

13 For the detailed version of the final report see Csajbók et al. (2002).

14 On the concept of the 'semi-autonomous social field' see Moore (1973) and Griffiths (2003).

had two great advantages from the point of view of the scavengers: it was close to the recycling depot and its wooded setting allowed for easy access to firewood.

Old Tóni had broken away from the more traditional Roma community of the neighbouring village probably because of a conflict with the community. The fact that he has not been there for many years, because he is afraid that they would pick a quarrel with him, certainly alludes to this. He has also made some obscure references to his wife's death, which happened several years ago and may not have been accidental – her tent caught on fire one night and the woman perished in it.

Feri, Old Tóni's son, and Mari got out of the original family ties in their childhood, since they were placed under state foster care. They became acquainted with one other in this, the state institution. After several failed attempts at re-integration into the family (their relatives tried to take advantage of them and took the money the state allotted to them), and in order to get a job and to make a 'living', they joined Old Tóni.

The culture of the original Roma community left its mark both on the family as a whole, and on each individual member's system of values and way of life. For example, Old Tóni usually supplemented his income from scavenging with basket-weaving, a traditional Roma trade. The way the entire family's existence was organised was, in fact, nothing but a 'small-scale' economic model of the greater traditional Roma community, but having to rely on scarce resources. Sometimes other relatives (for instance, Old Tóni's other son) visited the family, with whom they 'shared' according to the Roma traditions. Other Romas from Old Tóni's native village also go scavenging into the city; with these the family has contradictory relations. Their relationship is fundamentally driven by the competition for resources, but occasionally they get some information on a 'bigger loot' (for example, a large piece of scrap metal) just from these 'commuters'. The marks of the traditional Roma culture can be also discovered in the marital relations between Mari and Feri.

In their case, however, the values of the majority society have already overshadowed the traditional Roma value system in many respects. This can be caught in moments like, for instance, when they make a serious effort to meet the hygienic requirements of the majority.[15] It seems as if they had tried to distinguish themselves even by these means, from the more traditional, 'commuter' Romas whom they just refer to as 'smelly Gypsies'. The influence of majority values is more conspicuous in the blurry picture of a 'good life', depicted by Mari in a conversation. 'It would be nice, if somewhere ... on a farm, or maybe village, a small house and livestock, a garden and such things ..., to work a little bit, but ...'.

The livelihood of the family is basically ensured by the scavenging, which – contrary to the image the majority society holds – they pursue in a truly

15 Both the leaders of the recycling depot and that of the local Red Cross emphasised the fact that they are remarkably 'clean'.

'professional manner'.[16] In spite of all appearances, they scout the litter-bins and perform the selection and 'recycling' of waste materials on their territory quite rationally and methodologically (they do not cover the entire city). 'Recycling' means converting the selected materials into money, which in turn assumes extensive bartering relations. For example, they can sell the dry bread to those smallholders living close to the 'garage-line' who keep livestock in their yard. They take the scrap metal and paper to the recycling depot. These long-term business relations turn into personal acquaintances after a while, allowing them to exchange goods and services based on general reciprocity beyond the market exchange.[17] Thus Old Tóni and his folk do minor jobs sometimes for free for these acquaintances, and other times they get 'presents' (a bottle of wine, for instance) or maybe smaller loans other times, when they are short of money.

They usually do various odd jobs in addition to the scavenging. In autumn they collect the crops left on the fields after the harvest, other times herbs, they do garden work, bring in firewood, do similar jobs around the house for the acquaintances living along the 'garage-line'. Old Tóni used to help nearby shopkeepers load goods, or sweep the sidewalk in front of the shop. From time to time they visited the Red Cross, where they would get food, medicine, toiletries and cleaning supplies (in opened packages so that they cannot 'pass it on').

The way their entire existence is organised and their relationship with members of the majority may reveal the basic endeavour so characteristic of traditional Roma groups: striving for liberty and autonomy from the surrounding host society. Nevertheless, in their case this autonomy and liberty is extremely limited. On the one hand, they lack the emotional, psychological background and the appropriate social resources that could make this way of life possible, affordable only by members of a greater group. On the other hand, they must face discriminative prejudices continuously even in this narrow world. One may think of such humiliating 'niceties' as that in the neighbouring pub (with the owner of which they are on 'friendly terms') where they can get served only if there are no other customers present (they cannot even enter the pub, for instance, when there is a change of shift in the nearby factory) and can only use plastic cups; and continuing with the fact that concerns their existence directly and gravely, that is the constant possibility that some of their exchange partners may try to take advantage of their defenceless position (who feels guilt about making a few hundred forints off the scavenging Romas?), which turns true from time to time. Beyond all of these circumstances are those really 'tough' situations; for example, when a tree cut down next to the riding school, fell exactly on Old Tóni's tent – by accident.

This marginal way of life, balancing on the fine line between two worlds, the traditional Roma and that of the majority society, has a strong deteriorating effect on the family members' physical and mental health. It is only a matter of time before

16 On the traditional Roma trades and economics see Formoso (1986) and Havas (1999).

17 On the different types of reciprocity see Sahlins (1965).

some of them fall to an illness or some kind of accident (death by fire, freezing or railroad accident), as it has already happened during the last several years to some 'homeless' people who sought shelter in Old Tóni's neighbourhood.

As I mentioned above, the research study had some explicit legal aspects as well. The researchers got in contact with the family during the course of an investigation into a discrimination case. The local government brought an ordinance against scavenging – presumably under the pressure of the local street-cleaning company[18] – prohibiting and qualifying it as a misdemeanour. The local police started an investigation against the scavengers (most of whom were Roma) and imposed fines on them. This is the case[19] in which the family became the client of the Legal Aid Bureau of National and Ethnic Minorities (NEKI), where a member of the research group worked at that time.

The action of the NEKI succeeded in changing the practice of the police, and they no longer prosecute scavengers for taking away the waste – the last proceedings against a scavenger were at the end of 1999. These were the reasons that compelled the researchers to pay particular attention to the relationship between the family and the police.

The patrolling policemen encounter the family members on a regular basis, they know them by name and, under given circumstances, they have a relatively accurate picture of them, certainly more nuanced than that of the personnel at various state and non-governmental organisations operated by the majority, whose job is to know them well. Let a detective's words stand here to describe their point of view on the family: 'We have no more problem with them than with other people ... On the contrary, maybe less. ... Scavenging is primarily a source of income for them.' It is obvious to the detective that even if they are 'nasty' people – 'foul-smelling, filthy and infectious' – Old Tóni, his family and the other neighbouring scavengers *are not criminals* 'even though they may commit a petty offence or two at times', or larceny when they are short of money. The policemen generally think that scavenging attracted these people into the city, and they are now content with this lifestyle, 'they lowered their expectations', and 'they themselves are also responsible for the situation they are in', because they gave up their house in the neighbouring village, and at the same time do not want to move into the homeless shelter. Otherwise, it is easy to handle them when they are sober, but when they are drunk – especially Old Tóni – they often try to pick a fight with the policemen.

18 It is a fact that the sort of scavenging Old Tóni and his folks do is only the tip of the iceberg. The staff of the street-cleaning companies can acquire a considerable amount of supplementary income by informing their 'teams' – recruited from relatives and acquaintances – of the most valuable 'loot'. These teams haul away the used furniture, household appliances or the heavier scrap metal with trucks when there is a junk-clearance somewhere.

19 For the detailed description of the case see NEKI's *White Booklet, 2000* (2001), 48–51.

It may be in part due to these frequent meetings that some sort of a 'useful relationship' developed between the police and the family going beyond the official framework. The detectives offer small amounts of money (once a shabby bicycle) to them in exchange for information. Since Old Tóni and his folk happen to be in and out of different places – shops, pubs – in the city, they have easy access to information that may be useful to the police (for example, on who is stealing the bicycles around the railway station). If they can help the police, they can get money or some other form of a reward for their support. According to the police, this is only on an occasional and not a regular basis, and they are not considered informers. If the police need some information and the family is available to help, then the 'useful relationship' could work, and it is resumable at any time.

The picture drawn by the researchers on basis of the interviews shows that the members of Old Tóni's family are not afraid of the police, they know them by names (by the nicknames they have given them, of course). It happened sometimes under the 'scavenge-prohibition' that one or other policeman warned them of an outstanding warrant for their arrest (because they could not pay the fine for scavenging), or the police even dropped the case against them entirely.

Old Tóni and his folk confirmed what the police said about the 'useful connection' (except that they failed to mention the compensation they received from the police for the information). The researchers observed that they were not afraid of policemen; for instance, they never ran away from the litter-bins when seeing them appear.

There is another important aspect of their relationship with the police. The homeless people quite often have conflicts they cannot resolve among themselves, and they try to eliminate their opponent by telling on them to the police. This fact signals that the social mechanism or system of authority which could resolve their conflicts does not operate among homeless people; in other words, they do not have a real community.

The researchers drew the conclusion that among the institutions of the majority society Old Tóni's family has the closest relationship to the police despite the fact that they are not criminals.

Conclusions

If we had to summarise the morals of the two studies, we could say the Romas *really* are different. They behave differently in the courtroom from the non-Roma people; the homeless scavenging Romas who live in the countryside are really different from the non-Roma homeless scavengers living in the big cities. At this point, however, the majority of society and its institutions are incapable of doing anything else about this 'otherness' apart from *stigmatising* and *rejecting* it. If we want to change the latter (the stigmatisation and rejection of the Roma minority by the majority) then we have to understand the former (the Romas' 'otherness').

On the other hand, in a semiotic perspective, 'understanding' – that is, the way how we attribute meaning to signs and systems of signs – always presupposes communication (Kevelson, 1988c; Jackson 1995, 141–61). From this point of view, tolerance can be defined as the preliminary condition of understanding: a continuous effort to maintain the communication among the different members and groups of the society.

Chapter 5
'Une Certaine Idée de l'Homme, une Certaine Idée de la France': the Rhetorical Construction of Tolerance in French Political Discourse

Pamela Hobbs

Introduction

In 'Qu'est-ce qu'une nation?', French historian Ernest Renan, rejecting conventional definitions confounding the concept of nation with that of race, famously defined the nation as a political unit characterised by affective ties:

> A nation is a soul, a spiritual principle. Two things, which in truth are but one, constitute this soul, this spiritual principle. One is in the past, the other in the present. One is the common possession of a rich legacy of memories; the other is present-day consent, the desire to live together, the will to continue to contribute to the value of the collective heritage (1947, 903–4).

Renan's definition, which continues to influence contemporary scholarship on nationalism (see Snyder 1976, 20–24; Anderson 1991, 6), incorporates the idea that shared history results in the 'fusion' of ethnically diverse populations to create a common identity (Renan 1947, 890–892). However, this fusion is a process that occurs only over time; thus changing immigration patterns can fuel social and political unrest. In such cases, nationalism serves not to unite but to divide, as citizens who view immigrant populations as 'the Other' question their ability to become integrated into the national culture, a situation which may lead to the social and economic marginalisation and exclusion of immigrant groups (see Jennings 2000, 581).

Does nationalism offer a solution to this problem, or is it in fact the problem's root cause? I argue that nationalism has both positive and negative aspects which are discursively constructed, and that patriotic nationalism can be mobilised by the speeches of public leaders to combat racism and xenophobia by appeals to cultural values. This chapter examines the 8 July 2004 address of French President Jacques Chirac, in which he called upon the French government and people to take decisive action to combat the rising tide of racism, anti-Semitism, xenophobia and homophobia in France. My analysis identifies the rhetorical strategies by which historical events are organised to create a framework for the presentation of a French national identity that promotes tolerance and diversity and rejects racism and discrimination. My analysis thus demonstrates the role of political discourse in constructing the concept of nation as a system of positively valued inclusion.

Background

To the extent that their identifying characteristics are determined by the mental representations of citizens, nations are 'imagined communities' (Anderson 1991; see also Campbell 1992, 105; Wodak et al. 1999, 3). Yet in many parts of Europe, where changing patterns of immigration over the past several decades have resulted in ethnically diverse populations, the fragility of such mental constructs has become apparent. In France, the influx of immigrants from Africa and the Middle East during the last quarter of the twentieth century swelled the Muslim population of the country to five million people (Dewitte 2003, 90), bringing the French melting pot [*le creuset français*] to a boil. In 1989, in what came to be known as '*l'affaire des foulards*' ['the headscarf case'], three girls were expelled from a high school near Paris for wearing the *hajib* – the Muslim headscarf – to school, resulting in a media frenzy which Minister of Education Lionel Jospin attempted to defuse by announcing that the wearing of the *hajib* was to be permitted (Dewitte 2003, 89; Faroux and Chérifi 2003, 143). However, this only increased the furore, and thus *la guerre scolaire* [the school war] was begun (Fauroux and Chérifi 2003, 143).

The issues that were implicated were momentous: on the one hand was the principle of *laïcité* which commands a strict separation of church and state (Jennings 2000, 578); on the other was the *modèle français d'intégration*, the goal of which is to instil in naturalised citizens the cultural and patriotic values of the Republic (Jennings 2000, 582). Both of these interests were threatened by the perception that French Muslims felt themselves to be Muslim first and French only secondarily, a form of *communautarisme* that is antithetical to republican values (Jennings 2000, 583; Fauroux and Chérifi 2003, 73; Van der Valk 2003, 312). The anti-immigrant sentiment thus engendered, fuelled by rising unemployment, continued to simmer during the 1990s, and again reached a peak in the post-11 September election of 2002, when Jean-Marie Le Pen, the extreme-right *Front national* candidate, known for his anti-Semitism and his anti-immigration stance, received 16.95 per cent of the vote in the first round of voting, thus qualifying for the second round (Gattegno and Ridet 2002).

Le Pen's surprising showing was met with widespread dismay (Chayette 2002; Fauroux and Chérifi 2003, 143; Van der Valk 2003, 309). He was described on the editorial page of *Le Monde* as a 'sinister demagogue', and his interim victory was labelled 'an injury' to France (Colombani 2002); massive street rallies took place to protest his extremist positions (Service France 2002). However, the end result of these events was the further polarisation of public attitudes, and in March

2004, with the passage of a law prohibiting the wearing of 'conspicuous religious signs' (see Wagner 2005, 182–6) in the schools, the battle lines appeared to have been drawn. In such times, government response is critical to the preservation of public order and the restoration of national unity. Moreover, the response that is required is rhetorical, because national identities are discursively constructed and maintained (De Cillia et al. 1999, 153).

Data

The speech examined here[1] was delivered by French President Jacques Chirac on 8 July 2004, on the occasion of the impending national holiday of 14 July, the date upon which, in 1789, the storming of the Bastille marked the beginning of the French Revolution. First observed in 1790 as the '*fête de la Fédération*', the holiday plays a central role in the Republic's myth of origin. Annually celebrated by parades and pyrotechnical displays throughout France, it symbolises the triumph of the humanitarian principles of the Enlightenment over the tyranny of the *Ancien Régime*.

The speech was announced in a 1 July press release which stated that the President 'will express his thoughts on the necessity of fighting against intolerance and will invite the French people, in the days leading up to 14 July, to engage in vigilance and mobilisation to defend the values of the Republic' (Elysée, 2004).

By identifying the national holiday as the occasion for this speech, the President assured that it would receive national attention and wide dissemination by the media. In addition, the site chosen for the speech was highly symbolic of the topic to be addressed: Chambon-sur-Lignon, in the Protestant region of the province of Haute-Loire, is the only village to have received the title of 'Just Among Nations', conferred upon it by the state of Israel for the acts of its inhabitants in saving the lives of almost 5,000 Jews who were sheltered there during the Second World War (Pancho 2004).

Methodology

In analysing this data, I draw on the methodology of Critical Discourse Analysis, developed by scholars including Fairclough (1989, 1995), van Dijk (1993), Wodak (1995, 2001) and others, and specifically on the model of the discursive construction of national identity developed by Wodak et al. (1999). Critical Discourse Analysis

1 The text of the speech was obtained from the French government website *Présidence de la République Française* (<www.elysee.fr>). The text of the English translation was obtained from the website of the French Embassy, <www.amba.france-us.org.>; the portions of the translated text that appear herein contain some minor modifications involving word order and word choice.

focuses upon the intersection of discourse and social structure (Blommaert 2005, 25), and assumes a dialectical relationship between discursive events and the social and political contexts in which they occur (Wodak et al. 1999, 8). Moreover, political discourse, which operates 'as an instrument in the exercise of power, control and exclusion or, by contrast, as an instrument for achieving equality and democracy' (Van der Valk 2003, 314), is a key site for the implementation of this critical perspective.

In a comprehensive study of contemporary images of Austrian identity, Wodak et al. (1999) exhaustively analysed the lexical, syntactic and rhetorical dimensions of the discursive construction of national identity, identifying the macro-strategies by which political leaders and others construct national identities that reflect and promote personal or political ideologies, and the rhetorical figures, lexical units and syntactic devices by which these macro-strategies are realised (Wodak et al. 1999, 33–5). These include personal pronouns such as the inclusive 'we'; the use of the passive voice to obscure agency; the use of personification, metonymy and metaphor; the use of vagueness and euphemisms; and the use of argumentation schemes or 'topoi' which act as 'warrants' (Toulmin 1958, 98–101) connecting an argument to a particular conclusion. In this chapter, I apply this analytical framework to the data under examination.

Nationalism and discourse

The origins of nationalism are associated with the French Revolution and the social and political transformation that it precipitated (Ringmar 1998, 534; Snyder 1954, 80). The conviction that the revolutionary motto '*Liberté, Egalité, Fraternité*' applied, not only to certain classes or individuals, but to all citizens (Synder 1954, 80), resulted in a new form of group consciousness characterised by 'an expansion of affiliative beliefs, attitudes, and behaviours so as to include far more distant (indeed, purely figurative) kin, far more distant authorities, and far more inclusive commitments than those that are immediately available to or directly impinge on … [the citizen's] daily experiences' (Fishman, 1972, 6).

Anderson (1991, 5–7) encapsulated this powerful psychological response in his famed definition of the nation as 'an imagined political community'.

Yet the nation that is the object of this political love has no natural or stable identity (Bruner 2002, 1; De Cillia et al. 1999, 154; Campbell 1992, 105). A nation, as a symbolic community, is discursively constructed, and different national identities are constructed in different contexts (De Cillia et al. 1999, 154–5). What the nation is at any point in time is dependent upon the account of national character that has captured the public's imagination (Bruner 2002, 1). There is thus 'a never-ending and politically consequential rhetorical struggle over national identity' (Bruner 2002, 1), in which politicians, intellectuals, and the media play a part (De Cillia et al. 1999, 153). These rhetorical battles are politically significant because of the influence of conceptions of national character on the national community as a whole (Bruner 2002, 2): 'The conception of a community makes a certain kind of person possible, and the conception of a person makes a certain kind of community possible' (Ringmar, 1998: 538).

However, despite a widespread recognition of the role of discourse in the construction of collective identities, analyses of such articulations, until recently, have been rare (but see Augoustinos et al. 1999; Wodak et al. 1999; Condor 2000; Bruner 2002; Bishop and Jaworski 2003; Ricento 2003; Yamaguchi 2005).

The relationship between nationalism and history

National identity is strongly linked to national history. Nationalism seeks to construct the present as a rational continuation of a past that is pure and authentic, a source of greatness (Fishman 1972, 8, citing Bromage 1956, 29). This glorious past then serves as an example for the future (Nietzsche 1909, 16), inspiring the people 'to make new efforts, to overcome new dangers, and to achieve new (and even greater) greatness' (Fishman 1972, 8).

Nationalism's intuitive recognition of the power of these images of past greatness (Fishman 1972, 9) is vividly evoked by Renan: 'A heroic past, great men, glory … such is the social capital upon which rests a national idea' (1947, 904).

Such 'monumental history' is not mere cultural self-aggrandisement, but provides a powerfully motivating model for imitation, for greatness that was once achieved may again be possible to grasp (Nietzsche 1909, 19–21); thus national leaders may evoke past glories to exploit their unifying force. Citing calls to arms such as Napoleon's 1809 proclamation urging the Hungarians to join with him to defeat the Habsburg emperor in order to reclaim the language, the customs and the land of their illustrious ancestors, Fishman (1972, 9) notes: 'As we read these and similar words today we cannot but recognise their energising, mobilising purpose and effect. The past is being mined, ideologised, and symbolically elaborated in order to provide determination, even more than direction, with respect to current and future challenges.'

This force is 'necessary above all to the man of action and power who fights a great fight and needs examples, teachers, and comforters', for 'he cannot find them among his contemporaries' (Nietzsche 1909, 16).

Analysis

The speech examined here was delivered on the occasion of a national holiday, and thus belongs to the genre of commemorative speeches, the primary purpose of which is 'to retrieve the past for the present' (Wodak et al. 1999, 70). Speeches given by public officers on such occasions, while often viewed as largely ceremonial, enjoy a prominence that is derived from the fact that they constitute official acts whose purpose is to mark a high point in the nation's history. Accordingly, not only the subject and the occasion, but the political role and identity of the speaker, contribute to the production, interpretation, and reception of such speeches.

A nation's president, as head of state, is both the supreme representative of the national collective and the voice of the nation (Wodak et al. 1999, 72); the president is thus 'expected to address moral issues deemed to be important to the state in a solemn, dignified manner on relevant occasions' (Wodak et al. 1999). Yet when the issue to be addressed requires the condemnation of the behaviour of large segments of the population, the delicacy of the task requires the careful weighing of the words to be used. Moreover, speeches commemorating the birth of the Republic are conventionally expected to include paeans and panegyrics to French civilisation and French history. Indeed, praise of France is not only expected but mandatory, for a leader who fails to praise the nation on such a date cannot lead.

The President meets this challenge by developing a theme that assigns both praise and blame. The theme that he develops is that France is confronted with a choice between good and evil. However, rather than stating this explicitly, he evokes the history of Chambon, which he praises as embodying the authentic values of the Republic. His design is to hold up the actions of this village as an example for present-day France. In so doing, he uses a number of rhetorical devices which will be examined in detail.

Excerpt 1

Nous sommes, Monsieur le Maire vient de le rappeler, c'est vrai, ici dans un lieu chargé d'histoire et d'émotion. Ici, dans l'épreuve, s'est affirmée l'âme de la nation. Ici, c'est avancée et s'est incarnée la conscience de notre pays.
[We are, it is true, as the mayor has just reminded us, here in a place steeped in history and emotion. Here, in those terrible days, the nation's soul was awakened. This place was the embodiment of our country's conscience.]

Le Chambon-sur-Lignon est un lieu de mémoire. Un lieu de résistance. Un lieu symbole de la France fidèle à ses principes, fidèle à son héritage, fidèle à son génie.
[Le Chambon-sur-Lignon is a place of remembrance. A place of resistance. A place symbolising a France true to her principles, true to her heritage, true to her genius.]

Sur ce haut plateau aux hivers rudes, dans la solitude, parfois le dénuement, souvent dans l'adversité, des femmes et des hommes portent depuis longtemps les valeurs, ces valeurs qui nous unissent.
[On this high plateau, with its harsh winters, in solitude, sometimes destitution, often in adversity, women and men have long held the values, the values which unite us.]

> Dans ce qui fut l'une des régions les plus déshéritées de notre pays, bravant tous les périls, ils ont fit le choix du courage, de la générosité et de la dignité.
> [In what was one of the most deprived areas of our country, standing up to all the dangers, they chose courage, generosity and dignity.]
>
> Ils ont fait le choix de la tolérance, de la solidarité et de la fraternité.
> [They chose tolerance, solidarity and fraternity.]
>
> Ils ont fait le choix des principes humanistes qui rassemblent notre communauté nationale et fondent notre communauté de destin. Des principes qui font la France.
> [They chose the humanist principles which unite our national community and found our community of destiny. Principles which make France what she is.]

Chirac begins his speech with a personal reference, a use of the inclusive 'we' (Wodak et al. 1999, 45) by which he unites himself with his audience: 'Nous sommes … ici dans un lieu chargé d'histoire et d'émotion' ['We are … here in a place steeped in history and emotion']. This linking of history and emotion evokes a past that is not dead, but that lives on in the collective memory of the nation (see Halbwachs 1980). Moreover, by addressing the history of the village on the occasion of a national holiday, Chirac constructs the history of these local events as *the history of France*.

He opens his tribute to the village with the emotionally charged phrase, 'Ici, dans l'épreuve, s'est affirmé l'âme de la nation' ['Here, in those terrible days, the nation's soul was awakened']. In the lines that follow, repeated references to the place ('ici', 'un lieu') function metonymically to substitute the village for its inhabitants, whose acts are then attributed to a personified France: 'A place of resistance' ['Un lieu de résistance'], the village embodies 'the conscience of our country' ['la conscience de notre pays'], thus symbolising a France 'true to her principles, true to her heritage, true to her genius' ['fidèle à ses principes, fidèle à son heritage, fidèle à son genie'].

The personification of France ('la France', 'la belle France') is a standard convention of French patriotism with its characteristic emotional intensity. This personified France is a vividly experienced presence in which the nation's essential attributes are symbolically portrayed. Chirac exploits this symbolism by evoking several important topoi of French national identity as he praises the citizens of Chambon for adhering to 'les valeurs qui nous unissent' ['the values which unite us'], values which motivated them to make, at great risk to themselves, 'le choix du courage, de la generosité et de la dignité … de la tolerance, de la solidarité et de la fraternité' '[the choice of courage, generosity and dignity … of tolerance, solidarity and fraternity'].

The use of the word 'choice', which emphasises the voluntary (moral) nature of the citizens' acts, simultaneously draws attention to their political dimension. The notion of choice is rooted in the traditions of the French Revolution and the concept of the political community that it produced (Jennings 2000, 577). Schnapper (1991, 63) argues that '[n]ational identity is not a biological but a political fact: one is French through the practice of a language, through the learning of a culture, through the wish to participate in an economic and political life' (cited also in Jennings 2000, 577).

This description seems to echo Simone Weil, who stated that the quality of being French is 'pas un fait mais un choix de volonté' ['not a fact but a free choice'] (1949, 99). Moreover, in characterising this choice, Chirac conjures images of French civic virtues that continue to populate the nation's identity narratives, as exemplified by this description of French generosity from Giscard d'Estaing's book *Les Français*:

> It is a particular type of generosity, little known to the outside world. It proceeds from a mixture of hospitality and enthusiasm. Hospitality in the country dweller's sense of the term, which is to say that one opens one's door, or shares one's food, or sets out in the night to bring help to someone who is stuck in the mud, or has been caught in a snowdrift, and all with a simplicity, without fuss or ado, as if it were the most natural thing in the world. And enthusiasm – that French enthusiasm which has the inconvenience of setting off ad hoc revolutions, but which constitutes a genuine, heartfelt impulse, addressed to others, to their distress, to the hardship of their existence, as it is in other times to the glory of arms or athletic victories (Giscard d'Estaing 2000, 266–7.)

This French generosity, as thus defined, is nothing other than *fraternity*, the 'deep, horizontal comradeship' by which a people conceive themselves as one (Anderson 1991, 7). Yet Fraternity for France is more than fellow feeling: it stands, together with Liberty and Equality, as a timeless representation of the core values of the Republic. Chirac evokes the powerful symbolism of the revolutionary motto and its potent moral force when he states of the inhabitants of Chambon that '[i]ls ont fait le choix des principes humanistes qui rassemblent notre communauté nationale et fondent notre communauté de destin. Des principes qui font la France' ['They chose the humanist principles which unite our national community and found our community of destiny. Principles which make France what she is'].

Excerpt 2

> L'histoire des communes du 'Plateau' épouse celle du combat pour la liberté de conscience et pour la tolérance. Aux confins de la Haute-Loire et de l'Ardèche, cette vielle terre de protestantisme a subi, dès la révocation de l'Édit de Nantes, l'épreuve de l'intolérance religieuse. Pour y faire face, le protestantisme dut mener un douloureux combat, un combat pour la nation, un combat qui conduisit à l'inscription de la liberté religieuse dans notre Déclaration des droits de l'Homme.

[The history of the Plateau's villages and hamlets mirrors that of the battle for freedom of conscience and tolerance. On the borders of Haute Loire and Ardèche, this part of France, long an enclave of Protestantism, suffered, from the time of the Revocation of the Edict of Nantes, the ordeals of religious intolerance. To confront it, Protestants had to wage a painful battle, a battle for the nation, a battle which led to the inclusion of religious freedom in our Declaration of the Rights of Man.]

Parce que ces compagnes ont gardé vivante la mémoire de ces drames, elles sont devenues terre d'accueil, de partage et de refuge. Ici, persécutés, déshérités, réfugiés ont trouvé asile. Ici, juifs menacés de mort ont trouvé protection. Ici, maquisards et combattants de l'ombre ont trouvé abri.
[Because the Plateau kept the memory of those tragedies alive, it became a place of welcome, sharing and refuge. Here, the persecuted, destitute and refugees found asylum. Here, Jews threatened with death found protection. Here, Resistance and underground fighters found shelter.]

Cette terre d'asile est l'un de ces lieux où souffle l'esprit de résistance. Ce pays, qui a payé chèrement le prix de la liberté de conscience, a vu très tôt des femmes et des hommes se lever pour dire non.
[This place of asylum is one of those which breathes the spirit of resistance. The Plateau, which paid a heavy price for freedom of conscience, very soon saw women and men stand up and say 'no'.]

Guidés par des pasteurs et des enseignants admirables, villageois et paysans du 'Plateau', habitants du Chambon et des localités voisines qui ont partagé le même idéal, refuseront, pour reprendre le titre d'un livre édité ici même, au Chambon, 'les matins bruns'. Ils refuseront l'infamie de régime de Vichy. Ils feront de beau verbe 'résister' leur étendard. Ils transformeront chacune de leurs fermes en refuge. Quand d'autres, secondés par l'État français, commettaient l'irréparable, ici, des milliers de juifs, dont beaucoup d'enfants poursuivis par la menace d'extermination des nazis, trouvèrent hospitalité et refuge. Ils y trouvèrent le salut.
[Led by admirable clergymen and teachers, the Plateau's villagers and farmers, inhabitants of Chambon and the neighbouring hamlets who shared the same ideal, were to refuse – to take the title of a book published here in Chambon – 'les matins bruns' ['dark mornings']. They were to refuse the infamy of the Vichy regime. They were to make the fine verb 'to resist' their standard. They were to turn all their farms into refuges. When others, assisted by the French State, committed the irreparable, here, thousands of Jews, including many children hounded by the Nazis' threat of extermination, found hospitality and refuge. They found salvation.]

> Dans l'anonymat, la discrétion, dans le simple élan de la main tendue, de la fraternité et de l'humanité partagées, refusant la loi de la haine, 'le Plateau', 'Juste parmi les nations', le 'Plateau' a grandi la France.
> [Anonymously, unobtrusively, through the simple gesture of an out-stretched hand, through fraternity and shared humanity, refusing the law of hatred, 'the Plateau', 'Righteous among Nations', increased France's stature.]

In this section of his speech, Chirac engages in monumental history (Nietzsche 1909, 16–21) through a detailed and emotionally charged description of the history of the region which presents these historical events as a model for imitation (Nietzsche 1909, 20–21). In so doing, he continues to develop the theme of a choice between good and evil.

He evokes the Protestant history of the region in an extended *battle* metaphor which begins, 'L'histoire des communes du "Plateau" épouse celle du combat pour la liberté de conscience et pour la tolerance' ['The history of the Plateau's villages and hamlets mirrors the battle freedom of conscience and tolerance']. After citing 'the ordeals of religious intolerance' that the region's inhabitants underwent following the Revocation of the Edict of Nantes, he repeats the word 'battle' ['combat'] three times, with increasing dramatic emphasis: 'Pour y faire face, le protestantisme dut mener un doloreuse *combat*, un *combat* pour la nation, un *combat* qui conduisit à l'inscription de la liberté religieuse dans notre Déclaration des droits de l'Homme' ['To confront it, Protestants had to wage a painful *battle*, a *battle* for the nation, a *battle* which led to the inclusion of religious freedom in our Declaration of the Rights of Man']. He thus calls to mind the persecution of the Protestants which is part of French history, and which represents something that the nation was required to, and did, overcome, in order to become a democracy; and explicitly refers to the principle of *laïcité* which was adopted in order to protect Protestants against the monolithic power of the Roman Catholic Church (see Jennings 2000, 578). This history demonstrates that religious differences that divided the country and that were the source of major problems were (and thus, by implication, are) able to be resolved (see Nietzsche 1909, 19).

Drawing a connection between the region's Protestant history and the wartime heroism of its inhabitants, Chirac states, 'Parce que ces compagnes ont gardé vivante la mémoire de ces drames, elles sont devenues terre d'accueil, de partage et de refuge' ['Because the Plateau kept the memory of those tragedies alive, it become a place of welcome, sharing and refuge'], thus emphasising the role of historical remembrance in shaping the identity, and hence the conduct, of human groups (Halbwachs 1980, 51–2). In addition, his continued use of metonymy ('terre d'acueil, de partage et de refuge') acts to constitute a community of values that is stable over time.

A final metonymic expression introduces a more concrete description of the villagers' actions: 'Cette terre d'asile … où souffle l'esprit de résistance … a vu très tôt des femmes et des hommes se lever pour dire non' ['This place of asylum ... which breathes the spirit of resistance ...very soon saw men and women stand up and say "no"]. In poetic language, he describes how, '[g]uided by admirable clergymen and teachers' ['[g]uidés par des pasteurs et des enseignants admirables'], and refusing 'the infamy of the Vichy regime' ['l'infamie de régime du Vichy'], they made '[the] fine verb "resist" their standard' ['[le] beau verbe "resister" leur étandard']. He also incorporates a reference to a political fable published in Chambon in 1998 (Aissaoui 2005), which depicted a naïve onlooker's description of a society's incremental slide into totalitarianism, symbolised by its metaphorical title, *Matin brun* (*Dark Morning*), and which became a popular phenomenon after it was reviewed on the national radio station France Inter immediately prior to an interview of Jean-Marie Le Pen in April 2002.

In contrasting the acts of the inhabitants of the region in sheltering the Jews, and the humanitarian principles on which those acts were based, with the depraved criminality of the Nazi regime, with which the Vichy government was complicit, Chirac explicitly contrasts 'good' and 'evil' French actors. Yet without dwelling on the contrast itself, he foregrounds the actions of the villagers and farmers in an eloquent tribute that details their motivations, motivations which resulted in the village being honoured by the state of Israel, which conferred upon it the title 'Just among Nations'. These actions and motivations, Chirac affirms, increased France's stature ['a grandi France'].

Excerpt 3

Telle est la France à laquelle je crois. Une France capable du meilleur, fidèle à son histoire, à ses racines, à sa culture. Une France de l'audace et de la solidarité, qui surmonte ses peurs et se dépasse pour aller au-devant de celles et de ceux qui ont besoin d'elle, de son aide, de sa protection, de son soutien. Une France généreuse, qui refuse l'égoïsme, le repli sur soi, l'exclusion, la discrimination. Une France ouverte et accueillante, unie dans sa diversité, qui porte avec fierté son idéal de justice et de paix en Europe et dans le monde.
[This is the France that I believe in. A France capable of the best, true to her history, to her roots, to her culture. A France of courage and solidarity, who overcomes her fears and who reaches new heights by seeking out those who have need of her, of her help, her protection, her support. A generous France, who refuses to be selfish or inward-looking, who rejects exclusion and discrimination. An open and welcoming France, united in her diversity, who bears with pride her ideal of justice and of peace in Europe and in the world.]

De cette France fraternelle, nous devons être fiers. Nous devons la faire vivre et la défendre. Elle doit être pour nous un choix de chaque jour.

[Of this fraternal France, we must be proud. We must sustain and defend her. For all of us, every day, this must be the France we choose.]

> Ce choix, celui de vivre ensemble dans le respect de chaque différence, ce choix n'est jamais définitivement acquis. Le combat pour la tolérance et pour l'honneur est une conquête fragile et toujours recommencée.
> [This choice, to live together respecting every difference, is never made once and for all. Victory in the struggle for tolerance and for honour is fragile, with the battle always having to be fought anew.]

Having praised the citizens of Chambon, Chirac now holds them up as an example: 'Telle est la France à laquelle je crois' ['This is the France that I believe in']; in so doing, he positions himself as a moral leader, and moral teacher. Viroli (1995, 137) states, 'Patriotic politics is above all a politics of moral education'. Chirac uses the language of patriotism, of loyalty to and love of France, to create an account of French national identity that rejects discrimination and exclusion as antithetical to republican values. In this way he produces a kind of 'oratorical definition' (see Goodrich 1986, 192–3) designed to lead his audience to endorse the vision of France that he constructs, a France that is 'capable of the best, true to her history, to her roots, to her culture' ['capable du meilleur, fidèle à son histoire, à ses racines, à sa culture']. With this phrase, Chirac evokes the topos of French exceptionalism, an ideology that is built upon the notion that France's distinctive cultural and political contributions, as the birthplace of the Enlightenment and source of the Declaration of the Rights of Man, constitute it as a model for the rest of the world (see Ricento 2003, 613), and that is associated with Charles de Gaulle who, in the decades following World War II, laboured to restore France's global rank.

Moreover, in summoning for his audience the image of a France 'true to her history, to her roots, to her culture', Chirac at once conjures the nation's patrimony, a source of national pride, and the evocative personified France who stands for the best in all of them. In so doing, he appeals to the citizen's patriotic identification with these values, an identification which engenders strong feelings of attachment that he alludes to by his use of the word 'roots' ['racines']. Simone Weil, who wrote movingly about the importance of 'rootedness' ['l'enracinement'] and its critical importance to the ability of France to regenerate in the period following the Second World War, stated that certain modes of human thought and action can exist only in a particular national setting and vanish when a nation is destroyed; and that 'there exists, therefore, something to which a part of the soul of each French person is joined, the same for all, unique, real though impalpable, and real in the sense of things that one can touch' (Weil 1949, 138).

Chirac continues by cataloguing the qualities of this exceptional France: courage, solidarity, generosity, the willingness to help others and to be open and welcoming. He thereby produces a definition of fraternity which he announces with the hortatory phrase, 'De cette France fraternelle, nous devons être fiers' ['Of this fraternal France, we must be proud'], and which he immediately reinforces, once again evoking the idea of *choice*: 'Nous devons la faire vivre et la defender. Elle doit être pour nous un choix de chaque jour' ['We must sustain and defend her. For all of us, every day, this must be the France that we choose'].

The words 'un choix de chaque jour' ['a choice for each day'] recall Renan's famed definition of the nation as 'un plébiscite de tous les jours' ['a daily plebiscite'] (Renan 1947, 904; see also Jennings 2000, 577). Chirac expands upon this concept, stating that '[c]e choix, celui de vivre ensemble dans le respect de chaque difference, ce choix n'est pas jamais définitivement acquis. Le combat pour la tolérance et pour l'honneur est un conquête fragile et toujours recommencée' ['This choice, to live together respecting every difference, is never made once and for all. Victory in the struggle for tolerance and for honour is fragile, with the battle always having to be fought anew']. By acknowledging the fragility of shared visions of national character, he seeks to arouse the compassionate patriotism so vividly evoked by Weil (1949, 148–9):

> Compassion for fragility is always linked to love for true beauty, because we feel strongly that things that are truly beautiful should be assured an eternal existence, yet are not.
>
> One can love France for the glory that seems to assure her an existence extending far into time and space. Or one can love her as a thing which, being terrestrial, can be destroyed, and of which the value is thus all the more appreciable.

In thus presenting the beloved country as under threat, Chirac urges his audience to strengthen their commitment to its republican values.

Excerpt 4

Aujourd'hui encore, des actes de haine, odieux et méprisables, salissent notre pays. Les discriminations, l'antisémitisme, les racismes, tous les racismes, se déploient de nouveau insidieusement. Ils frappent nos compatriotes juifs présents dans notre pays depuis des temps immémoriaux. Ils frappent nos compatriotes de culture musulmane qui ont fait le choix de travailler et de vivre dans notre pays. Ils frappent, en réalité, tous nos compatriotes.
[Still today, odious and despicable acts of hatred are sullying our country. Discrimination, anti-Semitism, racism, all kinds of racism, are again spreading insidiously. They are striking our Jewish compatriots, who have been in our country since time immemorial. They are striking our Muslim compatriots who have chosen to work and live in our country. They are, in reality, striking all our compatriots.]

Ils atteignent nos écoles. Ils menacent nos enfants. Ils profanent nos lieux de culte, nos sépultures, nos symboles les plus forts.
[They are affecting our schools. They are threatening our children. They are desecrating our places of worship, our burial vaults, our most powerful symbols.]

> Tous ces actes, qui blessent les corps et choquent les âmes, disent l'obscurantisme, l'ignorance, la bêtise. Ils expriment le fanatisme, la volonté d'humilier, d'abaisser. Ils traduisent le refus de la différence et le rejet de l'autre.
> [All these acts which wound the body and shock the soul denote obscurantism, ignorance and stupidity. They express fanaticism and the desire to humiliate and abase. They reveal rejection of difference and of the Other.]
>
> Tous ces actes reflètent la part la plus sombre de l'âme humaine. Ils sont indignes de la France. Et, naturellement, je ferai tout pour que cela cesse.
> [All these acts reflect the darkest side of the human soul. They are unworthy of France. And I will of course do everything possible to stop them.]

Having eloquently praised the civic virtues that he seeks to encourage, Chirac now roundly condemns the vices that he seeks to deter. However, while he explicitly credits the citizens of Chambon with the values that he commends to his audience, he does not attribute the evils that he now deplores to any person or group, referring to them only as 'these acts'. He thus adopts a strategy of referential vagueness in which agency is obscured (Wodak et al. 1999, 35) through the use of the nominalisation 'acts' (Dunmire 2005, 491). This deletion of the actor(s) by topic transformation (Lerman 1983, 76–8) allows him to avoid directly accusing any of his immediate or wider national audience of the attitudes and behaviour that he attacks, thus allowing them to distance themselves from the reprehensible acts that he identifies. In addition, because he does not indict the behaviour of any specific individual, he can condemn these acts in the strongest possible terms.

The force of persuasive language stems in part from the fact that a word may have two types of meaning: a descriptive meaning and an evaluative or 'emotive' meaning (Stevenson 1944, 70–71; see also van Leewen 2007, 97–8). The emotive meaning of a word allows it to function as an implicit value-judgement which encapsulates a commendation or condemnation of the person, object, practice or situation that it designates (Hare 1952, 91). Here Chirac introduces the topic of intolerance with the metaphor of disease and contamination, warning that 'odious and despicable acts of hatred are sullying our country' ['des actes de haine, odieux et méprisables, salissent notre pays'], and are 'spreading insidiously' '[se déploient … insidieusement']. These negative labels precede the list of acts that he deplores (discrimination, anti-Semitism, and racism) to produce an oratorical definition that verbally marks them as stigmatised behaviour. Moreover, the strongly negative emotive meaning of the labels 'odious', 'despicable' and 'sullying', which is aptly illustrated by their common use in insults, acts to increase the force of his words, through the association between insult and psychological threat.

The topos of *threat* is further elaborated by his use of the verb 'strike' ['frapper'] to describe the effects of these acts: 'Ils frappent nos compatriotes juifs … de culture muselmane … en réalité, tous nos compatriots' ['They strike our Jewish … and Muslim compatriots … in reality, all of our compatriots']. This metaphor of physical attack, when used in connection with victims who are 'compatriots', signifies an attack on the nation, and indeed, Chirac signals that these acts endanger all aspects of French culture: 'Ils atteignent nos écoles. Ils menacent nos enfants. Ils profanent nos lieux de culture, nos sepultures, nos symbols les plus forts' ['They are affecting our schools. They are threatening our children. They are desecrating our places of worship and burial vaults, our most powerful symbols']. He thus frames these acts as embodying dangerous political beliefs which threaten the nation's cultural institutions (schools and churches), its past (burial places) and future (children).

Having described the acts in strongly negative terms, he now proceeds to describe the type of person who would commit them, while continuing to make use of the nominalisation 'these acts', which relieves him of the difficulties inherent in attributing them to a hypothesised actor or group and thus implicating some segment of his audience. Again making use of the language of insult, he states that such acts 'denote obscurantism, ignorance and stupidity' ['l'obscurantisme, l'ignorance, la bêtise'] and reflect 'the darkest side of the human soul' ['la part la plus sombre de l'âme humaine']. Then, speaking for the country as its moral and political leader, he pronounces judgement on these acts and affirms his commitment to prevent them: 'Ils sont indignes de la France. Et, naturellement, je ferai tout pour que cela cesse' ['They are unworthy of France. And I will of course do everything possible to stop them']. He then details, in a section of the speech not analysed here, his instructions to the nation's public officials – the Ministers of Justice and National Education, the police, judicial authorities, and all of the mayors of France – to combat 'these intolerable abuses' ['pour lutter contre ces derives intolérables'].

Excerpt 5

Face au risque de l'indifférence et de la passivité du quotidien, j'appelle solennellement chaque Française et chaque Français à la vigilance. Devant le danger, je les appelle au sursaut.
[In the face of the risk of indifference and passivity in everyday life, I solemnly call on every French woman and man to be vigilant. Confronted with danger, I call them to action.]

Devant la montée des intolérances, du racisme, de l'antisémitisme, de refus des différences, je leur demande de se souvenir d'une passée encore proche. Je leur dis de rester fidèles aux leçons de l'histoire, une histoire si récente. Je les invite à toujours rappeler à leurs enfants le danger mortel du fanatisme, de l'exclusion, de la lâcheté, de la démission devant l'extrémisme. Je leur demande de manifester avec force notre résolution, notre capacité à vivre dans la concorde et dans le respect.
[Confronted with growing intolerance, racism and anti-Semitism, the rejection of differences, I ask them to remember a past that is still near. I tell them to remain true to the lessons of history, such recent history. I urge them always to

remind their children of the mortal danger of fanaticism, exclusion, cowardice and abdication in the face of extremism. I ask them to demonstrate forcefully our resolution, our common capacity to live in harmony and respect one another.]

Je leur demande de toujours porter avec fierté notre héritage. Patrie des droits de l'Homme, la France a inscrit au fronton de ses édifices les valeurs universelles de l'Humanité. Elle a fait de la Liberté, de l'Egalité, de la Fraternité la devise de la République. Rappelons à nos enfants que toute l'histoire de la Nation française est jalonnée de ces combats, combats parfois terribles, les combats qui ont inscrit la tolérance et la protection du plus faible au premier rang de nos principes. Combats de ces grands esprits et de ces grandes consciences, qui ont forgé notre culture. Combats des plus humbles, souvent restés anonymes, dont l'engagement, parfois le sacrifice suprême, ont fait l'honneur et la grandeur de la France et des Français.
[I ask them always to bear our heritage with pride. France, the home of human rights, has inscribed on her public buildings the universal values of mankind. She has made 'Liberty, Equality and Fraternity' the motto of the Republic. Let us remind our children that the entire history of the French nation is punctuated with such battles, battles that were sometimes terrible, but which placed tolerance and the protection of the weakest at the forefront of our principles. Battles waged by the great minds, the great philosophers who forged our culture. Battles fought by the most humble, who have often remained anonymous, whose commitment, and sometimes supreme sacrifice, have done so much for the honour and greatness of France and the French.]

À quelques jours du 14 juillet, symbole de notre fraternité, j'appelle chacune et chacun au rassemblement pour qu'ensemble, fidèles à nos valeurs, nous sachions faire vivre une certaine idée de l'Homme, une certaine idée de la France.
[Just days before our 14 July celebration, the symbol of our fraternity, I call upon each and every one to join together, so that together, true to our values, we put into practice a certain idea of Man, a certain idea of France.]

Je vous remercie.
[Thank you.]

In this, the dramatic climax of his speech, Chirac issues a solemn call upon the nation to be vigilant. 'Confronted with danger,' he states, 'I call them to action' ['Devant le danger, je les appelle au sursaut']. With these words, he evokes General Charles de Gaulle's 18 June 1940 BBC radio appeal for the mobilisation of a Free French military force following Pétain's surrender. The speech, one of the most famous in French history, is commonly referred to as 'l'Appel au sursaut' ['the Call to Action']. By using this phrase Chirac thus combines a literal call to action with a historical allusion which recalls the threat that Nazi Germany posed to France's continued existence, while drawing an implicit parallel between recent incidents of racist and anti-Semitic violence and the horrors of the Nazi regime, thus heightening the effect of his warning. In this discursive context, the words 'vigilance', 'danger' and 'risk' elaborate the topos of *threat*, while the opposition of 'action' to 'indifference' and 'passivity' restates his theme of the choice between 'good' and 'evil'.

It is notable that, both here and in the personal exhortation that follows, he uses the third person ('them'), instead of 'you'. By this strategy of avoidance of second-person reference (see Lerman 1983, 81–2), he again uses distancing to avoid accusing his audience of the thoughts or actions which he criticises, and to allow them to accept his counsel while separating themselves from the blame that his words connote. At the same time, his repeated use of the self-referential 'I' emphasises his personal responsibility and unmediated involvement in the task at hand.

In the following sentence, he recycles the word 'devant' ['confronted with'] to list the acts that he condemns, which are thereby constituted as synonymous with 'danger': 'Devant la montée des intolerances, du racisme, de l'antisémitisme, de refus des différences, je leur demande de souvenir d'une passée encore proche' ['Confronted with growing intolerance, racism, anti-Semitism, the rejection of differences, I ask them to remember a past that is still near']. He thus introduces the topos of *history as teacher* (Wodak et al. 1999, 36, 40), which he develops by telling his (distanced) audience to 'remain true to the lessons of history' ['rester fidèle aux leçons de l'histoire'] and to 'to remind their children of the mortal danger of fanaticism, exclusion, cowardice, and abdication in the face of extremism' ['rappeler à leurs enfants le danger mortel du fanatisme, de l'exclusion, de lâcheté, de la démission devant l'extrémisme']. Through his use of the tutelary phrases 'I ask them' and 'I tell them', he foregrounds his role as a moral leader who commands their cooperation in defeating the evils that he decries. He then states, 'Je *leur* demande de manifester avec force *notre* resolution, *notre* capacité à vivre dans la concorde et dans le respect' ['I ask *them* to demonstrate forcefully *our* resolution, *our* common capacity to live in harmony and respect one another']. In this sentence, the shift from the distancing 'them' to the inclusive 'our', a variant of the 'national we' which constitutes the French people (Wodak et al. 1999, 131), implies the assent of *all those who are truly French* (see Ricento 2003, 619). Having sounded this chord, he summons the emotional persuasion of patriotic nationalism, charging his audience to 'always bear our heritage with pride' ['toujours porter avec fierté notre heritage'], and extolling France's role in embracing the principles of liberty, equality and fraternity and promulgating the Declaration of the Rights of Man: 'Patrie des droits de l'Homme, la France a inscrit au fronton de ses édifices les valeurs universelles de l'Humanité. Elle a fait de la Liberté, de l'Egalité, de la Fraternité la devise de la République' ['France, the home of human rights, has inscribed on her public buildings the universal values of mankind. She has made Liberty, Equality and Fraternity the motto of the Republic'].

As he continues, he now shifts from addressing a distanced, third-person audience to the immediacy effected by the use of the inclusive 'we': '*Rappelons* à nos enfants que toute l'histoire de la Nation française est jalonnée de ces combats, combats parfois terribles, les combats qui on inscrit la tolerance et la protection du plus faible au premier rang de nos principes' ['*Let us remind* our children that the entire history of the French nation is punctuated with such battles, battles which were sometimes terrible, but which placed tolerance and the protection of the weakest at the forefront of our principles']. He thus metaphorically joins the entire nation in the effort to construct a vision of France that will strengthen the social bond, a vision that constitutes French history as a battle for the establishment of human rights. Continuing to develop the topos of *battle*, he invites his audience to align themselves with those who have historically engaged in this battle, 'the great minds, the great philosophers who forged our culture' ['ces grand esprits et … ces grand consciences qui ont forgé notre culture'], and 'the most humble, who have often remained anonymous, whose commitment, and sometimes supreme sacrifice, have done so much for the honor and greatness of France and the French' ['[l]es plus humbles, souvent restés anonymes, dont l'engagement, parfois le sacrifice supreme, ont fait l'honneur et la grandeur de la France et des Français'].

As did the phrase, 'Je les appelle au sursaut', the phrase 'la grandeur de la France' calls to mind Charles de Gaulle, whose political philosophy during his presidency, centred on the development of the French economy and foreign policy, was known as 'le politique du grandeur' ['the politics of grandeur']. A towering figure in French history, due to the role that he played during the Second World War, de Gaulle is a 'symbol of France's fidelity to herself' (Weil 1949, 166). Having evoked the image of the man who 'incarnated the survival of [France's] honour' (Pompidou 1972), Chirac echoes de Gaulle in the powerful appeal to patriotism that concludes his speech:

> À quelques jours du 14 juillet, symbole de notre fraternité, j'appelle chacune et chacun au rassemblement pour qu'ensemble, fidèles à nos valeurs, nous sachions faire vivre une certaine idée de l'Homme, une certaine idée de la France.
> [Just days before our 14 July celebration, the symbol of our fraternity, I call upon each and every one to join together, so that together, true to our values, we put into practice a certain idea of Man, a certain idea of France].

He frames his appeal with a reference to the occasion, the holiday that is 'symbol[ic] of our fraternity', and again repeats the ritual phrase 'J'appelle', by which he constitutes himself as the nation's moral leader. After calling upon the distanced third-person audience to join together, he shifts to the inclusive 'we', which he fortifies with the phrase 'so that together, true to our values' ['pour qu'ensemble, fidèles à nos valeurs'], thus invoking the topos of *allegiance*, to share in the realisation of the lofty principles that 'put into practice a certain idea of Man, a certain idea of France' ['faire vivre une certaine idée de l'Homme, une certaine idée de la France'].

These stirring words immediately call to mind the revolutionary tradition that 'produces a distinctive conception of what it means to be a member of the political community and the nation' (Jennings 2000, 577). Commenting on this tradition in *Les Français*, Giscard d'Estaing notes 'the quasi-religious character that [the French] give to their political confrontations', and quotes an unnamed French diplomat who attributed this attitude to the Revolution, explaining, 'To replace the former order, it was indispensable to provide a new definition of mankind, and to give it a pretension to universality' (Giscard d'Estaing 2000, 51). He agrees, adding 'We do indeed have the habit of confrontation about a conception of mankind, and of making it a political subject … . It's what gives interest … to our political debate, but it's also what gives it a bitter edge. One doesn't compromise on one's conception of man!' (Giscard d'Estaing 2000, 51).

They also call to mind the opening pages of de Gaulle's *Mémoires de Guerre* (*War Memoirs*), in which he explores the patriotic sentiments that motivated his public service, and which begin with the line, 'Toute ma vie, je me suis fait une certaine idée de la France' ['All my life, I have had a certain idea of France'] (1954, 1). This well-known phrase is highly evocative, and is associated in the minds of many with the narrative description that follows, in which de Gaulle writes of being instilled with patriotism as a child by being taken to view French monuments, in a passage that is reminiscent of Michelet (1946, 263–4) and Rousseau (1916, 186–8). In thus evoking the greatness to which France is heir, Chirac seeks to inspire the nation through contemplation of its past.

Discussion

Notwithstanding its intrinsic appeal, Anderson's definition of the nation as an 'imagined political community' raises the implicit question: Imagined by whom? How does this imaginary entity enter the minds of those who come to constitute it? The answer is that it is transmitted through discourse, primarily in narratives of national culture (Wodak et al. 1999, 23; see also Hall 1996, 613–614). However, '[a] national identity is not simply a narrative or set of narratives', but 'an ongoing discursive negotiation of what it imaginatively means to be a member of a nation' (Bruner 2002, 7).

Constructions of national identity build on history; yet history itself is biased and incomplete, particularly as it exists in the collective memory (De Cillia et al. 1999, 154). Thus Renan (1947, 891) observed 'Therefore the essence of a nation is that all of the individual members have many things in common, and all have also forgotten many things.'

In their use in the public sphere, narratives of national identity construct a relationship between the (imagined) past and images of the present and future 'in order to overcome a quite modern kind of fragmentation and loss of identity' (Fishman 1972, 9). Such images are deployed in times of crisis for their energising effect (Fishman 1972), in order to promote social mobilisation and create support for government policies (Snyder 1976, 25; Bruner 2002, 8).

In the speech examined here, Chirac, responding to the rising tide of racism and intolerance in France, attempts to articulate a model of what it means to be a French citizen that will motivate citizens to reject these negative sentiments, and the behaviour that they incite. He thus implicitly evokes the concept of *civisme* [good citizenship], an important principle in France's republican political ideology. However, in order to avoid the capital mistake of directly accusing his national audience of *incivisme*, he seeks to renew in them a vision of the glorious past that will inspire its emulation. His choice of historical periods is thus surprising. The Second World War represents a troubled era in France's past, and the history of the period is composed of two contradictory stories: the first, the French surrender to the Nazis, entails the shame, not only of defeat, but of the collaboration of the Vichy government with Hitler's criminal design, while the second celebrates the heroism of the Resistance and the Free French forces led by General de Gaulle. Yet by choosing this seemingly problematic narrative, and by overtly avoiding its negative aspect to focus on the exemplary and courageous acts of the inhabitants of Chambon, Chirac provides himself with the means to contrast the negative nationalism of prejudice and exclusion with the patriotic nationalism of inclusion, and to thereby appeal to the revolutionary ideals that found France's imagined political community.

There is no consensus among scholars as to either the scope of the attitudes encompassed by the concept of nationalism or the factors that serve to distinguish it from patriotism, a closely related concept. Anderson contrasts nationalism with racism, viewing the concept of race as 'a system of negatively valued exclusion' and nation as 'a system of positively valued inclusion' (Condor 2000, 177, citing Anderson, 1991). Nevertheless it is clear that nationalism (ordinarily) has an ethnic component. Indeed, Fishman (1972, 8) sees ethnocentrism as intrinsic to nationalism, noting that 'a basic component of nationalism is its stress on ethnocultural characterisation and on the authenticity, purity, and nobility of the beliefs, values and behaviours that typify the community of reference.'

Similarly, Ringmar (1998, 534–5) argues that the Enlightenment created an association between nationalism and democracy, the latter being defined as the idea that rule should be not only 'by the people', but 'by *our* people', that is, by people who are like 'us'. Under this definition, intolerance and discrimination appear to be virtually guaranteed by certain constructions of this collective 'us'.

Some definitions of patriotism distinguish it from nationalism in terms of the *focus* of the respective concepts. Thus Viroli (1995, 1) defines patriotism as love of country, and nationalism as the cultural, linguistic and ethnic oneness of a people. Snyder (1976, 43; emphasis in original) draws the identical contrast, stating, 'Patriotism is concerned with the people's love for a *country*; nationalism refers to the historical sentiment of a *people*'. Yet Snyder (1976, 48) notes that patriotism 'can easily be exaggerated into an extreme form' that is very negative – that is, chauvinism or jingoism (see also Tolstoy 1905). In this form 'patriotism breeds nationalism, nationalism nurtures militarism, militarism encourages imperialism, and imperialism stimulates rebelling nationalism in the very people who it subjects to its control' (Snyder, 1976, 53).

As a result of these inconsistent and diverging definitions, Condor (2000, 178) questions the usefulness of the claimed distinctions between patriotism and nationalism in understanding how national identity is constructed through discourse.

It thus seems closer to the truth to concede that nationalism and patriotism are multi-faceted concepts which sometimes overlap, and which have both positive and negative aspects and manifestations. Accordingly, for the purposes of this discussion, I will use the terms 'negative nationalism' to denote enthocentrism, defined as identification with a particular racial or ethnic group, resulting in the classification of non-group members as 'the Other'; and 'patriotic nationalism' to denote love of country, defined as the sentimental attachment to the nation, particularly as symbolised by popular representations of its history, traditions and culture. Viroli applied similar definitions in arguing that patriotic nationalism (which he terms 'patriotism') provides a powerful weapon against negative nationalism (which he terms 'nationalism'):

> Precisely because it competes with nationalism on the same terrain of passions and particularity and uses rhetorical rather than purely rational arguments, patriotism is a formidable opponent for nationalism. It works on bonds of solidarity and fellowship that like feels toward like to transmute them into forces that sustain liberty instead of fomenting exclusive aggression. It does not say to the Italians or Germans who want to remain Italian or German that they should think and act as citizens of the world, or as lovers of an anonymous liberty and justice; it tells them that they should become Italian or German *citizens* committed to defend and improve their own republic, and to live freely in their own way, and it says so by using poignant images that refer to shared memories by telling meaningful stories that give colour and warmth to the ideal of the republic (Viroli 1995, 8–9; emphasis in original).

Chirac's speech is an example of the use of patriotic nationalism to mobilise citizens that is striking for its use of 'poignant images that refer to shared memories', because the memories that he evokes are not solely of the nation's virtues and glories but also of its vices and failures. In developing his image of the current crisis as a choice between good and evil, he presents a moving portrait of individual acts of courage and surrounds these acts with powerful cultural symbols and cherished ideals, in order to recreate a high point in the history of the nation, and to urge his audience to make the choice that motivated those heroic acts. In so doing, he follows a path sketched out by Nietzsche (1909, 17): 'For his orders are that what has once been able to extend the conception "man" and give it a fairer content, must ever exist for the same office.'

Conclusion

The foregoing analysis has identified the rhetorical strategies used by French President Jacques Chirac in his 8 July 2004 speech in an effort to heal the social rift in France through an appeal to patriotic nationalism. This use of patriotic nationalism is a well-recognised means of promoting social mobilisation (see also Fishman 1972, 9; Snyder 1976, 12–13; Bruner 2002, 8). In evoking the emotional symbolism of the personified France and the liturgy of the revolutionary motto, Chirac created vivid images of the Republic which appealed to national pride, while his fervent praise of the wartime heroism of the inhabitants of Chambon drew implicit contrasts between their acts and the genocidal racism of the Nazi regime – and, by extension, between racism, anti-Semitism and xenophobia and 'authentic' French values.

Yet just four days after this speech, a young woman accompanied by her 13-month-old infant was attacked on a train north of Paris by six assailants who believed her to be Jewish (Durand and Tourancheau 2004). Since then, France has experienced increasing signs of social unrest, including the widespread urban riots of November 2005, and a tear-gas attack on a mosque (Samuel 2005). Among the results of this chain of events have been a questioning of both the government's response to the changing conditions in the country, and the continuing vitality of the republican model itself (see also Jennings 2000; Fauroux and Chérifi 2003). However, Laurence and Vaisse (2005, 1), in an article discussing the November 2005 riots, argue that 'the real problem' is not the republican model, but 'insufficient mobilisation of the French people to make it a reality'. Their analysis serves to emphasise the importance of the role of public discourse in promoting national unity, for it is ultimately through discourse that national identities are produced and transformed (De Cillia et al. 1999, 153). Accordingly, Chirac's speech, while failing to miraculously alter the current of events, stands as a model for emulation by France's civic and religious leaders in the struggle to re-establish social and cultural equilibrium. In the words of Giscard d'Estaing (2000, 338):

> The day when [the French people] have the perception of belonging to the same human group, formed and wrought by a common history, and constituting a fragile cultural and demographic isle in the vast ocean which mounts around them, they will have more than enough strength to find the evolution necessary to their adaptation.

Chapter 6

Shifts in the Concept of War: New War Terminology and its Legal Consequences

Hanneke van Schooten

Introduction

In issues of war and peace, the question of which rules apply and which do not depends on the legal status of the situation: is a country in a state of war or in a state of peace? A state of war exists only after a declaration of war. This declaration is the dividing point between war and peace. If a country is in a state of war, the war of law binds the belligerents, as well as particular rules of domestic law that refer to a state of war or a time of war. However, the distinction between war and peace has become blurred. Owing to the prohibition of interstate force in the 1945 United Nations Charter, the terms 'war' and 'declaration of war', contained in Article 96 of the Dutch Constitution, have fallen into disuse. As a result, no declarations of war have been made, while the number of interstate hostilities not amounting to 'war' has greatly increased since 1945. Conflicts have been described as 'police actions', 'operations', 'missions' or 'armed conflicts'. The new terminology often leads to confusion. The meaning of the terms and categories used is unclear, the legal consequences are uncertain. Uncertainty about the legal status of an 'armed conflict' or a 'peacekeeping operation' can be observed in case law. The absence of the old, clear-cut categories affects citizens who are involved in warfare. This became crystal clear in several cases brought before Dutch courts concerning military actions during the Gulf War, Operation Enduring Freedom in Afghanistan, and the peacekeeping operation in Iraq.

In this chapter, the fundamental shift in the concept of war, new war terminology and new war categories will be highlighted. The legal consequences of these new terms and categories will also be discussed. To gain insight into these consequences, the Eric O trial (2005) in the Netherlands, will be analysed. This case illustrates the effects of the unclear legal status of hostilities during the peacekeeping mission in Iraq, as well as the Court's confusion about the applicability of legal rules in the case. The opposite standpoint, resulting in polarisation between the Public Prosecution Service [*Openbaar Ministerie*] and the Courts about the question of what rules had to be applied will be central. Finally, problems will be surveyed and conclusions will be drawn.

A fundamental shift in the concept of war

The declaration of war

Decisions about war and warfare deeply affect the lives of citizens. This holds in particular for the declaration of war (Article 96 of the Dutch Constitution). The reasoning behind the 'declaration of war' can be found in the work of Hugo Grotius, the seventeenth-century Dutch jurist and humanist. In Grotius' view, war and peace are to be distinguished as two mutually exclusive legal states. There must be a clear dividing point between war and peace: the declaration of war. Grotius' famous phrase '*Inter bellum et pacem nihil est medium*' is the basis for the idea that the declaration of war constitutes a precondition for the legitimacy of a war (Grotius 1993, 852). As the declaration of war initiates the legal state of war, the law of war binds the belligerent parties.

Since the period after the Second World War, when domestic law became dominated by the 1945 UN Charter's prohibition of interstate force, many changes have taken place and still are taking place in the domain of war and peace. The attacks of 9/11, resulting in the 'war on terror', contributed to the dynamics of this era. New anti-terrorism laws draw the attention. There is an ongoing debate on the question of whether security should be included in the Dutch Constitution as a fundamental human right.

Article 96 of the Dutch Constitution (until 1953, Article 57) is important in this context, and is consequently the focus of this chapter. The meaning of Article 96 has changed fundamentally, whereas the textual amendment to the Article – in the 1953 constitutional revision – was minimal. In 1953, the Dutch expression '*de oorlog verklaren*' (to declare war) in the former text of the Article was rephrased as a passive construction; that is, '*in oorlog verklaren*' (to declare [that the Kingdom is] *in* a state of war).[1] The Charter of the United Nations (1945) was the cause of this minimal textual change. In the former Article 57 of the Dutch Constitution, the formulation 'to declare war' was constitutive in character. The declaration itself – a governmental decision that needs the prior approval of Parliament (Werner and van Schooten 2002, 43–62) – initiates *de facto* and *de jure* a state of war. This means that a war actually starts at the moment it is declared and, at the same time, the legal consequences – the law of war – take effect.

It is obvious that the change in the meaning of Article 96 was in line with the international developments concerning the prohibition of force between states as a rule of positive law after the First World War.[2] The Kellogg-Briand Pact

1 The text of Article 96 reads as follows: 'A declaration that the Kingdom is in a state of war shall not be made without the prior approval of Parliament.' In Dutch, the Article reads: '*Het Koninkrijk wordt niet in oorlog verklaard dan na voorafgaande toestemming van de Staten-Generaal.*'

2 In this respect, the League of Nations (1919) marked a new period, characterised by a general striving to check the arbitrary use of force by single states. The legitimacy of war

(1927/28) explicitly condemned war as an illegal act of aggression between states.[3] The UN Charter stated the prohibition of force in a stronger formulation (De Jong 1990, 102). The Netherlands and other UN member states are obligated 'to refrain in their international relations from the threat or use of force against the territorial integrity or political independence of any State, or in any other manner inconsistent with the purposes of the United Nations' (Article 2(4)). The most important exception to the prohibition of the use of force is the right to self-defence of a member state of the United Nations against an armed attack by another state (Article 51). The fact that the UN Charter leaves some room for a declaration of war in the case of self-defence means that such a declaration does not bring about a state of war, but merely records its existence (van Schooten 2001, 329–44).

Should the declaration of war in Article 96 of the Dutch Constitution be understood in this restricted sense? Has the meaning of the declaration of war thus changed from a constitutive statement that starts a war *de facto* and *de jure* to a mere declaratory statement, the legal recognition of an already existing situation (state) of war? It seems that these questions are to be answered in the affirmative (van Schooten 2005).

Since the Dutch Council of State [*Raad van State*] stated that the term '*in oorlog verklaren*' (to declare [the Kingdom to be] in a state of war) in Article 96 of the Constitution

> did not include the preparatory military actions, not even if those actions were to result in a situation that the Netherlands would become involved in a war with another country. Prior approval of the States General [*Staten-Generaal*], i.e., Dutch Parliament, for putting troops and weapons into action is therefore not required under Article 96 of the Constitution.[4]

New terminology

Owing to the prohibition of force in the UN Charter, the terms 'war' and 'declaration of war' fell into disuse.[5] As a result, no declarations of war have been made since

became a central theme. The Treaty of the League of Nations did not yet, in general terms, prohibit war between members of the League.

3 General Treaty for the Renunciation of War as an Instrument of National Policy, 1928.

4 *Kamerstukken* II [*Parliamentary Documents*], 1985/86, 192 90 (A) 6, (my translation; my italics).

5 *Notitie inzake het VN-embargo tegen Irak* [*Government Memorandum concerning the UN embargo against Iraq*] *Kamerstukken* II [*Parliamentary Documents*] 1990/91, 21 664 (25), 9, states: 'Since the Second World War, the declaration of war at the beginning of an armed conflict between states has passed into disuse in international relations.'

the Second World War,[6] but the number of interstate hostilities *not* amounting to 'war' has greatly increased since 1945. Conflicts have been described as 'police actions', 'operations', 'peacekeeping missions', 'peace enforcements' or 'state building missions', or have been treated as civil wars in which the foreign party became involved to restore democracy (Van Schooten 2007). This euphemistic terminology veils the reality of war acts that take place during peacekeeping missions, peace enforcements, etc. It conceals the truth of actual warfare behind words connected to peace. The new terminology (Jackson 1995, 151–2)[7] came into being in international politics. By using the new terminology in political discourses, the legal concept of war was banned – as the prohibition of war in the UN Charter prescribed – but the actual warfare did not stop at all (Jackson 1985, 177–9). This confusing situation ended in several legal questions about the status of the missions mentioned, and the consequences of it for the laws of war.[8]

For this reason, in each of the four Geneva Conventions (1949), it was explicitly stated that these Conventions would be applicable not only after a declaration of war, but also in the case of 'any other armed conflict' between two or more States, even when the 'state of war was not recognised' by one of the parties. For the same reason, in 1952, the Criminal Law in Wartime Act [*Wet oorlogsstrafrecht*] and the Dutch Penal Code [*Wetboek van Strafrecht*] were extended with identical provisions. Article 107(a) of the Penal Code states that the criminal offence of Article 102 – aiding the enemy in *wartime* – is also applicable 'in the event of an *armed conflict* that cannot be designated a war'.[9] Here, a new category, next to war and peace, is introduced (Van Schooten 2004, 169–83). However, the terminology in the Military Penal Code [*Wetboek militair strafrecht*] was never changed to make criminal offences committed in 'war' and 'wartime' applicable in an interstate armed conflict.

As stated above, the new terminology often leads to confusion. The meaning of the terms and categories used is unclear, the legal consequences are uncertain. Confusion about the legal status of an 'armed conflict' or a 'peacekeeping operation', for instance, can be observed in the relevant case law. The absence of the old, clear-cut terms and categories affects citizens who are involved in warfare. This became clear in several cases brought before courts (Jackson 1995, 97–8, 52; Jackson 1999, 6),[10] concerning acts during the Gulf War, Operation Enduring

6 There is one exception. In 1989, Iran formally declared war against Iraq, with whom it had been engaged in hostilities since 1981.

7 With respect to sense construction, Jackson points at the notion of 'collected images' that serve as a kind of paradigm, which involves not only a description of a typical action, but includes also a tacit social evaluation.

8 The laws of war – *jus in bello* – concern acceptable practices while engaged in war once it has begun.

9 Unless otherwise states, all translations are my own.

10 Courts interpreted certain groups as 'semiotic groups', just as Jackson defines such a group as 'a social and/or professional group' that distinguishes itself from other

Freedom in Afghanistan and the peacekeeping operation in Iraq. Among these cases, the Eric O trial, which illustrates the Court's confusion about new war terminology, will be described and analysed in the next section.

The Eric O trial: new terminology and confusion in the courts

The facts of the case

Eric O took part in the Dutch military mission in Iraq, which was named a 'peacekeeping operation'. His rank was sergeant-major and he was attached to the operational group Royal Dutch Marines. As the commander of the ORF Battalion (Quick Reaction Force), Eric O was ordered to recover a container that was stranded on Main Supply Route (MSR) Jackson between Al Khidr and As Samawa, on 27 December 2003. The goods in the stranded container (filing cabinets belonging to the forces) had to be protected against plundering by Iraqi civilians. Several incidents had occurred on MSR Jackson, such as hijacking of civil vehicles and the use of deadly violence by criminal gangs. Containers as well as vehicles had to be protected against hostile and criminal attacks. The situation on MSR Jackson was dangerous, unpredictable and explosive. The road was frequently patrolled. Patrols routinely anticipated hostile actions, a car bomb or an attack by ambush.

Commander O and his battalion – an armoured car with military personnel, an armoured ambulance with medical personnel, a hoisting-crane, and a flatbed trailer – arrived at 12:30 hours. Already at the moment of arrival, the situation was chaotic. The QRF Battalion was responsible for the security of the men who recovered the container. The armoured car and the ambulance were blocking the road in two directions, in order to get the work done. This led to a traffic-jam in both directions, and more chaos and agitation among the drivers. The agitation increased at that moment when a convoy of 25 American vehicles, flatbed trailers with prefabs, and an American convoy of 350 war prisoners from the direction of Al Khidr tried to drive through the blockade. However, both American convoys were stopped. Agitated groups of Iraqi people standing beside the road tried to approach the container. The QRF Battalion was busy, blocking the road, recovering the container, and communicating by radio. Only three men were left to perform the protection tasks. As a result, O had insufficient military personnel to adequately secure the persons who were hoisting the container onto the flatbed trailer. The situation was threatening. Finally, when the container stood on the trailer, at 2:00 pm, about hundred Iraqi people, standing in several groups, slowly approached the trailer, which was ready to leave. There was real danger that the Iraqis would surround the trailer, the trailer driver and his men. In this foreseeable situation, the Iraqis would stand between Eric O and the military men near the trailer, and

---

social and/or professional groups by the (often overlapping but still distinct) system of signification operating within it.

O would have lost sight of the situation. Radio communication was hampered by a malfunctioning radio. O noticed that several groups of Iraqis continued to approach the trailer, creating the dangerous situation of isolating the men near the trailer. O loaded his weapon slowly and visibly in order to show the Iraqis the gravity of the situation. The Iraqis were looking at O's action. However, they were not scared off and they continued to approach. At that moment, the Iraqis were at a distance of about 75 metres. O fired a warning shot in the air. The Iraqis still did not stop, but continued to approach slowly. O took his weapon again and aimed the barrel in the direction of the group of Iraqis. He did not aim at the group. He looked through the sight and saw the man standing at the far left of the group at the far right of the picture. Then he turned to the left, saw nobody in the sight, and fired a second warning shot, aimed at the mud several meters in front of the group, in order to splash the sand, and to frighten and stop the group. At that moment, the group turned around and ran off. One Iraqi man stumbled and fell on the ground. This man (A) was severely wounded. He was taken to the hospital in Al Khidr where his death was certified. Afterwards, A was transported to the General Hospital in As Samawah for post-mortem examination. The post-mortem report gave a description of an oval wound of 3 cm diameter in the middle of the back and a bloody wound where his left eye would have been. From this description, it was not completely certain that the bullet had ricocheted.[11]

Eric O was arrested as a suspect on 31 December 2003. He was directly flown to the Netherlands, where he was imprisoned and prosecuted for manslaughter on the basis of Article 307 of the Dutch Penal Code. Besides manslaughter, O was accused of deliberately breaching the official instructions [*dienstvoorschriften*] endangering life or leading to death, as stated in Article 136 of the Military Penal Code. These official instructions were laid down in the *Aide Mémoire for SFIR Commanders* (AM) and the Instructions on the Use of Force (IUF) [*Geweldsinstructies*].

The legal framework

The District Court's conclusion

What rules apply in a situation which is a military mission, and is called a peacekeeping operation, and is neither a state of war, nor a state of peace? The District Court in Arnhem (Military Division) rejected all demands of the public

11 These facts stem from the statements made by several witnesses, among them the crane driver, and from O's testimony. All statements were used by the District Court as well by the Court of Appeal. Both courts stated that the suspect did not give an unreasonable account of his actions and that the untruth of his testimony could only be established if the untruth of his testimony could be proved.

prosecutor, stating the following arguments for its conclusion.[12] The Dutch military mission in Iraq was based on Resolutions 1483 and 1511 of the Security Council, as well as on the missions as formulated in the Memorandum of Understanding (MOU) ratified by the UK and the Netherlands, among other states. The MOU declares applicable the Rules of Engagement (ROE) which are attached to the MOU. The ROE were written especially for the mission in Iraq. The ROE are clearly formulated and guarantee the military units in Iraq a sufficiently robust action.

The District Court stated that, in this case, the ROE applied. The ROE are official instructions in the sense of Article 136 of the Military Penal Code. The above-mentioned IUF and AM are only summarised versions of the most important rules and obligations set out in the ROE. The AM is a translation of the ROE for the level of the commander in the field, the IUF are a translation of the ROE for the soldier. Most important is that the IUF give the soldier autonomous power in case of self-defence; he can fire an aimed shot without further commands. Moreover, the AM regulates under what circumstances the use of force is permitted and refers to the ROE for further explication. The ROE were binding rules at the moment Eric O was charged.

The ROE give guidelines and rules with respect to the use of force. They are a means to control the use of force by military personnel, by way of formulations of restrictions or by allowing particular forms of force. O's warning shot was legitimised on the basis of ROE 151, which authorises 'the passing of warnings to any person by any means', if warnings are necessary for the execution of missions. This means that the use of a warning shot as an independent means of force (that is, separate from the warning shot as the starting point for deadly force) is allowed.

The situation of the accused was one of potential threat and a hindrance for the execution of the mission. The warning shot, fired to avert the threat, is legitimised by ROE 151, if the accused's action meets the requirements of *necessity*, *proportionality* and *subsidiarity*. The Court declared that O's conduct met these requirements. O's behaviour was necessary under the threatening circumstances, sketched by several witnesses (necessity requirement). He could not have acted in any other way, given the lack of military personnel in the threatening situation (subsidiarity requirement).[13] Nor did he act out of proportion, giving the warning shots in order to remove the threat and the hindrance for the mission (proportionality requirement).[14] The Court acquitted O of the charge.

---

12 *LJN*: AR4029, Rechtbank Arnhem [Arnhem District Court], 05/097011-03.

13 It is generally acknowledged in international law that, in case of self-defence operations (Article 51 UN Charter), the requirement of subsidiarity has to be fulfilled. The subsidiarity requirement means that the solution or action chosen is the less damaging one possible.

14 The requirement of proportionality means that actions need to be in proportion with the force used, in character, as well as in scale and intensity. See Minister of

The Prosecution Department appeals against the court's decision

The prosecutor appealed against the Arnhem District Court's decision. The attitude of the Public Prosecution Service was later qualified by the Arnhem Court of Appeal as 'an attitude with a particular tenacity'. The public prosecutor's closing speech was long and consisted of 25 pages. The arguments concentrated on the term 'official instruction' [*dienstvoorschrift*] and the use of the ROE as an official instruction. The Advocate General, the public prosecutor of the Court of Appeals, argued that the term 'official instruction' as defined in Article 135 of the Dutch Military Penal Code had been interpreted in such a broad way – declaring the ROE as applicable rules – that the Court went beyond the legal basis of the facts of the charge, which is a violation of the legality principle; that is, the rule of law. Furthermore, the Advocate General held to his demand of manslaughter, Article 307 Dutch Penal Code. To clarify the legal status of the Dutch mission in Iraq, the public prosecutor distinguished five situations as different categories of war:

a. a state of war in which the Netherlands is involved as a belligerent;
b. a state of war in which the Netherlands has not accepted war, but its allies have; in this case, the Netherlands is only in a state of war if it has empowered its military units to use force, based on the state monopoly on (the use of) force;
c. a state of internal armed conflict between two or more sovereign states, or two or more sovereign states, on the one hand, and one or more parties with sovereignty claims, on the other;
d. a state of external armed conflict between two or more sovereign states, or two or more sovereign states, on the one hand, and one or more parties with sovereignty claims, on the other;
e. a state in which two competing parties without sovereignty claims fight each other, which has led to an internal state collapse, in which Dutch military units intervene on behalf of the UN or for the purpose of the International Criminal Court (ICC), for the enforcement of or for the purpose of on-site investigation.

The public prosecutor stated that, with respect to the situation of the Dutch troops in Iraq, only category e. was applicable. On the basis of this argument, the use of force was excluded.[15] In this way, the accused was not a 'military component of a party involved', but an 'expert on mission'. The public prosecutor answered the question of whether the Netherlands, as a military party, was involved in a conflict

---

Defence in his Letter to Parliament: <http://www.mindef.nl/actueel/parlement/kamerbrieven/2005/1/20050310_enduringfreedom>.

15 Here, the Public Prosecution Service referred to two cases in which the Court had rejected the existence of 'time of war' and its consequences; that is, the applicability of the Dutch Penal Code and the Dutch Military Penal Code.

in Iraq in the negative. If this statement is correct, what exactly *is* the legal status of the Dutch military units in Iraq, the Advocate General asked.

The public prosecutor concluded that the ROE were not applicable. The status of the Dutch military units was that of 'regular trooper' responsible for 'non-military potential tasks'. For that reason, the law of the common and general Dutch Penal Code was applicable. Therefore, the charge on appeal was again manslaughter.

The Court of Appeal's conclusion

The Arnhem Court of Appeal (Military Division), like the Arnhem District Court, concentrated on the applicability of ROE 151 for the mission in Iraq. In its conclusion, the Court of Appeal repeated the essential arguments already stated by the District Court. The ROE, as official instructions, were applicable for the following reasons. The word *dienstvoorschrift* is defined in Article 135 Military Penal Code, which states: '*Onder dienstvoorschrift wordt verstaan een bij of krachtens algemene maatregel van bestuur dan wel bij of krachtens landsverordening onderscheidenlijk landsbesluit gegeven schriftelijk besluit van algemeen strekking dat enig militair dienstbelang betreft en een tot de militair gericht ge- of verbod bevat.*'[16]

Once again, the Court of Appeal concluded that the actions of the Dutch troops were legitimised by Resolutions 1483 and 1511 of the UN Security Council. In Resolution 1511, passed on 16 October 2003, it is clearly stated that the Security Council 'authorises a multinational force under unified command to take all necessary measures to contribute to the maintenance of security and stability in Iraq.' In Resolution 1483, adopted on 22 May 2003, the Security Council welcomed 'the willingness of Member states to contribute to stability and security in Iraq by contributing personnel, equipment, and other resources under Authority'.

On the basis of these Resolutions, a number of states, among them the Netherlands, and the UK as lead nation, entered into a Memorandum of Understanding (MOU) with respect to participation in the Multinational Division (South East) (MND(SE)). This agreement was signed on 8 July 2003 on behalf of the Netherlands by the Minister of Defence. In this agreement, the ROE, laid down in Annex F, were declared applicable.

For the evaluation of the Eric O case, ROE 151 is essential. The MOU and Annex F are qualified 'confidential'. This means that, in principle, ROE 151 cannot be made public. However, the Dutch military units were actually familiar with the ROE. They were instructed about the ROE and had practised them. In this context, the 'need to know' principle had been used. The substantive meaning of ROE 151 had been recorded in the conclusion of the District Court, discussed in public, and published on the Internet. Moreover, ROE 151 had been discussed

16 'An official instruction is defined as a written decision of general application by virtue of an order in council or a national ordinance or a national decree concerning any military service interest and consisting of orders and prohibitions directed at the soldier.'

during the public hearing of the Court of Appeal. Under these circumstances, the Court of Appeal was of the opinion that the confidential nature of ROE 151 had to give way to transparency, also external transparency, an essential requirement for a fair trial, all the more since the conclusion of the Court of Appeal would not be comprehensible without information on knowledge of ROE 151.

Based upon this argumentation, the Court of Appeal was of the opinion that the ROE met all the requirements of an official instruction specified in Article 135 Military Penal Code. The fact that the ROE were in English was not a hindrance. The Court of Appeal's ample argumentation concentrated on the clarification of what rules were valid with respect to this specific military mission. In this context, the meaning of the words 'use of force' was analysed and elaborated. The ROE were rightly declared valid rules, being an Annex to the MOU, an agreement signed by the Netherlands. In this respect, the ROE count as valid rules, under a ministerial regulation. The Minister can exercise his power on the basis of Article 9, paragraph 2, under a, of the National Decree on Military Criminal and Disciplinary Procedure [*Rijksbesluit uitvoeringsbepalingen militair straf- en tuchtrecht*]. In this sense, the ROE constitute a written decision of general application [*besluit van algemene strekking*], concerning the interest of military servicemen and women and including prohibitions, orders, and the division of powers.

According to the Court of Appeal, the ROE were evidently applicable, valid rules for the mission in Iraq. Therefore, it concluded that a breach of the legality principle (that is, the rule of law), by going beyond the basis of the charge, had to be rejected. This basic principle had not been violated since ROE 151 was applicable. ROE 151 states: 'Passing of warnings to any person, aircraft, vehicle or vessel by any means in circumstances where MND(SE) forces or elements under MND(SE) protection or the mission are threatened or where the passing of warnings is necessary for purposes of execution of the mission is authorised.'

The warning shot fired by O could not be regarded as substantially imprudent, negligent or careless. The Court of Appeal stated that, in general, shooting in the ground under the existing circumstances, was not more dangerous than a shot fired in the air. Based upon these arguments, the Court of Appeal, too, acquitted Eric O of the charge.

Critical considerations

After the final conclusion, some remarkable comments can be noted. Under the obiter dicta, the Court of Appeal strongly criticised the Public Prosecution Service as well as the Minister of Defence. Firstly, the Court of Appeal stated that judges in the Dutch legal system, in conforming with Article 12 of the General Provisions Act [*Wet algemene bepalingen*], are obliged to take a reticent attitude with respect to the creation of new rules. Making new laws is solely reserved to the legislator. Within the separation of powers, the legislature has primacy over the judiciary. For this reason, the judge could not answer the legal questions posed by the Public

Prosecution Service about the legal status of the situation in Iraq. Is it or is it not a state of war? If it is not a state of war, what then is the legal status? The Court of Appeal pointed out that these legal questions have to be answered by the Public Prosecution Service itself, in mutual deliberation and agreement with the military experts of the Ministry of Defence. The answers have to function as the basis of a balanced policy for instruction and prosecution. Unfortunately, there had not been such deliberation between the Public Prosecution Service and the Minister of Defence. Next, the Court of Appeal observed (much to its regret) that, in the Eric O case, the Public Prosecution Service had evidently been *insufficiently* prepared for the question of how to react to the described shooting incident. This had led to a far too severe assessment of the case and permanent damage to the serviceman involved.

The Court of Appeal noted that, in the meantime, a further elaboration of ideas had been initiated within the Public Prosecution Service, leading to a different procedure: a soldier who fires will no longer be regarded as a *suspect*, as a matter of course in accordance with the existing 'Instructions for Police Officers concerning the Use of Force' [*Instructies positie politiefunctionaris bij geweldsaanwending*]. However, the Court of Appeal made the direct and clear statement that, in the comparison with similar rules, such as the 'Instructions for Police Officers', the fact that a military action during an international mission is *of a totally different order* had been completely ignored.

The Court of Appeal came to the conclusion that the Public Prosecution Service had prosecuted Eric O with an attitude of excessive tenacity. The public prosecutor's statement about the District Court's breach of the principle of legality, the rule of law, was unjustified. Moreover, the Court of Appeal concluded that the Public Prosecution Service had a rather one-sided view on the principle of legality; it had been applied only to the detriment of the accused. In doing so, the Public Prosecution Service had ignored that, first and foremost, the function of the principle of legality is the protection of rights of citizens. In similar cases, in the future, the Public Prosecution Service's attitude could result in the absence of the necessary legal certainty for soldiers on international missions acting under dangerous circumstances. The Public Prosecution Service was told to work on its 'situational awareness'.

Meanwhile, a debate had been taking place in Parliament about this issue. The Minister of Defence reacted to this debate in a letter to Parliament in which he stated that, meanwhile, regular deliberations had taken place between the Public Prosecution Service and the Ministry of Defence. These deliberations involved (1) operational and legal questions concerning the Dutch rules for the use of force, (2) policy deliberations concerning the armed forces between a representative of the Arnhem Public Prosecution Service, the Legal Affairs Directorate of the Ministry of Defence and the heads of the Legal Affairs sections of the armed forces, and (3) a military three-way discussion between the chief public prosecutor in the district of Arnhem, the Legal Affairs Director and the Commander of the Dutch military police [*Koninklijke Marechaussee*]. Furthermore, prior to all international missions, the Public Prosecution Service would henceforth be informed about the applicable rules on the use of force, the rules concerning the legal status of troops on missions and the mandate for the operation.

Final remarks

New war terminology and new categories of war, emerging from political practices, resulted in confusion and legal uncertainty about the status and the consequences concerning military personnel participating in international peacekeeping missions. The trial of Eric O is a case in point. The Court of Appeal's severe criticism towards the Public Prosecution Service and the Ministry of Defence about this subject underline the problematic character of the lack of legal knowledge and the unanswered question of what rules apply in international missions. The discrepancy between the Public Prosecution Service and the judges of both Courts about the question of what rules did apply was striking. The Public Prosecution Service stubbornly insisted on the charge of manslaughter (Article 307 of the Dutch Penal Code), whereas the judges declared Article 151 of the Rules of Engagement (ROE) applicable, the rules on the use of force. The polarisation increased when the Public Prosecution Service stated a breach of the principle of legality, and used the principle *against* the accused. The Court of Appeal strongly criticised the Public Prosecution Service's peculiar interpretation of this basic principle that is meant to protect citizens and is not to be used against them.

Another important part of the prosecution's case were the five categories of war, combined with the question about the legal status of these five situations. Since the judiciary, as one of the separate state powers, is not allowed to intervene in the tasks of the legislature, it could not answer the question. The Minister of Defence is the institution empowered to scrutinise these categories and legal questions and to establish clarity on this point. With respect to the mission in Iraq, the Minister has since (partly) fulfilled his task by referring to rules for similar situations in which force is used: the 'Instructions for Police Officers'. Owing to this, a soldier sent out on an international mission can no longer be a *suspect* in the way Eric O had been a suspect. However, in a critical reaction, the Court of Appeal pointed at the substantial difference between the tasks of a police officer and those of a military unit on an international mission. Military missions in dangerous circumstances are of a totally different order, the Court stated.

In the case of Eric O, the court exposed the lack of clarity about the question of what rules apply with respect to new categories of war. As a result of the dispute about the question of which of the two conflicting rules apply in a 'peacekeeping mission', it was shown that the general rule 'Thou shalt not kill' (Article 307 of the Dutch Penal Code) was turned into a rule with a completely different perspective: 'Killing is authorised in "war" situations' (Article 151 ROE). This meaning became manifest, not just by testing the act of killing against the rules, but against the specific situation – 'war' practice – in which the act took place. Summarising, it may be stated that new war terminology has emerged from political practice, and its legal consequences have become clear in the practice of a war situation. It is not so much the Constitution or legislation, but *practices* that have played a predominant role in the shifts in the concept of war since the 1945 UN Charter.

PART II
Case Analyses of Diversity and Tolerance

Chapter 7

Branding Barcelona: Semiotic Considerations in Contemporary Sovereignty[1]

John Brigham

Introduction

For hundreds of years Catalonia has been part of Spain. It is the part that borders France, on the Mediterranean. For at least as many years before that, Catalonia was an independent nation-state with a commanding presence at this strategic and commercial point in Southern Europe. Today, the geographical point on the Mediterranean seems less important. The strategic presence and commercial dimensions of power include other important things like access to technologies and to labour. But, in the strategic struggles for power today, hype and style have commanding significance. Barcelona is the centre of Catalonia and, among other things, it has a lot of style. Like warships, manpower and industrial might before it, style is a weapon in the struggle for sovereignty.

Style is the link between semiotics and sovereignty here. Significant elements of all nationalist movements involve semiotics.[2] How we understand the symbols of sovereignty is a key to what a sovereignty movement means and what it stands for. The symbols of sovereignty are relevant locally and they have global dimensions. This is particularly true where symbols or 'soft' power are able to operate beyond the reach of the nation and in ways that would not be permitted for military or even

1 My debt and gratitude for being supported in thinking on this subject are many but particular mention should be made of Christine B. Harrington (New York University), Clara Velasco Rico (Universitat Pompeu Fabra), Ira Strauber (Grinnell College) and Richard Mohr (University of Wollongong); all members of the 5th International Roundtable for the Semiotics of Law, 'Law, Tolerance and Diversity', 17–20 May 2006, Boulogne sur Mer (France), Convenor: Anne Wagner.

2 The chapter calls attention to 'semiotic sovereignty' and as part of the development it will mention two other relatively new concepts, 'semiotic democracy' and 'semiotic disobedience'.

some economic forms of power. At least this seems particularly true of Barcelona, where nationalism as a movement for Catalonian sovereignty is very strong.[3]

Places or groups raising issues of sovereignty within larger national units have long fascinated students of politics. The contested sovereignties that I am most drawn to as places to study are Western and generally progressive. In this, among other things, they tend to resist neo-liberal global integration at the same time that they depend on a commanding global presence. The conception emerges from experience with Catalonia and the Basque Country in Spain. It also applies in some ways (and not others) to Puerto Rico and has dimensions that link it to movements in Belgium, Italy and the UK.[4]

This chapter is about how Barcelona presents itself to the world. This region downplays rigid claims for autonomy while elevating language, culture and style. Style is the key to the brand that is Barcelona. In this strategy, Barcelona, or 'BCN', has positioned itself very successfully in the global clash of sovereignties. It is a centre for art and culture, a destination, a cool place, a brand.

Catalonia and nationalism

With Catalonia and sovereignty as the subject, the place of this 'semi-sovereign' people on a map seems like a good starting point. But there are biases and challenges that make the map seem old-fashioned in the context of this inquiry, more connected with the traditional struggles for sovereignty than this newer development. Catalonia is a historic culture that remains prosperous and assertive. It is imagined as a separate place but on a map it is a corner of Spain.

If it is a map of Spain, then the map is not the territory imagined by Catalans. The boundaries of the Pyrenees and the Mediterranean are dramatic but they cordon off Catalonia as part of Spain more than they define a separate country. Driving through Spain to the northwest the divide between Catalonia and Spain is imperceptible and the roads one takes on such a trip are Spanish. Going to the sea or over the Pyrenees one feels boundaries, but these are the boundaries claimed by the Spanish nation. This is true on the map (Figure 7.1) but for Catalans there is something else – an ethos of separateness, of being distinct and different.

Catalan is the official language. Catalan was banned under Franco. The language is often spoken about, as if to speak this language is a matter of identifying with

3 From Bronwen Morgan, ' ... Gaelic(s) in Wales and Scotland as a viable second language – catalysed by some legal requirements for holding civil servant jobs, etc. Apparently the languages were almost dead. It would be interesting to know more about the politics of it' (23 October 2005).

4 In this project I draw from work on 'the other countries' of law in the US and 'domestic colonialism' outside the US. These are the sub-national jurisdictions that have significant political sovereignty or cultural autonomy. They appear in the US in the form of Indian Reservations and the island colonies, including Puerto Rico.

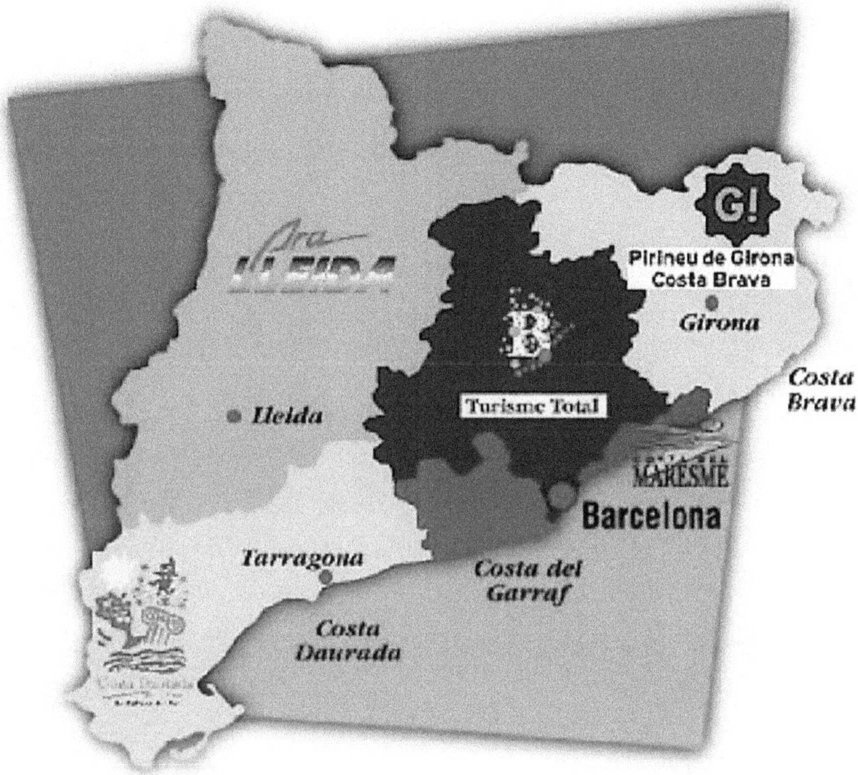

Figure 7.1 Conventional map of Catalonia within Spain

the struggle for liberation. As Jacqueline Urla has noted for Basques, it is also true for Catalonia that cultural nationalism '… has been premised on defending oneself from the hegemony of Spanish' through exclusion and denial (Urla 2003, 6). Within Spain, Spanish is the language of hegemony against which both Basque and Catalan national identity struggle. Thus, Spanish bears a relation to nationalism in Catalonia and the Basque Country and has the opposite meaning for Puerto Rico. In Puerto Rico, Spanish and an island identity are key elements of sub-nationalism. Spanish is the language of resistance, the language under perceived threat.

But the movement for linguistic, cultural and economic autonomy has its reactionary, corporate and oppressive dimensions. Catalonia is prosperous and those who speak the language run the region. While there are elites from the rest of Spain, Spanish is widely spoken by less prosperous immigrants from Latin America as well as the rest of Spain. Though there is formal and cultural pluralism, Catalan is the language of local power. In this context, things Catalan (the government, the local news, literature) have the upper hand these days.

Figure 7.2 Gaudi's Sagrada Familia, Barcelona

Here, the setting that once commanded the Western world is very attractive. Though southern it is not on the periphery of Europe. Connected to commerce for centuries, its culture has adopted technology and the liberal acquisition of new knowledges that is the hallmark of modern culture.

The identity of Catalonia is linked not only to its language but also to an old culture with considerable vitality. It is hard to think of Catalonia without attention to Barcelona, the Mediterranean and to Gaudí. There are also strong artistic expressions that span centuries of influence. Picasso and Miró appear in images identified with the place.

Some of the architecture of Catalonia is justly celebrated as the most important in the world. The early twentieth-century work of Antonio Gaudí combines a primitive mysticism, a reaction to modern life and deep religious belief . Gaudí's buildings are shrines represented again and again as symbols of Barcelona and the Catalan aesthetic (Figure 7.2).[5] This combination of taste and sentiment, as some dictionaries define aesthetic, is a way of viewing the world. From the outside it becomes a way of imagining and perhaps entering the world. The aesthetic, in the case of what it means to 'brand' Barcelona, is at the forefront of the presentation of place and it is highly significant for matters of sovereignty.

Figure 7.3 Sculpture in the Science Museum, Barcelona

Catalonia is a place where the aesthetic combines aspects of life that are often separated. A case in point is science and beauty. The science museum, which is at the base of the old amusement park of Tibidabo, is at the same time scientific and artistic. This announces a particular kind of modernism, one that engages emotionally with what in much of the rest of the West is considered separate. I am fascinated in looking back at a picture I took from within the museum where a fossilised tree is dramatically situated within a five-storey atrium to become a spectacular organic sculpture (Figure 7.3).[6] Not only does the building support the tree with arms of 'Corten' steel, the kind

5 The Sagrada Familia; photo by John Brigham, Spring 2005.

6 Science Museum, Barcelona; photo by John Brigham, Spring 2005.

that rusts naturally, it covers it in a mantle of coloured glass that, while part of the building, also serves to return the colour of fall to the skeletal tree.

In thinking of Catalonia and Barcelona this discussion moves from language to style – from something difficult to know to a way of looking at things that marks them easily. The exclusiveness and depth of linguistic diversity is mirrored in the equally obvious but much more accessible style of Gaudí.

Semiotic/global

Nationalism has always had its international dimensions. The US, France, Spain and the Netherlands were key players in the struggle with the UK and the emerging international significance of democratic struggles in France and Haiti influenced the outcome and amplified the consequences of the American revolution.

Nationalism from the eighteenth century onwards has been seen in 'traditional' terms, which emphasised the physical control of territory. Military control was paramount and sovereignty depended on the ability to dominate a territory and its people by force. Control of territory was the basis on which wealth was accumulated and sovereignty was traditionally understood in these terms. Force was fundamental and the symbolic was epiphenomenal. Today, in some parts of the world the relationships appear to have been reversed and perception and image drive the accumulation of wealth that lays the foundation for national identity.

So, while the existence of a larger global or international setting is similar to revolutions of old, struggles of the sort described here reverse the order of things. The symbols become more important where the order of things places markets above military force in some contests for sovereignty.

Semiotics provides a perspective from which to focus on the contemporary representations of nationalism.

While force and violence are still factors, other economic and social agents have come into play more dramatically. Economic forces such as banking and marketing now plays roles as important as the military.

One of the alternatives to traditional nationalism is evident in the role of branding and the prominence of design. Design is the symbolic space created by conscious effort and influenced by a visually aware community.

The significant work on the nature and consequences of Basque and Catalan struggles deserves to be noted (Urla 2003). In addition there is important literature that addresses nationalism comparatively (Dowley and Silver 2000) and in the context of current ways of understanding nation and identity (Buchanan and Pahuja 2004).

The global setting gives meaning to symbols and the positions they put forth. For instance, self-determination and self-governance are values recognised around the world. To the extent that symbols appeal to those values, they have meaning that goes beyond the immediate cases. Any analysis of sub-nationalism should include references to places such as Hong Kong, the nations of the former Soviet

Figure 7.4 Poster urging a vote against the European constitution (2005)

Union, Africa and Quebec. The experience in these places and how they have been analysed are important to both the context of struggle and the nature of the analysis.

The European context is important to the emergence of Catalan nationalism (Chakravarty 2001). The prosperity and stability of Europe today feature a politics of ballots and negotiations, a context within which different power relations can contest without the volatility of 75–100 years ago. Or so it seems. Looking at Figure 7.4,[7] we can see that in this poster flags and symbols of ethnicity and nationality are placed in a map of Europe to advocate a vote against the European constitution. The vote took place in 2005. Here, the Catalan flag is next to the Basque Nationalist flag. It is presented in a context of local diversities and anti-global sensibilities.

Sub-national struggles for sovereignty must exist in the context of international economies and free market logic. Semiotics has been associated with politics in a body of literature developing over the last twenty years about the concept 'semiotic democracy' (Fiske 1987). Semiotic democracy is like democracy generally; it is not what we have but what we might have if people participated in the semiotic constructions. It has been associated with movements to loosen the constraints of intellectual property and with others that seek to 'jam' the culture (Lessig 2004).[8]

The effort here is to understand the semiotic context for at least one nationalistic movement, that of Catalonia, because Catalonia and Barcelona seem very well positioned to use various semiotic aspects of the international system as leverage in the struggle with Spain. Here, aspects of politics depend on semiotics and are

7 Photo by John Brigham, Spring 2005.

8 See also, 'Semiotic Disobedience,' Sonia K. Katyal (2006). 'The objective of semiotic disobedience is to correct the marketplace of speech by occupying and transforming the semiotic "codes" within advertising.'

Figure 7.5 Parts of Europe, photo by John Brigham

manifest as semiotic sovereignty. It is hoped that this perspective will help us to understand what is happening when semiotics intersects with politics.[9]

The scholarship of Arlene Davila (2000) concerning the global dimensions of Puerto Rican culture will be applied to the Catalan case (and to a lesser extent that of the Basques) in order to show how design considerations play in these contexts. Puerto Rico is the sort of place where nationalism resists the hegemonic character of the international economy. In addition, I note foundational work on semiotics like that of Terry Fisher (Rosenberg 2003),[10] suggesting there is something he calls 'semiotic democracy', and Sonia K. Katyal's interesting mutation of this concept into 'semiotic disobedience'. Both perspectives draw on dimensions of semiotics that illuminate contexts over the signs of power and transfer attention from positivist aspects of politics.

While some still find talk of symbols to be epiphenomenal. Here, symbols, like those that lend glitz to Barcelona (Sagrada Familia, Picasso, the Olympic venues) are treated as essential elements of what it means to be sovereign.

Semiotics and sovereignty

Symbolism coexists with nationality and nationalism. Flags and other symbols of sovereignty represent national power and are understood in terms of the material

9 There are clearly many reactionary or liberal capitalist sub-national or emerging national regimes. They will not be dealt with here because the dynamic being explored is the tension between the progressive aspirations of global democracy and the linguistic parochialism that at one time depended on the global democratic movement for support.

10 On Terry Fisher and semiotics, see <http://blogs.salon.com/0000014/2003/07/08.html>.

and jurisdictional spaces. The symbols matter more than just as representations of something real. Because the symbols, and the map, really are the territory, we offer an analysis of them as a feature of sovereignty.

National symbolism

The place to begin in a semiotic study of how a nation is represented is with the flag. The origin of the Catalan flag has a variety of interpretations; yet, at the level of national identity, you do not hear much confusion (Figure 7.5). Four blood-red stripes on a yellow background – the stripes represent fingers, bloody from struggle, the yellow a golden field. While red and yellow are also the Pope's colours, and this may figure into the origin narrative, the flag and the stripes are ubiquitous symbols of more than local pride.

In the Catalan flag, the blood-red stripes evoke a history of rebellions. The Basque flag, charged with centuries of struggle, calls to mind the dangers of that struggle throughout Spain and the community of Basques at home. The Puerto Rican flag is already a compromise from that of Borincua, with its star, stripes and red, white and blue colour scheme. Examples abound in any place that has sought to symbolise its independence.

There is more than flags, of course. Other images or logos may appear because a place is compelling. Automobiles provide important space for expression, with the bumper being significant. Corporations and television stations have logos for the letterhead, the screen or the website.[11]

In addition to the flag, the people of Catalonia have their donkey, ubiquitous on licence plates and bumpers. The Puerto Rican autonomy movement points to the tiny tree frog, the coqui. Puerto Rican nationalists also use the pitirre, a small bird capable of attacking hawks or other predators (such as the American eagle) as a symbol. In the Basque Country no animal is so prominent.

Images and sovereignty

At the Amherst College Symposium on *The Empress Josephine: Art and Royal Identity* that was curated by Carol Solomon Kiefer (Kiefer 2006), a number of scholars tackled the elements of style embedded in sovereignty. Nicola Courtright spoke about the Medicis' mentions of 'the art of sovereignty (Courtright 2005) and Katia Dianina spoke of the Hermitage as 'a liminal space where art and authority mix' (Dianina 2005). Professor Dianina also spoke of the Medicis and the 'art of sovereignty'. In Russia, Catherine the Great contributed to the creation of national sovereignty by ordering that all the best paintings be gathered (even if in private hands) and placed in the Hermitage.

11 The little logo displayed at the left of a web address is usually called an icon.

Some symbols remain relatively timeless and unchanged over hundreds or even thousands of years. Peace, for instance, was associated with women[12] two hundred years ago and the reference makes some sense today. Other symbols associated with authority and the power of the state change. Medieval formal gardens were masculine because they represented the nation and the control of nature. Gardening today is both more pastoral and more likely to be closely associated with local life and nature than nationality and control. In modernity gardens became feminine. In a similar vein, the image of the sovereign female form remained deeply problematic. The masculine gardens were losing their gendered meaning. There was the dramatic pressure for a queen to be virginal because (as with Elizabeth I) her body was identified with the State. The desire to perform this particular Elizabeth has appealed to many important contemporary actors (Kate Blanchett, Gwyneth Paltrow, Helen Mirren, Judy Dench). The second Queen Elizabeth has been troubled by her image. Investing a great deal in a 1950s domesticity that was popular at the beginning of her reign, she has outlasted it and while there is clearly a downside to the dysfunctional elements in her family it is possible that this Queen has become modern and may even be popular again.

In representing kings and queens, artists will often place them high up and their subjects below. The elevated throne is, of course, also important, along with distinctive royal paraphernalia. In the case of Jacques-Louis David's *Coronation of the Empress Josephine* (1806–07), royal authority is presented through rays of light falling on the central figures. The light creates a sort of aura, which becomes a visual manifestation of the power that emanates from the monarch.

The semiotic façade

'Façade' is a wonderful word. The 'ç' is not common in English and has not been part of Spanish for over 100 years but it is essential in Catalan. Called a 'c-cedilla' in Old Spanish and French and a 'ce-trencada' or 'broken c' in Catalan it denotes a soft 's' sound where a 'c' would normally get a hard 'k' pronunciation. Wikipedia nicely references the important word 'Barça' which is the diminutive and most common way to refer to the football club, Barcelona. Perhaps if distinctive regalia were not enough to distinguish friend or foe of this hugely popular club a mistaken reference to 'Barka' would surely reveal an opposing fan or, worse, some sort of spy.

'Façade' is one of the few words where the 'ç' is used in English. That would be one reason for the title of this section. Another is that the word also captures contemporary notions of how symbols mask reality. In some senses, 'façade' is not quite the right term. The symbols I am interested in are not the hollow symbols that traditional positivist theory speaks about.

So, façade is part of the story. Symbols mask but they also constitute, or vice versa. The periodical put out by the Rhode Island School of Design (RISD), *View*, for spring 2006 features the engagement of designers with social issues. Since it is

12 When peace is legitimised it legitimises the authority of women.

an institutional publication there is a tendency to treat the designers as the givens that need to be reminded to engage with social issues. But we can also see and say that the social issues of the day have their semiotics, their design, even if some designers are not paying attention.

In the case of Catalonia we are calling attention to the semiotics in a sense more similar to markets. People are drawn to the semiotic façade of Barcelona. It is hip. It is sexy. It sells, and in all the hype there is political power, especially given the global integration that we see today.

Nationalisms and sub-nationalisms are all about semiotics (Riley 2006; Wright 1999). It is almost too easy to make the point. Flags, graffiti, parliaments, currencies – real or imagined – are the stuff of national and sub-national identity. But the signs and symbols are usually for those who are part of the community. They tug at the heart and other psychological points.

Symbolism is an effort to subsume and incorporate diversity. It represents history in a manner that can be managed and it translates culture into forms that are simple, catchy and non-threatening (Silbey and Cavicchi 2005). Some things, like buildings and flags, may be associated with shared sovereignty while money and parliaments suggest unitary systems. It is closely associated with branding.[13]

Battles of identity and sovereignty are complex and though they may be manifest through brands and taste, their capacity to affect either is limited. In March of 2006 *The New York Times* presented the story of Catalonian champagne, or Cava. When followers of a separatist leader, Josep-Lluis Carod-Rovira, called for a boycott of Madrid's campaign to host the 2012 Olympics, Spaniards responded with a campaign to boycott Catalonian goods, in particular Cava.

The way the symbols are articulated with reference to other social and political forces has all sorts of implications. Every manner of regime has its own banner and though there are differences, I would hesitate to say it is because of the flag. In order for there to be a jurisprudence of semiotics we need to identify the implications of the sign. It cannot be done in the abstract.

Jurisprudence and images

There is legal authority in the image. Because of this it follows that there is or ought to be jurisprudence too. The theory draws on the connection between image and authority suggested above and developed here in terms of Catalonia. The nature of design in its contemporary manifestations in Spain and the current aspects of nation, also in the particular Spanish context, constitute the jurisprudential sphere.

---

13 From Wikipedia, 'A brand typically includes a name, logo, and other visual elements such as fonts, colour schemes or symbols. It also encompasses the set of expectations associated with a product or service which typically arise in the minds of people.'

Figure 7.6 Placa España – symbol of imperial Spain

Paradoxically the ontological inversion makes ordinary perception, that a flag is worth dying for, for instance, more true than bourgeois formulations might have it. Thus, we say of a nation constituted by a globally significant style that it has the kind of power that was once reserved for military force. Where the flag 'represented' but the bayonet carried it, here we suggest that the brand exemplified by the manifestations of Gaudí, the images of the Barcelona Olympics or the BCN of the airport have made the bayonets passé.

Visualising sovereignty

The use of design seems less often discussed in the context of sovereignty than say, language or ethnicity. For one thing, design seems superficial. We are taught to think of it in the sense of 'façade' that we have just considered. To associate design with political identity and sovereignty is somewhat less obvious than associating design with geography, sport, or even ethnicity. But ultimately, sovereignty is made up of all these things and, ultimately again, it is real.

National symbols, like flags, uniforms, even political architecture, gain their authority from just being rather than being produced. Design, almost by its nature calls attention to the producers. The Plaça España, represented in Figure 7.6, is a symbol of Imperial Spain and the contemporary nation.[14] But the graffiti that obscures 'Plaça España' on the Barcelona subway is a clear indication that the

14 Photo of Plaça España by John Brigham, Spring 2005.

destination is problematic, from a Catalonian perspective. The plaza is itself an expression of the monumental Spanish (as in Madrid) conjunction of very large late-nineteenth- and early twentieth-century buildings juxtaposed with a bullring. It seems old, tired and very much from the past as it sits in the middle of Barcelona's present that celebrates Gaudí, Miró and Picasso.

It was in another space, an *okupa* or squatter building, that in 1997 I became aware of the depth of meaning federalism has in Spain. The subject of the session was prison and the particular Catalan dimension was the Spanish system of national prisons which has responded to pressure, some of it criminal, for autonomy with imprisonment away from the region.[15]

An Internet logo for the Catalan government incorporates an almost Victorian version of the ubiquitous red stripes, with the website name ('gencat') written in a modernist font and the Internet address 'www.gencat.net' as a logo around which to articulate the character of the semiotic façade.

Like law and institutions, design abstracts the relations of power, reifying and generalising them. The coherence and authority associated with symbols of nation operate as law and although there are not as many varieties of symbol as there are rules of law, the authority of law depends on those aspects of authority that give it meaning.

The authority of design

Design compels, seduces, excites and satisfies. As perhaps with the primal images associated with sex or eating or shelter, design signals what we want. A car that appeals by dint of design may lead us to want it even, sometimes, against other facets of meaning. Here the issue is the authority of design.

Like the matters of governance delineated and developed by Foucault, design is a different aspect of politics. It does not punish, it does not command but it can be a dominant consideration influencing human action.

Rick Mohr presented a paper to the 2nd International Roundtable in Oñati on the meaning of the Basque herald. He drew attention to the levels of meaning in the traditional symbol of a people living as a family.

Although design as we are speaking about it draws on more than language, the written and spoken word has an interesting relationship with design. The Basque language has a distinctive font that makes it look different. Imperial languages such as English, Spanish, Russian, Arabic and Chinese stand against or threaten to subsume languages such as Gaelic,[16] Catalan, Ukrainian and Persian.

---

15 Talk by Roberto Bergalli on imprisonment and politics with particular attention to the Spanish case.

16 From Bronwen Morgan: 'I'm struck here by the resurgence of Gaelic(s) in Wales and Scotland as a viable second language – catalysed apparently by some legal requirements for holding civil servant jobs etc. ... apparently the languages were almost dead.'

The reactionary signage in Quebec during the early years of nationalism subsumed design under the authority of language. The 1992 Barcelona Olympics were a showcase for the Catalan capital. They were brought to the city by its native son Juan Antonio Samaranch and contributed substantially to the authority of Barcelona as a cultural capital and a sophisticated place. The drawing out of the dimensions of jurisprudence in design is examined in Davila (2000), Balkin (1998) and Williams (1987). Davila argues that marketing and branding intercede in and moderate, if not transform, our nationalisms.

Design is a new jurisprudence. In Barcelona good design is attractive and smart, but like the problems of linguistic hegemony it marginalises difference, produces hype out of proportion to substance and distracts us from material conditions.

Imaging nation

The jurisprudence of the image is a matter of relations between other constituted spaces and the nature of those spaces.

While there are design projects like the Olympics and strategic initiatives like non-stop flights to New York, some of the imaging of nation is spontaneous and reflexive.

The reaction against the European Constitution and the nationalist movements in the Basque Country and Catalonia generated great symbolism but very little electoral power. Can these nationalisms be viable alternatives to the imperial umbrella, given the issues of global integration versus sub-national communities in Spain, Europe and the US?

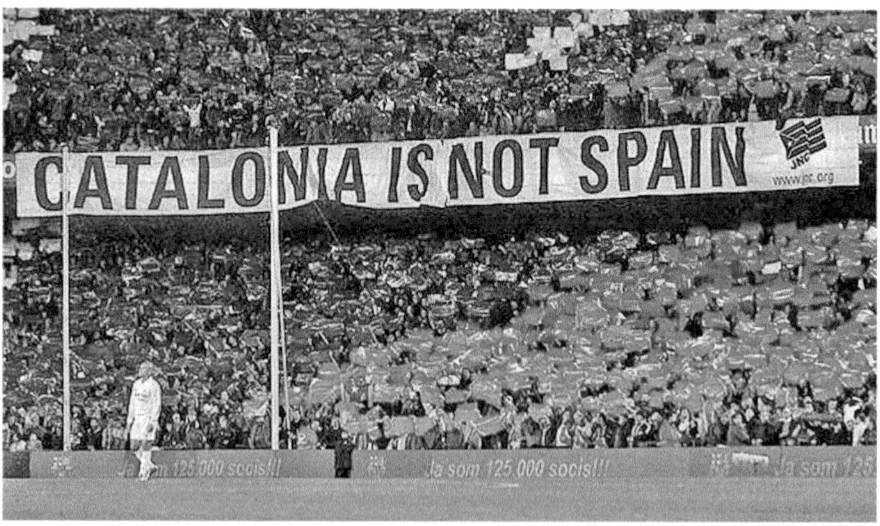

Figure 7.7 Separatist flag in English displayed at a Barcelona football match

The Catalan slogan 'Catalonia is not Spain' is used widely in its English form and thus dramatically associates the movement for a Catalan nation to the global English-speaking culture. The slogan was associated with Barcelona's football (soccer) team, Barça (Figure 7.7). It is reflected in the quote from Sir Bobby Robson, who took the team to major European success in 1996–97: 'You have to understand Barcelona is a nation without a state, and Barça is its army.'

At the same time as some of the most important developments taking Catalonia and BCN to the next level were unfolding, whole sections of the city were collapsing due to a massive structural mistake in the construction of a metro line.

These failures of policy would not be included in the meaning of the design for export but the cohesion and ambition of 'Gencat' would be identified internally as part of the problem and the glorious bars on the Catalonian insignia would likely themselves assume a different meaning for those who lost their houses due to government incompetence.

Marketing place

This section looks at elements of design that link Barcelona to the global economy. One of the most dramatic links is to New York City. This link involves a shift away from Madrid. We look for the commodification of sovereignty in design.

Culture and sovereignty

In Barcelona, there are cultural dimensions that come from Spain that are hundreds of years old and there are cultural dimensions from the Mediterranean city state which is the ancestral home of the Catalans that are over a thousand years old.

Tennis and soccer (football) are sports originally from England that have been adopted throughout Spain and particularly in Catalonia. Like Catholicism, soccer is a national commitment. Unlike religion it divides more than it unites, though perhaps not at the deepest level. The current success of the Barcelona football team, Barça, is perhaps the strongest expression of national identity, if not sovereignty, as the team won the Champions' League cup in Paris on 18 May 2006.

Spanish television is different from Catalan television. Spanish television is about the church, violence and romance. TV3 is about science and progress and art.

Catalonia and New York

I have said above, in laying out the tradition of autonomous movements in Spain, that the hegemony of Spanish (and French for Basques) and Madrid has been the focus of resistance. Where there is active repression from the Spanish state, resistance is an obvious dimension of sub-nationalism.

Figure 7.8 catalonia-is-not-spain.live.com

Without turning attention entirely away from that part of the nationalist struggle it is interesting to note in the context of design that new efforts to circumvent Madrid are increasingly important.

The Catalan government has set up an outpost in New York using the King Juan Carlos Center at New York University and the Institut Ramon Llull. Its cultural feature is a cultural connection between Barcelona (and by definition Catalonia) and New York City.[17] In their logo, design and text are serendipitously joined (Figure 7.8).

Barcelona by design

Design is the global language of the market. It is the feature of branding that at once grates and yet, in the context of this discussion, can be said to illuminate the dimensions of sovereignty considered here. A case worth considering was a design exhibition presented at the Architecture Museum in New York City during the period covered by this chapter. The exhibition was about the penetration of design in the physical structures and social fabric of Barcelona. Featuring map and product at the same time, 'Barcelona in Progress' billed itself as 'presenting Barcelona's dramatic post-Franco transformation through the present ... a framework for the progressive urban trajectory … and a global context for evaluating developments in large-scale metropolitan planning.'

One image from the exhibition is a stylised bicycle. It represents the idea that the city is like a bicycle. The dominant symbolic structure of the bicycle evokes movement. You have to keep pedalling or you will fall. Called 'BARCELONA PROGRÉS' in Catalan, the exhibition's web presentation is striking for its appearance in Catalan and English with no obvious Spanish component.[18] Though the backers are seldom featured, in this case they are the Adjuntament de Barcelona, Hines, Insitut Ramon Llull, Barcelona Regional, Collegi d'Arquitectes de Catalunya and the Consulate General of Spain in New York.

---

17 See The Catalan Institute of America's website at <http://www.friendsofcatalonia.com/>.

18 <http://www.bcn.es/urbanisme/barcelona_progres/welcome.htms>

The element of commodification – nation as product – submerges history and class and provides ease of movement, altering traditional legal relations.

Conclusion

In most things political the middle is a compromise, a place from which to avoid the poles. But in the area of linguistic nationalism the middle is radical. It is a contested place because it requires the negotiation of opposites. In the case of this chapter the middle is exemplified by the challenge of keeping alive the value and attractions of linguistic nationalism and good design when faced with the problems of hegemonic language politics and the absence of progressive resistance and warmth in the commodity form, at least historically.

What we are doing here?

One of the pleasures of Barcelona design is also a challenge in this chapter. The whole point is that Catalonia in general and Barcelona in particular are places that have been very good at depicting themselves with style. They have created a national brand that is highly sought after. The style is first rate and this why it matters. And, in Barcelona, the urge to present things beautifully is linked in many cases with the desire to make these efforts intelligent as well.

The power of all this is most significant with regard to nationalism as it affects the Spanish nation as has been constituted for the last 500 years. In the case of Barcelona, the rest of Spain cannot help but feel the emergence of this glitzy nouveau region since the controls of the old regime have been removed. And while it fights at every step to resist the independence that style brings, the government in Madrid seems powerless to stop such crucial elements of independence as direct air links between Barcelona and the capitals of the world.

Today the shrugs of inevitability and impatience at the rough sound of Catalan have largely replaced the martyrs' blood depicted in the flag of Catalonia. Such is the power of the new brand that it circumvents the forces that might be marshalled against it and operates at a whole new level.

The good and the bad

A prominent locution in the world of international film is 'the good, the bad and the ugly'. The title for the Sergio Leone film runs together conceptually and on reflection is associated with a global aesthetic phenomenon associated with music and image and personified in the internationally significant character of Clint Eastwood.

But, in the case of Barcelona, there is no ugly. It is not even clear that in the international market it matters that there is any 'bad' in the late twentieth-century image of the Catalan capital. Barcelona is the antithesis of ugly and at the level that the symbols operate it is given that there is no bad. This is the power of branding and the significance it has not only for selling drinks with no nutritional value but also political entities without attention to what lies beneath the surface.

There is a lot that does not fit with the Barcelona brand and it can make for difficult politics at home and abroad. In the winter of 2004–05 it was discovered that the city, in building a new subway line, had caused the fracture and eventual demolition of around 300 residences in the Mount Carmel (Carmelo) section of the city. Residents were furious and took on the arrogance of the city and provincial governments. Much of the politics looked less like the elevated aesthetic of the Olympics and more like the sad displacements forced on dependent people by arrogant and authoritarian governments. It was not a story easily conveyed to tourists or investors. But to those watching closely it challenged the brand and the image of progressive modernity that it sought to convey.

In the end, the branding is not so bad if you can see through it, but where it is successful this can be challenging because by its nature a brand is not complex. And, while we do not think of branding in terms of lives lost, to the extent that the consequences of local nationalism are forms of domination and closure with real effects, the unfamiliarity of branding in this area is its own challenge.

Chapter 8
Legality beyond the Scope of Policy

Sarah Marusek

Introduction

The wielding of power can be found in even the most mundane of places. In parking spaces, the power to displace is contrasted by the power to occupy. Likewise, the power of belonging yields the power of right as it is tied to the power of property. Therefore, the parking space is a contested site that uniquely constructs and engenders socio-legal notions of belonging and power. The creative architecture of the parking space renders this space a text from which the notion of a right can be interpreted according to formal and informal forms of law. Formal law may construct and regulate the space in order to foster legal methods of usage. In contrast, informal law, operating as the social norm, comports with legal dictations of usage to enforce expectations of belonging. Both types of law interact to show us the contested nature of a right according to the two primary governing tools: identity and property. In parking spaces, ascriptions of belonging, right and property can be translations of power policed by the parking police, parking office or simply by other parkers.

Parking spaces are constructed according to formal types of policy. One example is the American handicapped parking space. The policy of handicapped parking legally designates who belongs, who has a right to park in this space, and who can exert a formal claim of ownership on that space by demonstrating specified qualifications. However, the actual street-based law of the handicapped parking space is not confined simply to legal policy. The distinction between the two means that policy can be distinguished from law. In everyday parking lots where handicapped spaces exist, the general non-disabled public governs these spaces according to the jurisprudence of visible disability ubiquitously recognised in the form of a wheelchair. In this sense, it is the effect of law's power that is often more expansive than the study of policy suggests or allows. This expansive approach to studying law considers the social ramifications of legality unaddressed by the stated scope of policy and is termed as the constitutive approach to law (Brigham 1997; Harrington 1985). Fundamental questions of tolerance arise that the constitutive approach to law is able to address while the study of law solely as stated policy cannot fully imagine. Such limits include the following questions: to what extent does law enforce or discourage tolerance? What is the nature of law in terms of who is constituted by policy? Is the constitutive approach to law strictly policy-based or does it include considerations of law as it is shaped, interpreted, and reconstructed according to the variety of social contexts? Therefore, the study of law according to the limitations of policy formation and impact can be limiting in scope because the restrictive application of policy according to a policy's stated affected groups cannot consider the full range of the policy's impact.

In this chapter, I will assert that the constitutive approach to law includes more than just parties designated by a policy as being affected. Or in other words, the narrow tailoring of law to strictly address those written into policy crucially misses the everyday wielding of power in which many variables of law and legality outside of the stated policy contribute to the experienced interpretation of policy. In doing this, I will look at the nature of a right as disputed in the terrain of the American handicapped parking space in order to examine the local everyday governance of such parking spaces according to American disability policy. I will argue that a truly constitutive approach to law includes rather than discounts the participation of the mass public. The dismissal of the unspecified mass public as the unaddressed periphery of policy actually promotes a level of intolerance in the study of what law and where law can be found. A truly constitutive approach to law is, in contrast, a tolerant approach that can fully examine how policy as law really works, illustrated by the everyday fusion of formal and informal law operating as power. In this sense, the constitutive approach to law considers the reality of unmentioned parties impacted by a stated policy. This expansive view encourages a tolerant approach to the study of law that is not limited in scope by the limitations of stated directives of policy.

To make my argument, I will examine legal scholar Thomas F. Burke's work (2004) on disability policy from his article 'The Judicial Implementation of Statutes: Three Stories about Courts and the Americans with Disabilities Act'. Burke focuses on court involvement with the Americans with Disabilities Act (ADA) of 1990 through the eyes of legal scholars, disability activists, politicians and the disabled themselves. He develops the reactions of the above to the ADA through the themes of backlash, symbolic politics and statutory construction. While a thorough survey of the ADA, Burke's view of the constitutive approach is problematic. Even as Burke insightfully addresses the impact of ADA policy on disabled people, he dismisses the impact on and influence of the ADA on the *non-disabled* mass public. Arguably, this latter group is ultimately responsible for enforcing disability policy in everyday places where formal law is an immediately absent force. Constitutive law reminds us that law is made by everyday actors interpreting what the law really means. To construct my argument, namely that the non-disabled mass public must be considered in how disability policy is translated as law, I will refer to the work of socio-legal scholars Thomas Dumm (1999), Robert Cover (1992) and Barbara Yngvesson (1993).

In *A Politics of the Ordinary*, Dumm (1999) asserts that which is ordinary is political (1999). Using this expansive sense of law, I will draw upon Dumm's illuminating work on the politics of the ordinary to show that the banality of ordinary occurrences is underexplored territory in which structures of power that are less obvious but very telling of how power is wielded, can be revealed. Accordingly then, the mass public are political actors in ordinary spaces involving the disabled, such as the parking lot where both disabled and non-disabled drivers park. Next, I will look at law according to Robert Cover's idea of the violence of law in 'Violence and the Word' (1992). Cover tells us that there is violence in the word of law. Drawing upon Cover's premise, I will consider the implicit aspect of violence presented by the selective interpretation regarding the impact of disability policy. Lastly, I will examine the context of law created, interpreted and implemented in everyday, ordinary places as Barbara Yngvesson's work in *Virtuous Citizens, Disruptive Subjects: Order and Complaint in a New England Court* attests (1993). According to Yngvesson, we can see that the mass public is a constitutive force of law in how law itself is created and constructed in the everyday arena of legality by everyday people. My conclusion will illuminate why prioritising the study of law's effect to those explicitly targeted by policy is intolerant. This foundational exclusion of those affected by the policy, yet unconsidered by the policy's scope, creates a problematic tension that the constitutive approach to law demands us to rethink while begging the larger questions of interpretation and enforcement of legality in the everyday.

The mass public: real policy-makers

The full picture of the law involves policy, the interpretation of that policy as rights, and the enforcement of those rights. Although a wonderful approach to the parameters of the ADA, Burke's constitutive approach to law (2004, 123–39) is limited to the role of policy where the formal construction of and reaction to law prioritises the response of those written into the law. This is problematic because the everyday view of policy as law by people who are *not* explicitly considered to be part of the policy, can be just as important in constitutive analysis. An example of this would be the 'eyes upon the street, eyes belonging to those we might call the natural proprietors of the street' in Jane Jacobs's (1961, 35) discussion of safety and the uses of sidewalks.

While Burke (2004) does recognise that there is more to law than simply that which is written into policy, the role of interpreting and enforcing law is nonetheless up to the formal realm of legislation and judging. He states (2004, 124):

> Indeed for many statues, we must even consider the attitudes of the mass public, who though uninvolved in litigation, may have a decisive impact on processes of implementation. It is the behavior of this much larger cast – litigants, potential litigants, and seeming bystanders – that provides the context in which legislators and judges interact.

Burke (2004, 132) then insightfully speaks of the misplaced focus of interpreting law through formal institutions by saying: 'but this focus misses perhaps the most important aspects of judicial implementation of statutes, the mechanisms by which laws and litigation penetrate the larger society, the routines of nongovernmental organizations, and the everyday consciousness of citizens.'

His attention to the 'everyday consciousness of citizens' is intuitive in addressing the constitutive approach, although also limiting because of the following premise: 'My chief point is to highlight how many readers of statues there are – not just the judges, legislators, and bureaucrats, who populate most studies of the court-Congress interaction but also defendants, plaintiffs, lawyers, administrators, journalists, *and even the mass public*' [italics added by this author] (Burke 2004, 136).

Although Burke's central premise alludes to an atypically inclusive interaction with the law by emphasising the numbers of readers of law that exist, this possibility for expansion stops with the token acknowledgment of '... even the mass public'. This phrasing of '... even the mass public' is a limiting characterisation that does not address the views of the non-disabled public as the majority of inhabitants of everyday places, spaces and arenas where law is enforced without the presence of formal persona or procedure. To discount this quotidian faction of governance is to discount the full constitutive picture of law. In everyday parking lots where disability policy is abstractly present as law, the non-disabled public actually govern the disabled more on grounds of visible legitimacy and less on the dictates of policy *per se* (Marusek 2005). Furthermore, the symbolism of the ADA is heightened as a form of law for those 'excluded' from its protections, the presently non-disabled. This is symbolic for those who not only passed the actual law and the disabled who are directly impacted, but also for those it less ostensibly but just as tangibly affects.

The presence of handicapped parking spaces is quotidian, yet consistently invokes debates of legitimate occupancy according to parking-based identity and right, temporary claims of property, even murderous rage. Who parks where and why is a source of tension for drivers who repeatedly perform the banal task of finding a place for their cars. The semiotics of this terrain constructs a visual sense of right, where legitimate belonging is based upon the visual representation of proof of rightful occupancy (Johnson, 2005; Silbey and Ewick 1998; Anderson, 2005). The regulation of that proof, and of the right to park, reveals a sense of law that harkens beyond the confines of the legal text.

In fact, this sense of law challenges the formal law of parking policy by evoking the Constitution as the penultimate protector of equality and equal rights. In a complex tango between the formal law of policy, the heralded law of the Constitution and the everyday unwritten rules of parking, social law as constitutive law emerges triumphant. Expected practices and accepted behaviours dictate law as norm, particularly in such parking spaces as the Handicapped Parking Space where the governance of such spaces is dependent more upon the identity of the parker than on the legality of spatial occupancy and accompanying qualification.

Without recognising this attention to where law is really, the examination of policy is intolerant of those who are not formally written into the law itself yet informally enforce or resist its implementation. The everyday interpretation of the

ADA rests with the mass public, who may include in its ranks both the disabled and the presently non-disabled. Here, the everyday consciousness of citizens is central to the constitutive approach to the ADA where those same everyday people who do not have the least notion of what the policy details of the ADA are find themselves in the position to either support, refute or ignore who parks in a handicapped parking space. The trouble with focusing our attention on formal settings such as the courtroom or litigation-driven organisational setups is that we fail to acknowledge the realities of everyday life where the enforcement of law is put into action. This may be the case when considering the current enforcement of American immigration policies where informal groups, such as the Minutemen Project, who take it upon themselves to enforce who belongs and who does not at the US's southwestern borders.

Therefore, the constitutive approach to law as articulated in Burke's article (2004) is rather intolerant and really not all that constitutive as it places too much emphasis on the formal aspects of law and not enough on the translation of law in everyday spaces by non-policy actors. His approach concerning the impact of law is restrictive because it addresses the reaches of law which are formally constructed through courtroom decisions, policy, and immediately felt as reactions by those directly impacted by the law. I would argue that the law does not end where Burke (2004) thinks it does, but is much more encompassing in its many various interpretations and implementations precisely at the level of the mass public. As socio-legal scholars and political scientists, how diverse are we in our thinking if we do not consider the full impact of legislation on those who are not the stated targets of the legislation but in fact participate, and arguably *are* those who enforce or resist such legislation each and every day? In other words, we must acknowledge the extent of who is tolerating those who are legally tolerated. Does this tolerance rest solely within the stated parameters of policy?

As Austin Sarat (1990) reminds us, the law is all over. Keeping this in mind, the interpretation of what is law is tied to the unique circumstances of its enforcement. The formal articulation of law is tied to the social agenda of law revealed as the constitutive approach to law. In other words, how law is constituted is through its interpretation and its enforcement in informal settings. Here, Burke's work (2004) is useful not only to illuminate the formal parameters of the ADA, but just as importantly to show the limitations of the reaches of policy in settings where everyday interpretations of that policy by the mass public who, vaguely familiar with the details of that policy, actually change its meaning. It is this version of 'policy-making' that is worthy of further examination. While Burke asserts that 'there is a place for the study of policy and how it is made'[1] in considering the connection between policy and the everyday constitution of law, the study of law should not end with the study of policy.

1 This is from correspondence that I had with Thomas Burke during the summer of 2006.

Power of the everyday

Power can be found in observing the ordinary, as this is where politics can be found 'to the extent that normalisation reduces the unpredictability and unknowability of the ordinary, it operates as a form of politics', as Dumm suggests (1999, 6). The examination of power dynamics intrinsic to both handicapped and non-handicapped parking spaces, it is precisely this banal, ordinary, normalised place that invites observations of a political nature. In parking spaces, identity is characterised by a legal sense of right to park, designated by parking stickers, parking tags or licence plates. In these spaces, right is represented as a physical claim of property. Such physicality invites questions of belonging, be they individual or community-based, as well as of a public/semi-public/private determination. Although the distinctions of these spatial confines are legally reproduced, the social implications of these different types of space beckon further consideration into questions of belonging accentuated by race, class, gender and ability. Discrimination of place through property invokes a sense of identity that exposes the politics of injustice. Accordingly, the meaning of place carries implications of right versus might and raises constitutive considerations of jurisprudence that foster remedies of street-based justice. Dumm further asserts that 'to think about the ordinary as a contested space in which practices of representation occur links it to the forces of normalization and events' (1999, 6).

The representations of belonging presented by and inherent with the parking space render it an ideal place where politics occurs. Therefore, this politics of the ordinary can be found in the everyday interpretation and enforcement of disabled parking policy as the variety and ways in which law is constructed at the local level of the mass public is on city streets and in parking lots. Perhaps in this way, disability parking policy could best be understood in the banality of parking lots. Dumm (1999, 19) reminds us that 'We need to understand that the uneventfulness of the ordinary is the inevitable ground from which we may come to a better appreciation of events … [where] the relentless *presence* of the ordinary, even in, or especially because of, its elusive character, becomes the source of its validity.'

The ordinariness of disability policy is the street sign of reserved handicapped parking space picturing a white figure in a wheelchair upon a blue background. Tied to this is the conflicting ordinariness of the non-disabled driver either affirming this legal reserve of space by parking in a generic space or rejecting the legal command and unlawfully parking in this handicapped parking space. Signals work with signs as important methods and tools of acknowledgment implicated in the 'project of resistance that I increasingly identify with the ordinary', as Dumm describes (1999, 161). The recognition of the politics of ordinariness in everyday parking lots actually reveals the constitutive nature of law that changes in meaning as debated by the mass public.

These new perspectives on authority, space and jurisdiction invite consideration of the parking lot as socio-legal apparatus of place, position and occupation operating in everyday practice according to legal premises, but also social observation and political rationale. The parking space is a location of everyday governance. It is this framed social setting that is ripe with jurisprudential implications for property and right. Just as bodies of law both characterise and depend upon a sense of place, in a community, law is a function of the perception of a right and the protection and enforcement of that right. When discussed in terms of belonging, identity and property, the everyday practice of parking a car is a debate between local social practices and formal law. The right to park is a contested act between the driver and the governing power of the parked-upon space. The parking space can be viewed as an estuary of legitimacy, where private rights mix with public notions of occupation. The parked car is an inanimate representation of the driver that invokes aspects of either marginalisation or privilege. The occupation of this contested space is a site of social and legal governance created by formal as well as informal law. Formal law in this sense is law according to the courts, the Constitution and congressional statutes. On the other hand, informal law can be the mimicry of formal law, where everyday people copy the techniques of boundaries, practices and enforcement. This type of governance is used to invoke a notion of power that interprets rights according to social norms. The public knowledge of such norms creates and fosters a sense of law with expectations of enforcement. Both the expectation and the actual enforcement according to this expectation reveal a level of governance that is an extension of law. It is this constitutive approach to law that invites further exploration into the banality of everyday life.

The enforcement of everyday rights is often not according to formal law, but instead often takes on its own character of social law. Tickets, towing and appeals often match more mundane acts – handwritten notes angered by violation, keying, even tire-slashing. Resistance to this enforcement of formal and informal parking regulations is law on the streets, and with a nod to Michael Lipsky, with 'parking lot-level bureaucracy' (1980). Often violent, parkers can be victims and aggressors alike, receiving and directing anger at fellow parkers as well as at the personification of parking law, the parking control officer. The parking control officer is viewed as the most immediate presence of formal law that regulates rights while appearing as the face of social law, simply for being human. As a contested form of regulatory enforcement of regulatory design of parking, the control officer is a key aspect in the politics of parking where ideas of public forum, private property, public need, individual entitlement, community protection, legal justification and social need are transformed. This mundane activity of parking invites a new look into where law can be found and what jurisprudence can look like.

Examining the parking space through issues of local enforcement reveals critical notions of property, rights and belonging that the study of law and politics promotes. The semiotics of the terrain carries signs of legitimacy, the designations of property and entitlement, and the construction of identity and belonging. Central to these considerations is the fundamental notion of resistance to enforcement. The constitutive approach to the laws of parking and the enforcement of those laws is a reflection of democracy through the courts as well as in the street. Local forms of jurisdiction contribute to the discussion of where and what law really is. Because it is not immediately present and is not immediately fully understood (in terms of extent of rights and enforcement), law at this informal level is formal in theory but in practice is constituted by those who enforce it and by those who contest its enforcement. How far does law reach? In this context, law extends to the fingertips of the arm of law and further to what those fingers can grasp. According to Dumm (1999, 18): 'the conflict (between the event and the normalized) shapes strategies of governance and the forms of violence imposed on people in their exercise of ordinary freedom.'

Cover (1992) relates well to Dumm (1999) as he details the relationship between violence, legal interpretation and everyday contexts. Cover (1992, 203) has an astute sense of law in the everyday and states 'legal interpretative acts signal and occasion the imposition of violence upon others'. Here, the interpretation of law is connected inextricably to violence in acts, reactions and responses. Cover (1992, 210) tells us 'every interpretive practice takes place in some context' and broadens the scope of his argument to say 'I would be prepared to argue that all law which concerns property, its use, and its protection, has a similarly violent base' where 'even the violence of weak judges is utterly real – a naïve but immediate reality, in need of no interpretation, no critic to reveal it' (1992, 210, 213). In this sense, weak judges are those drivers not explicitly written into the ADA parking policy for disabled drivers. These non-disabled drivers judge the legitimacy of disabled drivers' claim to handicapped parking spaces. As mentioned earlier, this judgement is based upon visibility.

Using this framework, we can connect the understanding of law to practices of its everyday interpretation. Cover (1992) tells us that institutional context ties the language act of practical understanding to the physical acts of others in a predictable, though not logically necessarily, way. These interpretations, then, are not only 'practical', they are, themselves, practices. This idea of practices is important to consider when thinking of the institutional context of policy where the practical understanding of policy becomes law. Cover (1992, 218) speaks further of this understanding 'of the relation, between the interpretation of the judge and the social organization required to transform it into reality, the *hermeneutic of the texts of jurisdiction*' (emphasis added by this author). Accordingly, 'legal interpretation may be the act of judges or citizens, legislator or presidents, draft resisters or right-to-life protestor' (Cover 1992, 224). Following this combination of attributes, the text of jurisdiction is in the hands of the non-disabled mass public as the social influence and judge of the legal interpretation involving disability parking policy. In this context, legal interpretation may also be the practices of non-disabled drivers protecting or rebelling against disabled parking policy by parking or protecting the specified occupancy of handicapped parking spaces. Cover (1992) makes an important distinction between the experiences of the perpetrator and those of the victim of organised violence found in legal interpretation. He states that 'between the idea and the reality of common meaning falls the shadow of the violence of the law itself' (1992, 238).

The creation of this shadow of the violence of law as Cover suggests can be tied to the reality that policy is interpreted differently in varying contexts. Barbara Yngvesson (1993) perceptively illustrates this reality in her study of how everyday people interpret rights and law in local courts. These boundaries and margins of where law is remarkably illuminates a fluid scope of empowerment both inside and outside the court. Her attentive characterisation of residents of the two neighbouring towns of Turners Falls and Greenfield, Massachusetts, as constitutive members of the community, is adept and powerful. The local translation of power by various members of a local community is a wonderful approach to the self-governing construction and habitation of legal spaces. Yngvesson's purpose (1993, 11) is to

> show that the court is not solely shaped by professionals but that the law, the court, and legal officials are formed in the exchanges of officials with victims, defendants, witnesses, and others about the meanings of words and actions that bring people to the courthouse. In these exchanges, and in collective practices that develop around them, 'cases' and 'courts' are constituted, as everyday acts and spaces are transformed into legal ones.

She eloquently locates '"law", "court", "cases", and "community" in everyday processes of complaint, conflict and cooperation … channeled in particular ways by dominant communal and legal understandings and practices' and speaks of 'agents who are both constituted by the law and who confront the law' (Yngvesson 1993, 12). She also speaks of the 'local vernacular of rights', 'governing capacity' of court clerks as intermediaries between citizens, and legal power to illustrate the reality of shifting space for legal interpretation in finding law (Yngvesson 1993, 47). She describes local identities which through the courthouse, act as 'a vehicle for affirming this identity publicly through the law' (Yngvesson 1993, 31). Yngvesson's attention to the interpretation of policy shows us the breadth of legal interpretation involving the locality of the mass public.

The jurisprudence of the parking space creates a type of governing that by nature is local. In spaces where formal law is evident, yet dominantly absent, social law becomes judge and jury. Right and its regulation are culturally dependent and politically malleable. The right to park is a special right, considered to be a presumption of expectation connected, literally, to the person driving the car. Jurisprudentially, this special right is enacted between individuals in everyday parking environments where social norm operates as 'the law' and formal law is distanced. Feeding the meter distances the threat of a ticket. The appeal of that ticket is the pronouncement of right. Yelling angrily at a driver who cuts you off and parks triumphantly in a coveted parking space is a more immediate regulation of right.

In continuing the debate of where the law ends and even how far it reaches, I extend similar questions to my own work. My own work suggests that parking policies are often less than transparent. I have argued that with the consequence in the enforcement of these policies as a form of power wielded intolerantly. The legal right of reserved handicapped parking spaces for legally disabled drivers is limited in its protection by the ADA. It is the contested right to park in handicapped spaces that shows the difference between formal policy-based law and socially informal law (Marusek, 2005). In this context, formal law dictates that this space is reserved for any driver displaying the formal Blue Wheelchair placard on his/her vehicle. In contrast however is social law, which asserts that this space is reserved for those drivers who visibly appear to be disabled as the legal placard is not necessary proof. The difference between the two types of law can be seen in the everyday enforcement of these spaces designated by the street sign of legal handicap which pictures a white figure of a person in a wheelchair against a blue background, referred to henceforth as the Blue Wheelchair. The Blue Wheelchair sign designates space as a spatial marker. In these handicapped reserved parking spaces, onlookers and drivers themselves act to enforce their version of *the law*; they base their judgement of legitimate occupancy of that space on whether or not that particular driver *looks* disabled or not. This legitimising appearance of disability often ignores the legal showing of the Blue Wheelchair displayed on the vehicle. In everyday parking lots where these spaces are located, everyday folks are the actual enforcers of the law in terms of who parks in a handicapped space. Here, they make their assessment on the presence or absence of physical disability. Little attention is paid to the parameters of disability and space provided by the ADA's legal framework. This visual-based justice is informal law and stands in contrast to the formal policy of the ADA's legal construction of disability. According to the ADA's definition of disability, a person is disabled if he/she can be *regarded* as being disabled. The quality of being regarded as disabled or not is semiotically amalgamated with the legal image of disability found in the Blue Wheelchair image. In a constitutive fashion, this legal picture of disability becomes the social expectation of what disability looks like; this picture is the foundation of informal law in everyday parking lots where the handicapped parking space and its occupancy are socially enforced. This consideration of constitutive justice is important in determining the rights of disabled drivers in common social settings and challenges the formal governance of the ADA as the primary protector of disability rights in everyday parking lots.

Conclusion

What is the meaning of this debate? On tolerance? On diversity? On law and who really counts? Are only those written into law the ones that matter? To look to see if we are tolerant or not, one must only witness the countless handicapped parking spaces that are overwhelmingly vacant, either out of self-preservation and fear of getting a ticket, or out of respect for those who need the closer space to leave it readily available for them. The creation of these spaces is evidence of tolerance through law, both for those who are handicapped and for those who one day may become handicapped. This tolerance is displayed everyday by people who do not park in those spaces, yet do not know the legal language of the ADA that details who can park in those spaces and why. In this way, the non-disabled mass public enforces the law, without really even knowing the law in a constitutive approach to the tolerance of policy. Tolerance of policy tells us that policy as law reaches into places unexamined by strict adherence to policy as written and/or formulated. The politics of ordinary acts and places and the policing of such politics reveals that law happens in the everyday arena of the mass public and beyond the strict scope of written policy application and impact.

Additionally, such policy can also be intolerant as the contribution of those making laws and impacting everyday people can not be ascertained. Moreover, we only have to look to the everyday implementation of law to find a tolerance-based approach to seeing how we interpret and remake law in everyday contexts. Each of these facets is present in the context of handicapped parking space determined by the ADA and affecting the disabled as well as the non-disabled in everyday common places where parking regulation occurs and is resisted. A truly tolerance-based look at law takes these expansive factors of interpretation and enforcement of 'even the mass public' into account. In conclusion, power is not solely wielding simply by policy-makers, judges, or even the targeted group of legislation, but through the localised interpretation of legality through everyday spaces and constructions by the mass public.

Chapter 9

On Sight/On Site: Visuality in Native Title Claims: Can We Even Speak?

Tracey Summerfield and Alec McHoul

Introduction

In 1997 a collaboration of around 50 artists, representing the Walmajarri, Wangkajunga, Mangala and Juwaliny peoples of the Kimberley/Great Sandy Desert region of North West Australia (Anker 2005, 91) tendered an 18 × 12 metre canvas as evidence in their native title land claim. Known as the Ngurrara canvas, it depicts country south of Fitzroy Crossing in Western Australia. It is described as 'like looking at a giant map or an aerial view of the country … depict[ing] waterholes (Jila), dunes and rangelands special to several indigenous groups' (ABC 2004).[1] An image of the painting adorned one of Perth city's metropolitan buses. The original hangs as a work of art in a private collection.

The Ngurrara canvas represents a possible bridge between cultural systems: a way for Indigenous people to 'map' their lands into a visual medium to meet the evidentiary requirements for establishing native title in an Australian legal system based on white knowledge systems. The canvas was one of the first canvases used in evidence to support a land claim (Anon. 2003), though some 26 years earlier, the Yirrkala Bark Petitions were presented to the Federal Parliament by the Yolngu people from Yirrkala in eastern Arnhem Land in the Northern Territory, as part of their claim for recognition of rights to land in the Gove Peninsula (Anon. 2003, Northern Land Council Land & Sea Rights 2005, Commonwealth of Australia n.d.).

The Ngurrara canvas should not be understood merely as an alternative form of mainstream European-style cartography, as is explained below. It represents more than just surfaces and boundaries, as does the Indigenous relationship to land generally. A website paraphrasing some of the Ngurrara artists (Skipper et al. 2002) puts this succinctly:

---

1 An image of the canvas can be seen at Andrew Meares, *Law Text Culture* 9, 2005. Available at <http://search.informit.com.au/documentSummary;dn=099219979163080;res =E-LIBRARY>. The image depicts Nyilpirr Spider Snell, of the Kimberly/Great Sandy Desert region of North West Australia, performing the *Kurtal* (the Snake Dreaming Dance) to the High Court in Canberra, Australia (Anker 2005, 91).

> When preparing for the first plenary session of their ... Native title claim they were faced with the perennial problem of how to bridge the gulf between two such different laws, languages and world views. Finally, they hit on a solution: instead of merely talking about their claim, they would collaborate in painting it. Then each claimant could stand on his or her section of country as represented on the canvas and speak it in their own language, pointing out different features or travel routes to illustrate what was being said, their words interpreted.

This was to 'remind those sitting on the High Court of the depth of [the] claim' (Anker 2005, 91, citing *Native Title Newsletter* 2002, 4). As Anker argues, the painting did more than merely map the claimants' country, appealing to a Western legal tradition in which maps and law authoritatively represent reality. The painting also represented their credibility and provided a means of communicating Indigenous knowledge to a non-Indigenous audience and legal system (2005, 92–3). Similarly the Bark Petitions were more than a mere plea to the Parliament; they presented Yolngu law itself, including traditional ownership to land, to white lawmakers.

Coupled with the strategy of bringing land to the decision-maker, in the form of the painting, has been that of bringing the decision-maker to land by holding parts of hearings 'on country'. These two possible meeting points between traditional and Eurocentric laws (one on sight, the other on site) are the focal points of this chapter.

Knowledge, evidence and the recognition of native title

Until the landmark case of *Mabo v Queensland (No 2)* (hereinafter *Mabo*), there was an insurmountable gulf between the ways in which the common law and Australian property law conceived of real property and the relationship of Indigenous people to land. There was no mechanism under the common law for recognising what has come to be known 'native title'.[2] In *Milirrpum v Nabalco Pty Ltd* (the Gove case), Justice Blackburn recognised that the people of the Gove Peninsula in the Northern Territory had a system of law which included conceptions of land, but the plaintiffs failed in their land claim because there was no doctrine of native title in Australian common law at the time.

Mabo incorporated the concept of native title into the common law of Australia, by recognising that native title pre-existed the Crown's radical title over Australian lands upon colonisation, and finding that it still existed unless extinguished by an act of the Crown. The Indigenous relationship to land was at last given a name in Australian law.

2 Though 'land rights' were able to be conferred under the *Aboriginal Land Rights (Northern Territory) Act* 1976 (Cth), they were, nevertheless, a construction of the statute, rather than recognition of pre-existing interests.

Subsequent to *Mabo* the *Native Title Act 1993* (Cth) (hereinafter *NTA)* established a system for recognising Indigenous peoples' native title.[3] Section 223 defines 'native title' in the following terms, reflecting the descriptions provided in *Mabo*:

> (1) The expression *native title* or *native title rights and interests* means the communal, group or individual rights and interests of Aboriginal peoples or Torres Strait Islanders in relation to land or waters, where:
>
> (a) the rights and interests are possessed under the traditional laws acknowledged, and the traditional customs observed, by the Aboriginal peoples or Torres Strait Islanders; and
>
> (b) the Aboriginal peoples or Torres Strait Islanders, by those laws and customs, have a connection with the land or waters; and
>
> (c) the rights and interests are recognised by the common law of Australia ....
>
> (2) ... *rights and interests* in that subsection include hunting, gathering, or fishing, rights and interests [emphasis in original].

Cases since *Mabo* and the passing of the *NTA* have illustrated that giving a legal name and description to the Indigenous relationship to land is not sufficient to protect that interest. The traditional owners must prove their continued relationship to that land, which can be physical and/or spiritual. The Justices in *Mabo* specifically noted that the contents of native title and the persons who have entitlement are derived from the traditions and customs of Indigenous people to whom that land relates[4] and this is reflected in s223 of the *NTA*. In *Yorta Yorta v Victoria* the High Court of Australia considered which of these traditions intersect with (and are therefore recognised under) the common law (439–440 per Gleeson CJ, Gummow and Hayne JJ). The majority find that the traditions recognised under the common law are those which, firstly, existed prior to sovereignty and, secondly, continue to exist as laws, as indicated by their maintenance and observance; that is, they must 'observe the same normative system that "burdened" the Crown's acquisition of sovereignty' (Strelein 2006, 88).

---

3 'Land rights' were established as a statutory granting of land by the *Aboriginal Land Rights (Northern Territory) Act* 1976 (Cth). This, however, did not establish any right to land for Indigenous people, except by grant.

4 Per Mason CJ and McHugh J at 1, Brennan J at 57–8, Deane and Gaudron JJ at 110 and Toohey J at 178. See also *Fejo v Northern Territory of Australia* (1998) 195 CLR 96 per Kirby J at 148 and *De Rose v State of South Australia* [2002] FCA 1342 (1 November 2002) per O'Loughlin J at ¶8.

Of course, the traditional rights and interests of Indigenous people exist irrespective of their recognition as 'native title'. Perhaps, then, one of the greatest difficulties for Indigenous people has been in describing the form and content of these traditions, to a legal system which itself has firmly entrenched ideas of land and the types of relationship that one can have to it. Coupled with two disparate systems of knowledge, evidence and power, in terms of what information counts, who can and should tender that knowledge and the mechanisms for explicating that knowledge, the barriers to recognition are almost (but not quite) insurmountable.

The dual barrier is perhaps best indicated by Graeme Neate, President of the National Native Title Tribunal, when he asks:

> What is to be done if the relevant Indigenous community understands their links to land differently from the statutory definition or if other information is available which would give a more complete and accurate picture of the links of a group and their traditional land but, in a strictly legal sense, is irrelevant to the inquiry? (2004, 25)

He presents the *différend* between white and Indigenous Australians' language of land, when he quotes Stanner's 1968 attempt to put the Indigenous relationship to land into words: 'No English words are good enough to give a sense of the links between an Aboriginal group and its homeland. … A different tradition leaves us tongueless and earless towards this other world of meaning and significance' (Stanner 1979, 230, in Neate 2004, 10). A *différend*, according to Lyotard's theory of justice, is any situation where the idiom of a victim of injustice cannot be heard according to the rules of the relevant tribunal (Lyotard 1984, 4–14). Stanner's remarks are poignant in this respect: being left 'tongueless and earless towards this other world of meaning and significance' is precisely what Lyotard was referring to via this concept. A possible proposition, then, is that where tongues and ears fail, sites and sights might *just* succeed. But can this slight shift to sight be sufficient to establish a relationship between white and Indigenous laws such that the latter cannot only be seen but also given precedence in their own right? The *différend* refers to idioms, to failed speaking and hearing practices. Does the glimmering of a shift to the visual mean mutual vision or a new blindness?

The significance of visual representations, as opposed to written forms of knowledge, was highlighted in the Yolngu Bark Petitions presented to the House of Representatives of the Australian Parliament in 1963. The petitions were presented as a response to the failure of the federal Government to negotiate with traditional land owners over mining of their lands and the removal of more than 300 square kilometres of their land for bauxite mining (Commonwealth of Australia n.d.). Galarrwuy Yunipingu of the Northern Land Council explains that the petitions were prepared as a bridge between Yolngu and Balanda (white Australian) systems of law: combining both written (typed) text on paper, in both English and Gumatj, with traditional bark painting. The designs depicted the Yolngu traditional relationship to land (Anon, 2003, 3). Yunipingu stresses the significance of the document by outlining the background to its creation:

> The thirteen clans came together, negotiated what should be included, and set about preparing this painting which was unique and unprecedented. It could be likened to the Magna Carta of Balanda [white] law because it was the first time Yolngu had ever set our law down for others to see (Yunipingu 1998).

The document's failure to protect the Yolngu interests, according to Yunipingu, was evidence of the *invisibility* to the Balanda of Yolngu law, leading to the realisation that the only way of fighting for land rights in Gove was through Balanda law (Yunipingu 1998). Hence the Gove case, noted above. We return in more detail to this crucial set of events in the final section of this chapter.

Still, white Australia has since given language to this relationship – 'native title' – but its form and content remain unarticulated and possibly inarticulable. We know from the definitions provided in *Mabo* and the *NTA* that it involves rights and interests in land or water, possessed under traditional laws and customs by Indigenous people with the requisite connection to those lands or waters from the time of settlement. But if white Australia has only recently given terminology to this interest, how easily can it be expected to understand the traditions and customs that will give right to these interests? In short, can these traditional laws and customs be articulated in the Australian common law system?

The range of issues for Indigenous people in their attempts to prove links to land has been widely canvassed. These issues include:

- The limits of the adversarial system (Neate 2004,16).
- The role of experts and the authority of witnesses (*ibid.*).
- The use of propositional logic in the examination of witnesses (Anker 2005, 97) and differences between standard and Indigenous English, questioning styles and speech norms (Anker 2005, 97).
- An inherent bias in favour of written evidence (Reilly 2000, Ketley and Ozich 2003, Neate 2004, 16, Anker 2005, 97).
- The reliance in the Western legal tradition on access to information, whereas access to Indigenous knowledge is selectively and cultural prescribed (Anker 2005, 97) (see for example *Ejai v Commonwealth* where the Supreme Court of Western Australia acknowledged the need to conduct proceedings in a culturally sensitive matter).
- The difference between abstract knowledge and particularised knowledge connected to places and rituals. Country is the basis of knowledge and corresponds to 'differentiated rights in country' (Anker 2005, 97).

These issues affect the court's reception of 'facts' that are required to establish native title and are essentially of an evidentiary nature. They reflect a conflict between the requirements for entering evidence into legal proceedings and the form and manner of presenting knowledge of culture and country for Indigenous people.

This conflict between the evidentiary requirements and the form and manner of presenting Indigenous knowledge was originally contemplated in the *NTA*. Section 82 provided, before the Federal Government's amendment in 1998, that:

> (1) The Federal Court must pursue the objective of providing a mechanism of determination that is fair, just, economical, informal and prompt.
> (2) The Court, in conducting proceedings, must take account of the cultural and customary concerns of Aboriginal peoples and Torres Strait Islanders.
> (3) The Court, in conducting proceedings, is not bound by technicalities, legal forms or rules of evidence.

Hence, the provision placed fairness, efficiency and the cultural issues for Indigenous people in providing evidence before the formal rules of evidence. It was, perhaps, a recognition that formal rules of evidence reflected a particular tradition of knowledge and authority, inconsistent with Indigenous traditions. This is not to say, however, that the Court could 'lapse into whimsical regulation of the evidence it admits'. It was limited by requirements of procedural fairness, the fundamental requirement that regard should only be had to 'relevant, probative and cogent' evidence, and the specific limits of subsection 82(1) (*Members of the Yorta Yorta Aboriginal Community v the State of Victoria & Ors* 1998, per Olney J, citing Neate 1997–98, 56). The provision did, however, provide at the forefront for the use of different processes for hearing evidence (Australian Law Reform Commission 2005, 503; see, for example, *Western Australia v Ward* 1997, where the power of the court to exclude attendance in the court room on the basis of gender was recognised).[5]

The Federal Government's *Native Title Amendment Act 1998* (Cth) reinstated the normal rules of evidence. The amended section 82 provides that:

> (1) The Federal Court is bound by the rules of evidence, except to the extent that the Court otherwise orders.
> (2) In conducting its proceedings the Court may take account of the cultural and customary concerns of Aboriginal peoples and Torres Strait Islanders, but not so as to prejudice unduly any other party in the proceedings.

The provision operates in tandem with the Federal Court Rules which give the Court some discretion in the making of orders on evidentiary matters, so that it can make an order 'relating to the presentation of evidence about a cultural or customary subject' (O 78 r 31(3)(f)) and might include evidence given 'by way of

---

5 Citing Yamatji Marlpa Barna Baba Maaja Aboriginal Corporation Submission E, 16 February 2005.

singing, dancing, storytelling or in any other way other than in the normal course of giving evidence' (O 78 r 32).

The amendment was considered in *Daniel v State of Western Australia*.[6] Nicholson J's view was that:

> By enacting s82 of the *Native Title Act* in 1998 and abandoning the prior provision that the court was not bound by the rules of evidence, Parliament evinced an intention that the rules of evidence should apply to native title applications except where the court order otherwise. That requires some factor for the court to otherwise order (para 39).

He indicates elsewhere that the appropriate approach is to first consider the evidentiary question by reference to the rules of evidence and then to consider if there is a discretionary basis for making an alternative order (para 26) (see also *Wilkes v Western Australia* 2003).

This clarifies subsection 82(1) and the first limb of subsection 82(2). But how should the court view the second limb? In *Sampi v State of Western Australia* (No. 2), Beaumont ACJ approached the provision by, firstly, considering the Indigenous applicants' cultural concerns and, secondly, considering any prejudice that might have been caused to the respondents, in terms of a denial of procedural fairness. The Court, here, was dealing with the question of whether evidence supporting a native title claim should be withheld from the respondents because the evidence was of a culturally restricted nature. On a balancing of factors, the Court ordered that the information be released to the respondents' expert anthropologists, with an undertaking that the evidence not be otherwise divulged.

Section 56 of the *Evidence Act* 1995 (Cth) provides that only 'relevant' evidence is admissible; that is, evidence which 'could rationally affect … the assessment of the probability of the existence of a fact in issue' (subsection 55(1)). A view (such as a visit on-country) or demonstration may be ordered by a judge if all parties have reasonable opportunity to be present and if the court believes that, amongst other things, the view or demonstration will assist the court to resolve the issues or understand the evidence (section 53). Neate explains that most evidence will be in oral or written form, but may include ceremonial activities and viewings of significant sites (2004, 62). Such visits are commonplace, at times constituting a significant part of the hearings (Neate 2004, 64–5).[7]

The effect of the 1998 amendment to the *NTA* and the reversion to normal statutory and common law rules of evidence is that cultural and customary concerns are no longer an obligatory consideration for the Federal Court, despite

---

6 Original citation 'Daniels v State of Western Australia' includes a corrigendum dated 6 March 2001 requiring that 'Daniel' replace all references to 'Daniels'.

7 Neate cites *Ward v Western Australia*, *Nankiriny v Western Australia*, *Neowarra v Western Australia* [2003] FCA 1402, *Daniel v Western Australia* and *De Rose v South Australia* as examples.

subsection 82(2). According to the Yamatji Marlpa Barna Baba Maaja Aboriginal Corporation, in a submission to the Australian Law Reform Commission's review of the Evidence Acts, the additional factor required to allow the Court to dispense with the normal rules of evidence 'remains an enigma with no judicial determination of what this entails', such that the existing law is effectively ambiguous and leads to uncertainty as to whether evidence is admissible (Australian Law Reform Commission 2005, 503).

In this sense, the older *différend* is re-instated and the clearly visually based alternative is downgraded. The Court has a discretion on the admissibility of evidence and such evidence may be accorded little weight if the Court believes that it has limited probative value (Ketley and Ozich 2003, 84–5). Ketley and Ozich provide an illustration of the effect of this discretion on the outcomes of native title trials, by reference to the *Yorta Yorta* and *Miriuwong Gajerrong* cases, in particular relating to the provision of oral evidence and evidence of ancestral and continuing connection to land (2003, 84–5).[8]

A significant case for us, *De Rose v South Australia* (hereinafter *De Rose*), illustrates that visits on country will not necessarily convince a court of the existence of native title. This is not to say that, in this case in particular, the Court did not take on-country visits extremely seriously in its pursuit of the question of spiritual connection to land on the part of the applicants. The Court took evidence at no less than 13 significant sites and, notwithstanding confidentiality matters (such that full details of the evidence could not be disclosed), even what remains in the judgment of the details of the visits shows a tremendous attention to detail. For example at the 'Apu Maru' site, we find the following kinds of specifics with their fine 'ethnographic' detail:

> 418 The Court initially convened near a large claypan. It was fenced and filled to capacity from recent rains. The claypan was surrounded by groves of eucalypts, mulgas and other trees. As well as the Court, the parties, their advisers and the transcript providers, twenty Aboriginal men were in attendance at Apu Maru. Three witnesses, Whiskey Tjukanku, Peter de Rose and Peter Tjutatja, were called to give evidence.
>
> 419 Tjukanku told the Court that this site was part of the *Malu*, *Kanyala*, and *Tjurki Tjukrpa*. He said that *Malu*, *Kanyala* and *Tjurki* travelled to Apu Maru from Yura and, when they arrived there, they created a sacred and secret song (*Imma*). Unlike the song that had been performed at Wantjapila on the previous day, the song for Apu Maru was for singing only – no dancing was involved. Tjukanku's story finished at Kulpitjara and he would say no more of the journey of *Malu*, *Kanyala* and *Tjurki*.

8 The cases referred to are: *The Members of the Yorta Yorta Community v The State of Victoria & Ors* and *Ben Ward & Ors v The State of Western Australia & Ors*.

The description of the site visits in this detail, along with similar ethnographic details provided by each of the applicants, accounts for hundreds of paragraphs of the judgment. For all this, and although convinced by the evidence of a relevant connection between the claimants and the claim area, O'Loughlin J did not find that there was a sufficient physical connection to the land to establish that native title existed. Referring to the knowledge that he discovered during the on-site visits, O'Loughlin J says:

> That knowledge would have, in turn, gone a long way towards satisfying me that there was a relevant connection between those people and the claim area were it not for the fact that there has been a virtual absence of all Aboriginal people from the claim area for twenty years or so (*De Rose* 2002, 381).

Although the claimants clearly had knowledge of the claimed land, they did not display sufficient present physical and spiritual connection, as required under section 223(1)(b) of the *NTA* and 'that breakdown [was] fatal to their claim' (*De Rose* 2003, 911).

On appeal, the Full Court noted that O'Loughlin J did not give sufficient weight to the claimants' 'strong evidence of spiritual connection' and 'he placed too much emphasis on the absence of physical contact with the claim area after 1978' (*De Rose* 2003, 316). The Full Court said that:

> Depending on the circumstances, it may well be possible for Aboriginal people, by their traditional laws and customs, to maintain a connection with land notwithstanding that they cease to reside there because of the influence of 'European social and work practices' (*De Rose* 2003, 328).

De Rose is but one judgment that points to a different connection to the land for traditional people(s) by comparison with standard European forms of ownership, interest and identification: and a different form of connection that, at least on appeal, was formally acknowledged largely on the basis of evidence taken from on-site visits. So these 'sitings' are indeed at least *potentially* critical for native title determinations, especially with respect to showing continuing spiritual connectedness to land.

White v Indigenous understandings of land

As indicated above, establishing native title under the NTA requires evidence of a continuing relationship, under observed customs and traditions, between Indigenous people and the land of claim. This entails the presentation of evidence concerning the claimant groups' cultures and customs, but it also requires a clear delineation of the land to which those traditions relate. The ability of Aboriginal claimants to map their relationship to land and water is a critical aspect of the process, from registration of the claim to establishing relationships to land (Reilly 2003, 3)

That the National Native Title Tribunal (NNTT) website provides guidelines for the preparation of maps and for describing the lands under claim is testament to the importance of mapping in native title processes. These are required in any native title application, proposed Indigenous Land Use Agreement (ILUA) and related public notices, to provide a degree of certainty of the boundaries of the area to any interested persons. The NNTT provides the following as the benefits for clear maps and descriptions:

- to identify the relevant areas, the people who have an interest in the area, who can be a party to an application and who must be a party to an ILUA;
- to provide public notice of an affected area; and
- to assist people searching the registers held by the Native Title Registrar (National Native Title Tribunal 2003).

Although the specific mapping requirements may vary, the map and/or description should be unambiguous and consistent, noting boundaries, inclusions and exclusions. Additional guidelines are provided for written boundary descriptions.

In *James on behalf of the Martu People v State of Western Australia*, a case involving the Ngurrara people, French J noted the differences in the ways that the courts and Indigenous people determine land boundaries:

> Although the Court has to set boundaries in order to define the area of native title determination, it is a fact that in the extremely arid region of the Western Desert boundaries between Aboriginal groups are rarely clear cut. ... Desert people define their connection to the land much more in terms of groups of sites, thinking of them as points in space not as areas with borders (para 5).

While Australian law permits a delineation between land boundaries and the connotative qualities of land, for Aboriginal people 'the land itself is a sign system' (Morphy 1998, 103).[9] The NNTT's mapping guidelines require information that is strictly of a topographical nature: positions on lot on plan; positions of physical features; geographic features; boundaries, geographic or grid references and reference datum.

Compared to white Australia's topographical representations of land, the Indigenous 'mapping' of land into a visual form (aside from when strictly required to apply to the native title requirements) has spatial, historical, cultural, conceptual and temporal dimensions. It is true that the paintings are maps of land, outlining

9 We intentionally refer to Aboriginal people rather than Indigenous people, here, because the anthropological material to which we refer is specifically describing Aboriginal culture. In Australia, the use of the term 'Aboriginal' typically refers to people of the mainland, with 'Indigenous' also including Islander peoples.

the land's topography and features (Morphy 1998, 107). But Howard Morphy, an anthropologist, warns that this is an oversimplification of their role (1998, 103). They represent the Aboriginal understanding of land, including its mythological significance, reflecting also the artist's social identity (1998, 103–7):

> Aboriginal representations of place and space are influenced by social factors as well as mythological conceptions. The relations between places involve the relations between groups as well as between ancestral beings, and features included in paintings can reflect both the social identity of the artist and the group to which he or she belongs. ... Making paintings of country is exercising rights of inheritance and ritual authority, and often implies rights in the land itself (Morphy 1998, 107).

As Ngarralja Tommy May, one of the painters of the Ngurrara canvas points out, the creation of the canvas represents proof, but not of an externality as is the purpose of evidence conventionally tendered (Anker 2005, 92). Rather, the painting *is* the country: 'We want them to understand, so that they know about our painting, our country, our *ngurrara*. They are all the same thing' (2001, in Anker 2005, 92).

In their work on 'Water Ways in Aboriginal Australia', Toussaint et al. discuss the use by Aboriginal groups of paintings and films to explain Aboriginal people's relationship to land (2005, 61). They note, as do others, that there is an interconnectedness and an historical embeddedness between Indigenous people and land: 'relationships to the cultural landscape ... cannot be recorded, analysed or understood by separating humans from their past, present or future environment' (Toussaint et al. 2005, 65; see also Anon. 2003). An ongoing and projective narrative rather than a static picture is the norm. If so, at least in terms of mutual justice, and the excision of the fundamental injustice – the *différend* – there is a fundamental flaw in some legal findings of supposed Indigenous 'disconnection' from the land in question. It is not limited to physical presence, let alone utility and does not have a linear temporality, as is the requirement for establishing native title following *Yorta Yorta* (*Yorta Yorta* 2002, 444–5; see also Strelein 2006, 84–91). Spiritual connection (to use a rough term) has yet to be codified, and may not be able to be codified; yet it remains 'on the books' as a justification for a claim. And sightings or sitings could be its evidentiary basis in a mutually just outcome. But that – mutuality of justice – would mean that Australian-European law would have to accept versions of what is just that are outwith its current understandings.

The need to establish native title rights has increased the production of visual images. However there has been a dual motivation: they are a means of mapping the relationship to land (as well as its sheer topography) as part of native title claims; but they also represent this process itself. This extends also to filmic production (Toussaint et al. 2005, 68). For example, the video documentary, *Jila*, traces the coming together of the peoples of the Great Sandy Desert to produce the aforementioned Ngurrara canvas as evidence in native title proceedings. Similarly, there have been exhibitions, such as *Native Title Business*, which not only reflect the use of artworks to support claims but also represent the nature of native title itself (Anon. 2003). Likewise, the 'Saltwater Collection of Yirrkala Bark Paintings of Sea Country', a collection of 80 works by 47 Yolngu artists, which demonstrate the Yolngu rights and responsibilities over 'land', extending to coast and sea (Yirrkala Print Space 2005). Towards the end of this chapter we will encounter a very different version of what 'the nature of native title' could be.

Going to country?

Given that the white system of mapping does not carry, within the image, a story of history, culture, mythology and ancestry, white arbitrators are unskilled in interpreting these visual texts. In such a context, there is a special significance to actually going to country. If taking the map to court does not always convey the Indigenous relationship to land, and if rules of evidence exclude some forms of evidence such as hearsay which are integral to Indigenous accountings for culture, then it is necessary to take the court to land in the hope that views, demonstrations and ceremonies will convey this connection. Neate argues that visits to country are valuable because they: (a) provide an illustration of knowledge of land and traditional attachment; (b) empower witnesses and improve their testament; (c) enable a more detailed description of the features and spiritual dimensions of the sites; and (d) enable the Court to witness cultural practices associated with the land (2004, 63–4). The value of such visits is apparent in the description of evidence provided in Federal Court judgments, clearly countering some of the evidentiary difficulties facing Indigenous witnesses; particularly those relating to language and the failure of the English language to be able to accommodate and represent Indigenous concepts, customs and relationships.[10] Visits to country at least enable the Court to witness these things first-hand, presenting it with these markers of difference, even if comprehension is beyond its capabilities. But the visit is not only a means of communicating, at whatever level. Evidence 'on country' also recognises the 'normative impact of being on country' for Indigenous people, enabling, for example, the tendering of evidence in situations where the claimant may only speak of country whilst it is beneath their feet (Anker 2005, 98,113).

The basis for Euro-Australian mapping is, fundamentally, the Mercator Projection. Any white Australian who has ever seen alternatives to this means of mapping has been astonished by the differences. It is seriously flawed by its attempt to impose flatness on a geoid – a slightly pear-shaped planet that resists flatness at every single one of its points. All official cartography relies of elements of this fiction – the white man's flatness over the Earth's depth and density. In a similar vein, the Torrens system of land title, which involves the abstraction of land holdings, is the culmination of a process of 'dephysicalisation' of real

10 For example, see O'Loughlin J in *De Rose v State of South Australia* 2002, in particular ¶379–429.

property in the common law (Anker 2005, 108–9), a far cry from the materiality of medieval property conveyancing practices, marked by the turning of turf or the exchange of objects which functioned as reference points within a localised knowledge loci (Anker 2005, 108–9).

Traditional customs and their representations in artworks do not necessarily observe this fiction. As Reilly reminds us, 'they predate circumnavigation, the drawing of state boundaries, and standard topographical map series' (2003, 3). They see instead. And they ask us to see *in return* – rather than to map in formal ways. The same is true for actually looking at country. It presents what white-fellas might call 'an experience', as unsettling as that might be for the court (Anker 2005, 113–114). You don't see the formal map any more but, say, a 'locale'.

The question for non-Indigenous Australians now is how a different form of seeing could be seen by and – most importantly – be taken into account by the non-Indigenous legal system. The earlier form of evidence requirements was at least a reminder of the need to see *differently* in those sitings and sightings. To not begin to understand – formally, legally – the original inhabitants of *any* land, as a matter of policy, is to fail in anyone's custodianship of that land. Otherwise what? Otherwise: the subjection of Indigenous people 'to a deeper process of colonisation by reducing them to a singular, unambiguous discourse known to the law' (Reilly 2003, 3); explicit racism beyond dispute.

The Bark Petitions

As mentioned earlier, the first instance of traditional visual materials being submitted as a bridge between Indigenous laws and Commonwealth law were the Yolngu Bark Petitions which were sent to the Federal Parliament by the Yolngu tribes of North East Arnhem Land in 1963. Could these constitute the original model of a possible mutual understanding about land and different forms of connectedness to it? In the lecture we also noted above, Galarrwuy Yunupingu marks the Bark Petitions as the first attempt by Indigenous people(s) to let their *law* be known to those who make white (Balanda) law, the federal government and those who carry it through, the judiciary. From his lecture, it becomes clear that these are not petitions in the easily recognised sense: requests that governments or other bodies act in a particular way within already-known parameters, frameworks and boundaries. Instead, for Yunupingu, they are explications of a quite different law and their purpose is to have that law recognised by the laws instituted since white invasion or settlement. They are a description of an ancient and alternative means of acting on, governing and relating to the land. In particular, they explicate a relation to country deep in the law of the Yolngu people of the Gove Peninsula. If something *is* that deep in their law, can it not, he asks, be accepted by another law *as being* so deep? If so, then there is no dispute.

Yunupingu illustrates this with his moving story of the sacred banyan tree:

> I suppose I was 16 when the news travelled urgently throughout Yirrkala that the sacred banyan tree at Nhulunbuy was going to be damaged by the mining company [Nabalco]. There was a rippling anger that shot through the old people. People called out in the high upset tones of my people when they are under threat. Old men I knew to be strong and courageous and afraid of nothing were shaken.
>
> We were led to the site by my father and a number of senior Yolngu men. I saw tears in my father's eyes. I had never seen this before. I quietly asked why are you crying? I am sad and I am angry he told me. We have tried very hard to teach Balanda about our land. We have tried to share this knowledge, free and open. And after all of that they cut that tree and it cuts me inside.
>
> I was shocked. I had never seen my father in the position of not being able to stop someone doing something to our country. His authority had been absolute and now this mining company and these Balanda were ignoring us.
>
> That tree is a special place – inside it are important things. It's like the heart of the country – our beliefs about our land reside in that tree and at the site of the tree, they reside in the rocks, in the water and in our minds. We know these things to be true.

How easy is it for someone not versed in this knowledge system to recognise the poignancy and centrality of this story to the legal matters currently described as 'native title'? Several things are crucial to Yunupingu's account that help us understand the centrality of sights (paintings) and sites (on-country hearings) as possible 'evidence' in native title claims:

1. At one point in his lecture he refers to his story as a *map*: one which plots out what has happened in the past vis-à-vis the connections and disconnections between the two fundamentally different types of law, noting the convergences as positive and the divergences as negative. for example, the acceptance by Parliament of the Bark Petitions was positive; the failure to institute the implied request for two-law integration was negative. The original evidence provisions in the Native Title Act was positive for similar reasons; its subsequent modification was negative. Yunupingu then goes on to narrate (map out) what could be a 'better' way to complete the mapping: a better way to make different laws coincide in practical ways.

2. This suggests that visual representations (in the form of both paintings and site visits) are effectively maps-that-are-stories. They are not static like cartographic maps, taking a snapshot of topography as it stands still at one moment. Rather, they are more like movies: they have a narrative that points our present back in time and forward in time to past rights and wrongs and to possible (and, for Galarruwuy

Yunupingu, 'better') futures. Better futures are those in which the two laws – or, in fact, many traditional laws and a single but ever-revisable Balanda law – sit together as equals in a partnership of mutual respect for their differences.

3. Yunupingu expresses a very distinct idea of what 'native title' is. From his position as a Yolngu lawyer, it is not something merely to be established by evidence in a Balanda court. Native title, he tells us, is 'us', 'in us', 'what is inside us'; it can't be taken away by another law without consent. That other law may think it has taken it away, but it cannot reach inside and drag it from the interior of a people's very being:

> Native Title is in the ground and the trees, the rocks and the water; it's in the songs and the dancing; it's in the painting; it's in me and it's in the land. I ask you to understand this. You can't separate us and you can't destroy it while there is one Aboriginal person still alive who knows the law. That is why we know we have always had our Native Title and land rights and we always will ... I cannot refuse that title because it is inside me. Land rights and Native Title cannot really be taken away from us. The Balanda just think they can.

4. From this point of view, sight and site events and objects are not simply proposed as 'evidence' to be taken into account by Balanda law. Rather they are proposed as meeting points, in the manner of agreements between different-but-related Indigenous peoples themselves when traversing each other's lands. Patrick Dodson Jagun's testimony to the *Rubibi* case is apt here:

> You respect those people. You respect the rights of those people to look after when you come to that country. If someone comes to our country, we've got to look after them so they don't go to places, like Kunin for instance. If they don't know where places are, in our law could be dangerous to them, we explain to them to keep away from those places. If they want to go fishing or hunting in the country, then we can explain to them where they can go. They're free to go but if they come from another place, we can show them or take them to those places, so they can go, they're free to go there. But they got to clear those things with people from the country (*Rubibi Community and Another v Western Australia and Others* 435–6).

In many traditional forms of law, then, there are means of negotiating, accommodating and understanding acknowledged adjacent forms of law. And these are incorporated into each mutually adjacent form of law respectively. What the Bark Petitions – and also the many visual forms of 'evidence' coming after them – may have been attempting, then, is not only to say 'this is our law' but also 'this is *how* our law and yours may establish acceptable patterns of adjacency'. If this is so, then the petitions generously gave up considerable ground. They offered the Balanda lawmakers a chance to be considered adjacent and, in the process, generously divulged matters that were not strictly their business in the first place. What would have been a suitable response by the then government, if Yunupingu is right, is something like a 'petition' in response: an acceptance of Yolngu law and an offer to negotiate the appropriate rules of mutual adjacency.

5. In all of this, the fact that the petitions tried to speak *and show* from *one law to another* is highly significant. It is a matter that has rarely been raised in legal circles about the status of 'visuals' which, until now, have been taken somewhat cartographically, somewhat in terms of formal evidence to claims for, at best, physical connectedness to country. They may have such a status for one law; but if Yunupingu is right, they may have another status altogether for another law: as proposals for what has become, over the centuries, a commonplace for Australian Indigenous peoples. In other words, if another law is acknowledged as adjacent to one's own, a mutual agreement has to be arrived at by appropriate exchange agreements. Every instance we have looked at clearly indicates that such olive branches have been held out at every turn by Indigenous groups to white lawmakers and jurists and subsequently misunderstood by them.

Conclusion: a surer footing?

One way of explicating this deep misunderstanding is via Goffman's notion of footing (1981). Footings are the very basis on which any human communications – legal or otherwise – can take place. On one footing (a Western legal footing), visual materials, sites and sights, are formal evidences to be used in reaching a judgment. Within the peculiar dream some jurists have of a completely rational legal process, they are something like the scientist's data, leading, in the end, to logically and empirically derived 'findings'. On another footing they are more like gifts: generously offered insights into (indeed material instances of) an original law and tradition opening itself up to a much more recent one in the form of story-maps. (And here, we must use a shorthand since our own grasp of the latter footing is bound to be nothing more than scant.) A basic rule of communication is, then, to find and accept the other's footing. And, as far as we have seen, this has never quite been achieved: hence the very deep misunderstanding referred to above. This is more than just a *différend* in the routinely encountered sense of injustice (the sense concerning idioms). It is a *différend* situated at the very basis of any possible communication: a difference between two distinct footings – with one clinging firmly to its own self-understanding and the other offering a gift of ungrudging exchange.

The question is: what, in the terms of such offerings, ought to be the appropriate response if the alternative footing is accepted as it must be? What sites and sights ought to be given in return such that some glimmering of adjacency (sometimes called 'reconciliation') can be established? It is not a question of what 'their' paintings and tours of country mean to 'us' – that question wore out long ago. It is now a question of how to respond to these ultra-generous offers and offerings in like-kind and in ways that make the responses binding upon white Australian law and tradition in perpetuity.

Chapter 10

Race, Class and the Supreme Court: *Rodriguez v. San Antonio Independent School District* (1973)

William Pencak

Introduction

The question of racially integrating US schools has been a major issue in both court cases and public life since the famous Supreme Court decision of *Brown v. Board of Education of Topeka, Kansas*. There, the court ruled that failure to integrate schools denied African Americans the equality mandated by the Fourteenth Amendment to the US Constitution in the clause that no state may 'deny to any person within its jurisdiction the equal protection of the laws'.[1]

Yet no court decision enforces itself: what *Brown* required was that school districts throughout the nation draw up a plan for integration, as well as calling into question whether current school districts were the appropriate units within which integration was to occur. The aftermath of *Brown demonstrated the limits of white America's toleration for its racially diverse population to achieve the full rights of citizenship as mandated by the Constitution.* As school districts and states dragged their feet, filing repeated cases in state and federal courts and publicly intimidating students and their supporters who tried to integrate schools, some lawyers and activists suggested that financial compensation to poor, predominantly black or Hispanic school districts to pay for better facilities and teachers would be an effective means of achieving equality of opportunity if integration did not occur (Ogletree 2004; see *Rodriguez* and *Serrano* decisions, below).

The Supreme Court ruled against this remedy in the case of *Rodriguez v. San Antonio Independent School District* of 1973,[2] using dubious logic heavily influenced by a mentality incorporating a 'deep structural' fear of Communism and the spectre of 'absolute equality' accompanying it. At this very time, conservatives were exploiting these fears to attack the black movement for reparations – which was asking for nothing of the sort, but rather limited contributions from churches

1 347 U.S. 483, 74 S.Ct. 686 – 1954. In this and all other footnotes I use standard US legal citation followed by a dash and then the date of the case.

2 411 U.S. 1, 93 S.Ct.1278 – 1973.

and the government to help fund projects to better the lot of the black population (Schuchter 1970; Bittker 1973).

Had Chief Justice Earl Warren, author and main driving force behind the *Brown* decision, lived another year and the Supreme Court ruled 5–4 the other way in *Rodriguez*, states would have been required adopt systems of taxation financially aiding not only minorities but the poor in general in their struggle to the middle-class status, which usually brings toleration and acceptance (Blinder 1973; O'Connell and Birdsall 2001; Oliver 2001). To be sure, some states with sympathetically inclined legislatures and supreme courts, such as California – see *Serrano* decision below – were able to use their state constitutions to this effect. But in general, the *Rodriguez* decision has seriously impeded the equalisation of educational opportunity in the US.

Cases in state courts in favour of equalised school funding

In 1968, Derrick A. Bell, Jr. and Charles E. Jones, black lawyers with the federally supported Western Center for Law and Poverty, a branch of the US government's Office of Economic Opportunity located in Los Angeles, decided to challenge the state of California's local, property-based system of taxation for funding schools. Their support of the complaint of John Serrano and 26 other parents bore fruit in 1971, when the California State Supreme Court ruled 6–1 that 'recognizing as we must that the right to an education in our public schools is a fundamental interest which cannot be conditioned on wealth, we can discern no compelling state purpose necessitating the present method of financing', in which each school district determined its own funding, thereby assuring wealthier districts would have better schools (Reinhold 1972).[3]

A similar suit was won in the Texas Supreme Court. Demetrio Rodriguez joined other Mexican-Americans in a lawsuit contending that Texas's funding of public schools through property taxes violated the equal protection clause of the Fourteenth Amendment on the basis of wealth. The state of Texas contended that it provided a certain level of support to all school districts, but that, in the interest of 'maximising local initiative', each school district could add to that based on local property taxes. Rodriguez's attorneys showed that Edgewood, one of seven

3 *Serrano v. Priest* (1971) 5Cd 584, 5. (Serrano I). In *Rodriguez*, the Supreme Court would deny that education is a 'fundamental interest' and construct the required interest – 'local control'. When the California legislature and Supreme Court in two subsequent cases – *Serrano v. Priest*, 18 Cal.3d 728 (1976) (*Serrano II*) and *Serrano v. Priest*, 20 Cal.3d 25 (1977) (*Serrano III*) – were able to use state law to set property taxes at a percentage of assessed value, which placed a heavy burden on elderly residents whose property had increased astronomically in value over the years, the reaction was the famous Proposition 13 of 1978, which limited property taxes to one per cent of assessed value and has yet to be repealed. See Smith (1998).

districts in San Antonio, was 90 per cent Mexican-American, and 6 per cent black. Despite the fact that property was taxed at the highest rate of any of the area school districts, there was comparatively little property to tax: Edgewood could only add $26 per pupil to the $222 provided by the State's Minimum Foundation Program, although the federal government added another $108 for a total of $356 per pupil. By contrast, Alamo Heights, the wealthiest of the seven districts, had expenditures of $594 per pupil with only $36 of federal assistance. No one contested any of these facts. Things were even more extreme in other localities: Texas' richest school district spent $5,334 per pupil in 1969–70, its poorest $342 (Reinhold 1972).[4]

The Supreme Court overturns the state courts' rulings

The Supreme Court reversed the Texas tribunal 5–4 in the *Rodriguez* case. Justice Lewis Powell's majority opinion rested on four points: that 'poor' people (or people living in poor school districts) do not constitute a class against which 'invidious' discrimination has occurred; that the correlation between the price spent on education and the quality of that education is uncertain; that 'absolute deprivation' of education would be required to show discrimination; and finally, that education is not a guaranteed constitutional right which permits the Supreme Court to intervene given the three previous arguments – 'strict scrutiny' that government policies do not violate the Fourteenth Amendment is not required when fundamental rights are not involved, rather 'rational scrutiny' – that the action undertaken (educational funding) is an appropriate means of achieving the goal intended. Since no discrimination based on the sorts specified in the Fourteenth Amendment had occurred, the case was not supportable.[5]

The Court's arguments went way beyond the principle of judicial restraint. In fact, taken together they can be viewed as an implicit pre-emptive decision against efforts to use the courts to equalise wealth in America by covering up the fact that certain racial and ethnic minorities suffered from educational discrimination that ensured, in general, the perpetuation of their poverty (Blinder 1973, 437; Cotton 1988, 237; Oliver 2001; O'Connell and Birdsall 2001). To begin, the Court deliberately misread the concept of 'equality' in two ways that were irrelevant. It thereby hoped to show that the plaintiffs had not thought through their case: 'The case comes to us with no definitive [note word] description of the classifying facts or delineation of the disfavored class.'[6]

---

4 *Rodriguez v. San Antonio Independent School District* 337 F. Supp. 280 (1971). Cited in the Supreme Court reversal, 411 U.S. 1, 93 S.Ct.1278 – 1973, 12–15.

5 *Rodriguez v. San Antonio Independent School District* 411 U.S. 1, 93 S.Ct.1278 – 1973; see 17, 30, 40 and 41 for 'strict scrutiny'; 17 and 48 for 'invidious discrimination'; 21 and 24 for 'absolute deprivation.'

6 *Rodriguez v. San Antonio Independent School District* 411 U.S. 1, 93 S.Ct.1278 – 1973, 21.

Thus, the Court easily showed that the plaintiffs could not be arguing that any or all '"poor" persons whose incomes fall below some identifiable level' could not be the dis-favoured class, since some poor people lived in school districts that were predominantly non-poor. The only empirical education outcomes case cited by the Court was a supposedly a 'recent and exhaustive study of school districts in Connecticut [that] concluded '[i]t is clearly incorrect ... to contend that the "poor" live in "poor" districts'.[7]

Apparently, in the long run the Connecticut Supreme Court did not agree, for in 1996 it ruled that students in the state capital of Hartford were segregated and denied equal educational opportunities because of race. With more deliberation than speed, the city and state took until 2003 to reach a practical desegregation agreement (*Sheff v. O'Neill* Agreement 2003).

The Court's second deliberate misreading of the plaintiffs' intentions then suggested they might have been suing on behalf of 'those who are relatively poorer than others'. This then raised the question as to what level the poor district's expenditures needed to be raised: equal to the best, equal to the average, or equal to some minimum standard? Again, the plaintiffs failed to prove what the Court considered an important point: 'We have no indication that the present level of educational expenditures in Texas provide an education that falls short [of what?], even if it were conceded that some identifiable quantum of education is a constitutionally protected prerequisite to the meaningful exercise of their "legal rights".'[8]

Halfway through the decision, after undoubtedly impressing logical positivists with his ability to split hairs on irrelevant subjects, Powell finally confronted the only sort of evidence that really mattered: the relative expenditures of poor and rich school districts. The Court argued here that 'the class [of people living in poor school districts] is not saddled with such disabilities, or subjected to such a history of purposeful unequal treatment, or relegated to such a position of political powerlessness as to command extraordinary protection from the majoritarian political process.'[9]

But for all its claims that the plaintiffs have ignored the key elements required to prove their case (such as defining equality or showing people in poor districts received inferior educations), the Court itself ignored the really important evidence that it, itself, even brought up in its decision – that the poorer school district was overwhelmingly Hispanic and black, and that the richer one overwhelmingly white. Given the Court's own previous rulings, it was, in short, unnecessary for the plaintiffs to show that poorer districts offered inferior educations on grounds of wealth because the court itself cited evidence to show that schools were segregated,

7 *Rodriguez v. San Antonio Independent School District* 411 U.S. 1, 93 S.Ct.1278 – 1973, 23.

8 *Rodriguez v. San Antonio Independent School District* 411 U.S. 1, 93 S.Ct.1278 – 1973, 10.

9 *Rodriguez v. San Antonio Independent School District* 411 U.S. 1, 93 S.Ct.1278 – 1973, 29.

and that was enough. The Court had already ruled on that point, unanimously, in *Brown*: 'Segregation with the sanction of law, therefore, has a tendency to [retard] the educational and mental development of Negro children and to deprive them of some of the benefits they would receive in a racially integrated school system.'[10]

However, the Court was confronted with a school district that demanded not integration, the remedy suggested in *Brown*, but reparations due not only to low expenditures, but to low expenditures that were proven – although the Court chose to ignore this – to have a racial as well as a class bias. Now it is interesting that this case arose while the question of reparations for blacks for sufferings during slavery and subsequent years of hardship was a lively political issue. The date of the Court decision followed the Black Manifesto of 26 April 1969 that James Forman presented for reparations from churches in Detroit, and extensive public debate and scholarly writing on the subject (Schuchter 1970; Bittker 1973). I believe the hidden major premise of the Court's decision was fear that underprivileged groups would use the Constitution and the Court to acquire reparations to compensate for the fact that insufficient wealth deprived them of their constitutional rights, and that acceptance of the legitimacy of using government money to eliminate legal inequities would lead to wholesale wealth distribution in the US. (Financial remedies when some rights are violated, as in instances of police brutality, for example, however, are unquestioned.) The Court therefore sought ways of pre-empting constitutional arguments to dispose of the issue of wealth redistribution should it later arise explicitly: thus, the Court argued that poor people, or children in poor districts, do not necessarily get inferior educations (as students in segregated districts do) and so are not entitled to any adjustments.

The Court spent half its decision arguing against two definitions of equality which had nothing to do with the main point of the plaintiffs' case. The plaintiffs insisted that poor school districts had less money to spend on education, that race was linked to class in the evidence, and that therefore the existence of schools that were segregated and poorly funded districts denied equal protection. Why would the Court bring up other definitions of equality that were clearly inapplicable to this case? I contend that it feared that acceptance of the plaintiffs' arguments might open the door to a significant redistribution of wealth – downwards for a change – which was precisely what the black reparations movement was demanding.

Related court decisions

But while making this argument, the Court could not repudiate its *Brown* decision directly, both for political and legal reasons. The American black and Hispanic communities would have exploded had they done so, not to mention the national and international outrage that would have occurred if the Court had repudiated

10 *Brown v. Board of Education of Topeka, Kansas* (347 U.S. 483, 74 S.Ct. 686 – 1954, 495.

school integration. Furthermore, the Court would have had to repudiate two decades of case law and abandon the principle of judicial conservatism that cases are to be decided on as narrow grounds as possible and not overturn a history of previous decisions unless there is a compelling reason. It therefore implicitly had to define the Edgewood school district as integrated – although it could not say so explicitly for then the *Rodriguez* decision would have fallen apart because in *Swann v. Charlotte-Mecklenberg Board of Education* the Court had already ruled that 'In a system with a history of segregation the need for remedial criteria of sufficient specificity to assure a school authority's compliance with its constitutional duty warrants a presumption against schools that are substantially disproportionate in their racial composition.'[11]

The Court ignored its own decision of two years before, somehow conflating *Brown* and *Rodriguez* to constitute 'the supreme law of the land'. 'Remedial criteria' constitutionally could require redrawing district lines but not redistributing taxpayer dollars. Creating a legal mess in a blatant effort for rich people to separate themselves from the poor and to hang onto as much money as possible, the Court would contradict that point too in *Milliken v. Bradley* the following year, in which it confined the poor in inner-city school districts by granting district lines the cachet of 'tradition' and 'history'.

In *Rodriguez*, the Court seems to be driving at the point, again contradicting its own ruling in *Swann*, that if so much as one white or non-white student attended a given school, or district, then it must be defined as integrated. Sounds extreme? In *Rodriguez*, the Court cited *Douglas v. California*[12] (in which only the indigent, rather than the merely impoverished, were entitled to free court-appointed counsel. It further cited *Williams v. Illinois*[13] where the only people who could be exempted from imprisonment as opposed to paying a fine were those 'absolutely' unable to furnish the cash. In *Rodriguez*, the Court ruled that 'unlike each of the foregoing cases, lack of personal resources has not occasioned an absolute deprivation of the desired benefit' of education.[14] Consistently, the Court ruled in another case involving the San Antonio school district, *Plyler v. Doe*,[15] that the state could not deprive the children of illegal aliens of education, as this constitutes absolute deprivation of a legal privilege.

On the other hand, in *Milliken v. Bradley* the Court, again 5–4, ruled that urban (that is, black) and suburban (that is, white) districts did not have to be integrated, using the argument that deliberate discrimination could only occur within a given jurisdiction, and evidence could not be presented that the state as a whole (in this case Michigan), its officials who were named in the suit, or school districts outside

11 402 U.S. 1, 91 S.Ct. 1267 – 1971, 10.

12 372 U.S. 535 S.Ct.– 1963.

13 399 U.S. 235 S.Ct. – 1970.

14 *Rodriguez v. San Antonio Independent School District* 411 U.S. 1, 93 S.Ct. 1278 – 1973; 21 and 24 for 'absolute deprivation'.

15 457 U.S. 102 S.Ct. – 1982.

of Detroit were complicit in Detroit's segregation. The majority's second principal argument stressed local control: 'that no single tradition in public education is more deeply rooted than local control over the operation of schools, the notion that school district lines may be casually ignored or treated as a mere administrative convenience is contrary to the history of public education in our country.'[16]

Finally, the Court maintained that restructuring Michigan's entire system of public education would be an administrative nightmare with an uncertain outcome.

The Supreme Court's only black justice, Thurgood Marshall, pointed to the implied major premises behind the apparently neutral rhetoric. Refuting the bugaboo of 'local control,' repeated like a mantra in the majority decision, Marshall noted that the state of Michigan, like every other state, in fact imposed its will on localities when it came to education (by establishing graduation requirements, for instance) and was entrusted with supervising it by a state constitution which did not mention 'local control' and 'tradition'. Furthermore, Marshall noted that what defines a 'locality' could be shaped as much by state policy as by the natural evolution of communities. 'The state must also bear part of the blame for the white flight to the suburbs which would be forthcoming from a Detroit-only decree and would render such a remedy ineffective.'[17]

Had historian Kenneth Jackson's book *Crabgrass Frontier* (1985) been published at the time, Marshall could have shown that states permitted banks to operate which denied inner-city mortgages to whites, all the while subsidising suburban highway systems and improvements, thereby creating the very 'localities' which the court's majorities defined as an autonomous and independent of state regulation.[18]

Now if the Supreme Court had reasoned in *Brown v. Board of Education* as it did in the San Antonio and Detroit cases, it could have argued that 'separate but equal' still gave black people some sort of education, or that 'history' and 'tradition' had kept white and black people apart, as indeed it had in *Plessy v. Ferguson*.[19] But then the plaintiffs in *Rodriguez* and *Milliken* did not make this connection explicit either, permitting the Court to state that 'whether the quality of education be determined by the amount of money expended for it', was 'unsettled and disputed', but in any case irrelevant: 'the Equal Protection Clause does not require absolute equality of precisely equal advantages'.

But no one was claiming that. So why did the Court toss in what seems like a gratuitous insult to the plaintiffs? Here is an instance of a tendency of legalistic minds noted by T.V. Smith (1941, 60–64): 'The more the law seeks formal objectivity the less justice it may be feared will be strained out. ... Social things do

16 *Milliken v. Bradley* 418 U.S. 717, 94 S.Ct. 3112 – 1974, 742.
17 *Milliken v. Bradley* 418 U.S. 717, 94 S.Ct. 3112 – 1974, 801–2.
18 *Milliken v. Bradley* 418 U.S. 717, 94 S.Ct. 3112 – 1974, 742–3.
19 163 U.S. 537, 3 S.Ct. 18 – 1896.

not lend themselves to precision and whatever principles we get that are precise do not lend themselves to social things.'

Anything carried to absurdity is senseless, and one of financial equalisation's strongest supporters, Berkeley law professor John E. Coons, admitted that the issue apparently raised the 'equal sewer problem: that is, if the Constitution requires equality in education, then why not in other local services such as fire or sanitation?' (Reinhold 1972).

Leaving to one side that it might be a good idea for everyone to have quality services in these areas as well, supporters of equalisation came up with several possible plans for implementation, none of which pointed toward the absolute equalisation of wealth the Supreme Court invoked as a spectre. One, the Hawaii solution, practised only in that state as of 1971 (and even today), simply treated the whole state as one school district and financed each school equally per pupil based on general state taxation. Coons' (Coons, Clune and Sugarman (1970), cited in Reinhold 1972) preferred solution was to set parameters within which districts could spend money, requiring that if they opted to increase local taxation to provide additional services they would have to share that money with poorer school districts that could only add programmes by increasing taxes to a much higher rate. Other plans would be versions of affirmative action: school districts that required more money to provide equal educational advantages would get it – for instance, poor school districts which would require higher pay for teachers as incentives or districts with schools for handicapped or specially advantaged students that drew from several districts (Stevens 1971; Reinhold 1972).

What I suggest is that in *Rodriguez* the court attributed to the plaintiffs, while ironically doing precisely the same thing itself, the abandonment of the reasonable arguments necessary for having a meaningful constitutional dialogue in favour of *reductio ad absurdum* statements. The Court dismissed the *Rodriguez* case because it implied that, taken to utterly illogical, but for the Court logical, conclusions, the plaintiffs were insisting on some kind of mystical absolute equality. The Court, to review, contended that the plaintiffs had no case because they were unable to 'definitively' define equality, which is both irrelevant and impossible. Second, the Court denied that a cheap education, even generally speaking, is a bad education, a denial which could have been disproven using any number of correlations such as percentages of college graduations and imprisonment rates of graduates in rich and poor districts. Third, the Court ruled that we cannot define the minimum education necessary for [well, for what?]. Well, whatever the minimum is, according to the supposedly unrepudiated *Brown* decision, such a minimum is *ipso facto* not met in schools with a minority population of 96 per cent.

Again, I think the Court made such arguments to raise and then quiet the spectre that someone was aiming for absolute equality of wealth or a substantial redistribution thereof through some form of reparations. To repeat the Court's point: 'the Equal Protection Clause does not require absolute equality of precisely equal advantages'.[20] No one was asking for that. Once again the Court adopted a worst-case paranoid scenario, irrelevant to the arguments put forth by the plaintiffs. But this gratuitous statement was a backhanded way of branding both people who wanted a different means of funding schools from property taxes, and implicitly the case for black reparations, with the spectre of Communism. How appropriate for what is known as the 'Nixon' Court', named in honour of the President who had begun his career as a congressman a quarter-century previously rooting out 'Communists'.

To recall, the black reparations movement did not suggest everyone should have equal wealth. Among the principal suggestions were the following: taking the money from the Vietnam War and investing it in social programmes; using federal funds to support black businesses and mortgages, which were in the form of loans, not gifts; and taxing churches to the tune of $15 for every black person in America. Of course, any form of reparations or wealth redistribution (the largely forgotten reason progressive taxation was adopted), like desegregation, will create problems and require adjustment of ideals to realities and comparative adjustment of ideals. But for the Court to equate the desire for practical progress to reduce inequality with the bugaboo of 'absolute equality' was obscene. Minorities' desire to educate their children decently – to better themselves in capitalist society – is subtly transformed into the spectre of Communism – absolute equality! To put it bluntly, *Rodriguez* should go down in history along with *Dred Scott v. Sanford*[21] and *Plessy v. Ferguson*[22] as one of the most monumental insults to people of colour in American history offered by our supreme judicial body. But at least in the earlier two decisions, the Court said what it meant. Here, the simultaneous handing down of this decision, combined with rhetoric condemning 'absolute equality' at a time when blacks were seeking reparations, is to make by innuendo an argument that would not stand the test of reason.

The extent to which the American political system is unwilling to deal with class inequities appears in the fact that the court did not technically overrule *Brown*. Political repercussions aside, the reason is clear: *Brown* sidestepped the issue of class as neatly (or sloppily) as *Rodriguez* ignored the question of race. *Brown* came close, but only that, to denouncing class inequities that were intertwined with racial ones: in part of his decision, Justice Warren said education was:

> The very foundation of good citizenship, ... a principal instrument in awakening the child to cultural values, in preparing him for later professional training, and in helping him to adjust normally to his environment. In these days, it is doubtful that any child may reasonably be expected to succeed in life if he is

---

20 *Rodriguez v. San Antonio Independent School District* 411 U.S. 1, 93 S.Ct. 1278 – 1973, 25.

21 19 How. (60 U.S) 393 (1857).

22 163 U.S. 537 (1896).

> denied the opportunity of an education. Such an opportunity, where the state has undertaking to provide it, is a right which must be made available on equal terms.[23]

Yet while everyone knew black-only schools were for the most part inferior in terms of curricula, libraries, facilities – to wit, expenditures – the inequality on which the Warren Court focused was psychological: 'To separate them [Negroes] from others of similar age and qualifications solely because of their race generates a feeling of inferiority as to their status in the community that may affect their hearts and minds in a way unlikely ever to be undone.'[24]
In Warren's famous footnote 11, he cites psychological and personality studies, rather than such things as, say, percentages of college graduates in all-black and all-white schools, percentages of prison inmates, life expectancy or average income. Had Warren expressed discrimination in terms of dollars and cents – money spent on pupils compared to average income – he would have opened the way for financial remedies for poor schooling in addition to integration. It is interesting to speculate whether Warren's concentration on psychological rather than economic disabilities was accidental or intentional.

Someone could have pointed all this out to the 1973 Supreme Court. I am sure someone did, since I am no constitutional lawyer. Someone could also have pointed out that 'the rich are different from you and me', as F. Scott Fitzgerald knew (1926, 2), and cited psychological studies to prove that class discrimination, whether as invidious as racial or not, still has profound effects. That is why the Court went on to foreclose the possibility that someone could, in fact, hope to win a future case by making the arguments the Court chided the plaintiffs for failing to make in *Rodriguez* – that is, by presenting studies to show that students from poor districts on average lived shorter and poorer lives than those from wealthy ones, that cities and states deliberately drew districts to keep the poor and the rich separate, that where blacks and Hispanics were the majority in school districts, these districts were funded less well than predominantly white districts. My own thought is that the plaintiffs' lawyers did not stress these points because they were so obvious, and that in any event the Court had no choice but to take inequality and discrimination granted, given the school district's racial inequities and its own pre-existing *Brown* and *Swann* decisions.

How did the Court pre-empt future suits based on these arguments? It tried to foreclose these possibilities by repudiating Warren's contention in *Brown* that education was a 'right' without – at least explicitly – repudiating the entire former decision. Powell stated 'Education, of course, is not among the rights afforded explicit protection under our Federal Constitution.' *Brown* still stood, on the

---

23 *Brown v. Board of Education of Topeka, Kansas* 347 U.S. 483, 74 S.Ct. 686 – 1954, 494.

24 *Brown v. Board of Education of Topeka, Kansas*, 347 U.S. 483 – 1954, 74 S.Ct. 686, 495.

grounds that a state cannot discriminate on the basis of 'race, religion, etc.' when people need to use public facilities or programmes, but 'this Court has never held that wealth discrimination [not mentioned in the 14th Amendment] alone provides an adequate basis for invoking strict scrutiny [of state or federal programs on grounds of wealth discrimination].'[25]

Given a different court, racial discrimination could have been correlated with wealth to effectively show discrimination – conscious, pervasive and invidious.

Three of the four dissenters (Justice White construed the case more narrowly) and possibly all four, might have been members of such a court. Thurgood Marshall, however, found an even deeper hypocrisy at work, although given the way 'Brother' justices refer to each other he did not quite put it that way. If 'education' was not a 'fundamental right', specified in the Constitution, neither were the rights to procreate, vote in state elections or appeal criminal convictions, yet they were 'instances ... [in which] the Court has displayed a strong concern with the existence of discriminatory state treatment'. Marshall argued that where other rights are 'interrelated with constitutional guarantees', they must be protected to 'ultimately insure the integrity of the constitutional ... guarantee itself'.[26] Marshall pointed out not only this inconsistency – that the Supreme Court dealt frequently with discrimination in areas not specifically mentioned in the Constitution – but the crucial link between education and American ideals: an uneducated person is, for the most part, incapable of enjoying his or her constitutional rights. But even Marshall did not bring up explicitly the high coincidence of racial and class inequality.

Defeated at the Supreme Court, reformers then turned to the states, many of whose constitutions did explicitly guarantee the right to an education. In the early 1970s, given the momentum of the 1960s reforms, supporters of equalised funding were sure that 'there are strong enough forces at work across the country to suggest that the decision is in fact only a setback, not a defeat, for reform' (Jenkins 1973b, 33).

Indeed, over the next several years, ironically starting in Connecticut, the very state the Supreme Court had cited to show that poor children did not necessarily live in poor school districts, state supreme courts ruled that education was a fundamental state right and hence the Fourteenth Amendment applied in their states, if not throughout the nation (Fellows 1974; Fellows 1977).

---

25 *Rodriguez v. San Antonio Independent School District* 411 U.S. 1, 93 S.Ct.1278 – 1973, 25.

26 *Rodriguez v. San Antonio Independent School District* 411 U.S. 1, 93 S.Ct. 1278 – 1973, 62–3.

The New York decision, 1982, confirming *Rodriguez*

However, the movement toward equalisation was given a sharp setback when in 1982 the New York State Court of Appeals ruled 2–1, in a case that had been pending six years, refusing to order the restructuring of school funding as had Connecticut and, later, New Jersey (Fiske 1977). The decision was especially significant because New York has always been regarded as a liberal state, in the forefront of social reform, and its Court of Appeals has enjoyed high judicial respect. Judges Hugh Jones and Moses Weinstein cited both the San Antonio and Detroit decisions as authoritative, which meant that all the courts were required to exercise with respect to school funding was 'rational scrutiny' – that the means of funding education rationally accomplished the intended goal – rather than 'strict scrutiny' – that a fundamental constitutional right was involved which the means adopted had to guarantee. Again praising the benefits of local control and citing the New York State Constitution of 1894, the two judges maintained that

> what appears to have been contemplated ... was a statewide system assuring minimal acceptable facilities. ... Interpreting the term education, as we do, to connote a sound basic education, we have no difficulty determining that the constitutional requirement is being met in this state, in which it is said without contradiction that the average per pupil expenditure exceeds that in all other states but two.[27]

The judges were patting New York State on the back for its average per capita expenditure at a time when its governor, Hugh Carey, was telling the legislature that 'financial inequities in education are more pronounced than any time in the state's history' (New York State Supreme Court 1982, B6).

Once again, the minority voice, of Judge Jacob Fuchsberg, pointed out the fatal flaw in the argument: 'Strict scrutiny may have been an appropriate test' for educational policy precisely because racial as well as class bias was present. He cited the 'undisputed fact', agreed to by both parties 'that the existing education aid formulae have an adverse effect', not only on pupils from impoverished families, but also on a large percentage of the nearly 750,000 'minority' students in the state, 83 per cent of whom resided in the cities bringing the lawsuit where higher rates of taxation still left many schools in terrible shape.[28] Fuchsberg was in effect saying that the New York Court of Appeals, like the US Supreme Court, looked at racial minorities only as poor people in order to nullify *Brown v. the Board of Education* (New York State Supreme Court, 1982).

---

27 *Board of Education, Levittown Union Free School District et al. v. Nyquist* 459 N.E. 2d 359, 365, 368, and n. 8.

28 *Board of Education, Levittown Union Free School District et al. v. Nyquist* 459 N.E. 2d 359, 376.

From 1982 to the present

Columnist Fiske in the *New York Times*, however, questioned whether the decision would be a 'fatal, or even a serious blow' to the movement to equalise funding. Pointing out that 28 of 50 states had recently revised their tax codes and methods of school funding, he predicted that, regardless of the courts, school reformers would win in the political arena. 'Special interest groups – the Spanish, women, the handicapped – are all more active in state political circles' (Fiske 1982). Yet looking back twenty years after the New York decision, have such liberal political forces predominated? The handwriting was on the wall when the Nixon Court ruled against Rodriguez; by 1982, the Reagan Revolution was in full swing (two years later he would carry New York). Political forces affect court appointments and elections, in which voters choose many state judges. It is sobering to realise that had one judge voted differently in any of the three cases – the San Antonio, Detroit and New York – the verdict would have been different. Does it matter? In 1993, half of the high school students in Edgewood, Rodriguez's district, dropped out before graduation, over four times the national average of 12 per cent. College preparatory classes were scarce, and good teachers left for better-paying districts. School districts in Texas varied in expenditure per pupil from $1,897 – the average being about $4,200 – to $73,000, the last a lightly populated, spread out, oil-rich district (Celis 1994).

When the *New York Times* ran its 50-year post-mortem on *Brown v. Topeka* it noted that 'in their most cynical moments, some civil rights activists suggest that the legal situation is actually worse than before Brown'. Realistic would be a better word than cynical, as elsewhere in the article the author noted that the percentage of black children in the South attending majority white schools had declined from 43 to 31 per cent between 1988 and 2000, and the overall national average in the latter year was 28.4 per cent. Their point was that the

> *Plessy* separate-but-equal regime guaranteed an 'equal' education, and when it was denied, as it uniformly was, black students had a legal claim for improving their schools. But since the Supreme Court decided in the *Rodriguez* case in San Antonio that there is no requirement to equalize financing, many minorities are now stuck with schools that are separate and unequal.

Thus concluded the fourth-from-last paragraph of the article, before a brief conclusion that 'the real lesson of *Brown* may be that to achieve racially integrated schools, we need less blind optimism – and more appreciation for how much hard work remains to be done' (Cohen 2004).

Missing from this article is the word 'class' and the idea that state and local rights have proven throughout American history not the guarantees of liberty against the central government's tyranny some of the Founding Fathers hoped, but rather obstacles to equal educational opportunity as well as a fair labour and wage policy, as employers can play states off against each other to offer the cheapest worksites as in no other First-World nation. Had one judge voted the other way in *Rodriguez*, the door would have been open to equalise school funding, as racial discrimination invariably accompanies class inequalities. But class discrimination is the one form of discrimination the US is not prepared to confront: George Washington's statement of 1790 to the Freemasons and Jews of America is still more a dream than a reality: 'All possess alike liberty of conscience and immunities of citizenship. It is now no more that toleration is spoken of, as if it was by the indulgence of one class of people, that another enjoyed the exercise of their inherent natural rights' (Schappes 1976, 77–84).

Chapter 11
Legal Terms across Communities: Divergence behind Convergence in Law

Le Cheng and King Kui Sin

Introduction

Although legal terms, on their own, are generally considered to have self-referential, self-closed meaning (Hart 1983; Teubner 1986), often independent of context, most of them, just as other signs, essentially acquire their meanings within a given context. As the context varies, the meaning of the same legal term as a sign may change correspondingly. Drawing on a corpus-based semiotic study, we argue that a legal term is just a sign within semiotic systems, and as such it does not carry any inherent meaning, and its meaning can only exist in the relationship with other signs or sign systems; in other words, a legal term only denotes in a particular temporal and spatial context.

According to semioticians, nothing is a sign unless it is interpreted as a sign (Peirce 1931–58, vol. 2, 172). Signs are found in the physical form of the sign vehicle such as words. Signs have no intrinsic meaning and become signs only when sign-users invest them with meaning with reference to a recognised code. The value of a sign depends on its relations with other signs within the system – a sign has no absolute value independent of this context (Saussure 1983, 80). In other words, the relationship between a sign and its value is relative or even arbitrary and the value of a sign changes when 'what constitutes it' (Saussure 1983, 119) changes.

Jurisprudence seeks to provide an explanation of how meaning was actually created rather than what meaning will or could be created (Jackson 1992). Semiotics, drawing on the private psychological processes in order to understand the sort of sense the decision makes, criticises the legal positivism, which 'takes as a fundamental assumption that law is a matter of rules and/norms which are applied to facts by way of syllogism' (Samuel 2005, 23) and which takes a judge's role as 'a deductive machine applying statutory axioms' (Samuel 2001, 43), as not being able to accurately account for all the deep structures in which legal discourse is embedded. A semiotic approach is also designed to uncover the basic structural elements of the meaning of a term and emphasises that the relation between signifier (such as legal terms) and signified (such as legal concepts) is subject to dynamic change. Legal semiotics aims to develop a unified principle of intelligibility regarding all aspects of the legal phenomenon (Landowski 1988,

79). Semiotics therefore offers a viable approach to jurisprudence, including the nature of legal terms.

However, it is not surprising that some scholars interested in the standardisation of legal terms argued that a legal term should have only one meaning on any occasion in a jurisdiction so as to avoid ambiguities and maintain the authority of the law (Chen and He 2005, 34). By using the data in China, including Mainland China, Hong Kong, Macau and Taiwan, we demonstrate the legal consequences brought about by the change of legal terms. We also try to defend legal terms as sign on the one hand and argue that, under the background of legal pluralism (Wagner 2005, 2008), it is necessary to tolerate terminological diversity in different spaces on the other hand.

Legal terms and time

Despite his emphasis on studying the language-state synchronically rather than diachronically, Saussure was well aware that the relationship between the signified and the signifier in language was subject to change over time (Saussure 1983, 74ff). Legal rules govern the legal relationships in a certain historical space. A legal term, as a constitutive element of a rule, is also characteristic of temporality. A legal term may come into being, and concur with specific historical conditions, and become invalid or cease to exist with the disappearance of such conditions. It is therefore natural that the same phenomenon is labelled with different legal terms and a legal term may be interpreted differently in different historical contexts. Legal rules are never absolute and have to adapt to societal developments (Wagner 2008, 3).

Considering the term '*de facto* marriage' in Mainland China, for instance, it is easy to notice changes in a relatively short period of time. A *de facto* marriage is one that meets the formal requirements of the Marriage Law and is otherwise valid, but has not been registered. The general rule is that *de facto* marriages are not legally binding. '*De facto* marriage' as a legal term was implicitly mentioned as the Marriage Law of the Chinese Soviet Republic (1934) stipulated: 'When a man and a woman cohabit, whether registered or not, it is taken as marriage'. *De facto* marriage took the cohabitation between a man and a woman as the only sufficient condition for marriage. It was closely related to Chinese traditional marriage ceremony but it had the potential to harm women's interests in the case of concubine or arranged marriage.

The concept of *de facto* marriage was explicitly mentioned for the first time by the Supreme People's Court in the Opinions on Enforcing Civil Policies and Legislations dated 2 February 1979, which stipulated if a man and a woman having no spouse cohabit in the name of the husband and wife without registration and they were also so considered by the public, *de facto* marriage was established. After the promulgation of the Marriage Law of the People's Republic of China

(1980), which remained silent as to *de facto* marriage, Article 24 of Regulations on Control of Marriage Registration (1984) prescribed:

> If citizens not reaching the legally marriageable age cohabit in the name of the husband and wife, or citizens conforming to the marriage conditions cohabit in the name of the husband and wife without marriage registration, their marriage relationship shall be null and void and outside the protection of law.

In the Several Opinions on Dealing with Cases Involving Cohabitation in the Name of the Husband and Wife without Registration issued in 1989 by the Supreme People's Court explicitly proposed the concept of 'illegal cohabitation'. Any cohabitation in the name of the husband and wife without registration was then illegal, even if they met the substantive requirements of marriage. The revised Marriage Law of the People's Republic of China, which became effective in 2001, differed significantly from the 1980 Marriage Law in that it established rules regarding invalid and revocable marriages. One survey by the National Women Union in 2000 indicated that *de facto* marriage still had the proportion of 4.6 per cent in urban areas and 7.5 per cent in rural areas (Liu 2002, 45), which had to be taken into consideration in the Marriage Law (2001). According to Article 8 of Marriage Law (2001), a marriage is not established until it has been registered. If the cohabiting couple obtains a marriage certificate prior to revocation, the union will be valid. Interpretation No. I of the Supreme People's Court on Several Issues in the Application of Marriage Law of the People's Republic of China further clarified the issue of *de facto* marriage in Article 4 and Article 5 as follows.

> If both the man and woman make up their marriage registration under Article 8 of the Marriage Law, the validity of the marital relations shall be calculated from the time when both parties conform with the substantial conditions for getting married as described in the Marriage Law (Article 4).
>
> For any man and woman who fail to go through the marriage registration formalities as prescribed in Article 8 of the Marriage Law but live together in the name of husband and wife, if they initiate a lawsuit in the people's court to request for divorce, they should be treated differently:
>
> (1) Before the Regulation on Marriage Registration was promulgated and implemented on February 1, 1994, if both man and woman meet the substantial conditions for getting married, the case shall be treated as *de facto* marriage.
>
> (2) After of the Regulation on Marriage Registration was promulgated and began to be implemented on February 1, 1994, if both man and woman meet the substantial conditions for getting married, the people's court shall inform them that they should make up the marriage registration before the case is accepted.

> If they fail to make up their marriage registration, the case shall be treated as dissolution of cohabiting relations (Article 5).

It can be seen that '*de facto* marriage' as a legal term did not coexist from the very beginning with marriage acts or regulations. It is a by-product of legitimate marriage. The same phenomenon became 'illegal cohabitation' with the promulgation of Regulations on Control of Marriage Registration in 1984 and the issue of the Several Opinions on Dealing with Cases Involving Cohabitation in the Name of the Husband and Wife without Registration in 1989, and it is now named 'cohabitation' under the present of Marriage Law (2001), which though explicitly prohibits a person having a spouse to cohabit with others. In other words, '*de facto* marriage', as well as 'illegal cohabitation', as a legal term is no longer effective and active in contemporary Mainland China.

Similarly, with the social and economic developments, the Partnership Enterprise Law of the People's Republic of China has undergone some changes, one of which includes the types and responsibilities of partnership enterprise (*hehuo qiye*) as indicated below.

> *1997 version*
> Article 2 'Partnership enterprise' mentioned in this Law refers to a profit-making organization established within the territory of China according to this Law with their partners associated under a partnership agreement, each making capital contributions, carrying out business operations, distributing profits, undertaking risks and bearing unlimited and joint liability for the partnership enterprise's debts.

> *2007 version*
> Article 2 The term 'partnership enterprise' refers to the general partnership enterprises and limited liability partnership enterprises which are established within China by natural persons, legal persons and other organizations in accordance with the law. A general partnership enterprise may be formed by general partners. The partners shall bear unlimited joint and several liabilities for the debts of the partnership enterprise. If this Law has any special provisions on the way in which the general partners shall bear liabilities, these special provisions shall prevail. A limited liability partnership enterprise shall be formed by general partners and limited partners. The general partners shall bear unlimited joint and several liabilities for the debts of the limited liability partnership enterprise. The limited partners bear the liabilities for its debts to the extent of their capital contributions.

The 2007 version amends and supersedes the PRC Partnership Enterprise Law promulgated by the Standing Committee of the National People's Congress in 1997. The Standing Committee has made some major amendments in the new law, one of which is that the concept of limited liability partnership is recognised under the new law and a partnership enterprise of limited liability may go bankrupt under the new law. When the constitutive elements of partnership change, it is difficult to imagine that the value (denotation) of the same term remains intact. The form of limited liability partnership, as indicated by its name, has the advantages of both limited liability and partnership; that is, the virtues of low operation cost, convenient management and flexible operation of the traditional partnership are combined with the limited liability which used to belong exclusively to company. The presence of limited liability partnership enriches the organisation of enterprises and also embodies Mainland China's keeping up with the international track, which indicates the globalisation of economy will bring its influence on the legislation in a jurisdiction.

From the two examples, '*de facto* marriage' and 'partnership', it can be easily concluded that different values may be attached in different historical contexts to the same legal term as a sign, which reflects the interaction between law and society as two separate semiotic systems. The value of a sign such as legal terms is not totally independent of other semiotic systems such as society; that is, whenever the society changes, the value of a legal term as a sign may change. The change in legal terms will in turn bring about different consequences.

Legal terms and space

Space is herein taken as an abstract concept rather than the physical space. We will find as discussed in the following sections that the same legal term as a sign may have different meanings in different jurisdictions, in different fields of law, or even in the same code by taking China as an example, a state with plural legal systems (broadly speaking, the Chinese Legal System, the Continental Law System and the Common Law system) and various jurisdictions (Hong Kong, Macau, Taiwan and Mainland China).

Polysemy across jurisdictions

In the communities which share the same language, the same sign may have different denotations because of the differences of legal systems. Even in the same legal system, the understandings of the same legal term may vary in various jurisdictions. Such differentiations are not only the embodiment of differences at the level of legislative techniques, but also the indicator of the differences of the objects that legislation governs.

For the very important concept '*budongchan*' ('immovable property'), we can notice the differences, though not so sharp, in the four jurisdictions in China; that is, there are different meanings (signifieds) of the same signifier *budongchan*.

> *Interpretation and General Clauses Ordinance (Cap 1) – SECT 3*, Hong Kong
> [original] 'Immovable property' (不動產 budongchan) means: (a) land, whether covered by water or not; (b) any estate, right, interest or easement in or over

any land; and (c) things attached to land or permanently fastened to anything attached to land;

Civil Code – Chapter III Article 66, Taiwan
[my translation] Real property is land and things which are constantly affixed thereto. The products of the real property, if they are not separated therefrom, constitute a part of the real property.

Civil Code-Article 195, Macau
[my translation] Imóveis (immovable property) includes: a) rural and urban property; b) water; c) trees, bushes and natural fruits when connected to the soil; d) the integrative parts of rural and urban properties.

The Guarantee Law of the People's Republic of China – Article 92 – Mainland China
[my translation] The real property described in this law refers to lands and such affixed objects on the ground such as buildings and forest woods.

Polysemy in the same jurisdiction

A sign has no absolute value independent of its context (Saussure 1983:80). When contexts change, the value may also change. We can even notice the different values to the same sign in the same ordinance, as shown in Section 79A of Criminal Procedure Ordinance of Hong Kong (Cap 221).

'child' (兒童) means a person who:

(a) in the case of an offence of sexual abuse:

(i) is under 17 years of age; or

(ii) for the purposes of section 79C, if the person was under that age when a video recording to which section 79C applies was made in respect of him, is under 18 years of age; or
(b) in the case of an offence to which this Part applies, other than an offence of sexual abuse:

(i) is under 14 years of age; or

(ii) for the purposes of section 79C, if the person was under that age when a video recording to which section 79C applies was made in respect of him, is under 15 years of age.

Co-reference

As mentioned in the introductory section, some scholars ideally expected monosemy of legal terms in an absolute sense. Even if a legal term has only one core meaning in a given context, it may be subject to various interpretations because of vagueness, whether intentional or unintentional, in normative texts (Bhatia et al. 2005). Moreover, we can even notice in reality two different terms are used to signify the same legal concept. One of the typical cases is that '*hetong*' and '*heyue*' are simultaneously used in legislation to refer to the same legal concept '*contract*' as indicated in Table 11.1.

Table 11.1 Coexistence of 'hetong' and 'heyue' in various legal jurisdictions

Jurisdiction	Corpus (accessed on 10 August 2007)	Legal terms		Retrieval method
		hetong	*heyue*	
Mainland China	China Laws Retrieval System <http://202.99.23.199/home/begin.cbs>	229	0	Text
Hong Kong	Bilingual Laws Information System <http://www.legislation.gov.hk/>	16	1588	Key words
Macau	Macau Laws Network <http://www.macaolaw.gov.mo/>	4677	1561	Key words
Taiwan	Taiwan Laws and Regulations Database <http://law.moj.gov.tw/>	279	13	Title

Discussions

Any 'fixing' of 'the chain of signifiers' is both temporary and socially determined (Coward and Ellis 1977, 6, 8, 13). Legal terms as signifiers also have the inherent temporal and (socially) spatial nature. Legal terms are usually associated with meaning differentiation with daily language and terminological monosemy; that is, the legal meaning of a term is explicitly different from that in the daily language, a legal term can only have one meaning in a specific jurisdiction and there should not be more than one legal term to signify the same legal concept. In other words, legal terms are expected to be free from temporal and spatial constraints.

A sign must have both a signifier and a signified. One cannot have a totally meaningless signifier or a completely formless signified (Saussure 1983, 101). The first principle of language as sign is arbitrariness (Saussure 1983, 67, 78); that is, the relationship between the linguistic signifier and signified is arbitrary: the link between them is not necessary, intrinsic or natural (Saussure 1983, 67). It helps to account why there is no one-to-one link between signifier and signified and signs have multiple rather than single meanings, even in legal domain. Legal rules govern the legal relationships in a certain historical stage. A legal term, as a constitutive element of a rule, is also characteristic of temporality. A legal term may come into being, and concur with specific historical conditions, and become invalid or cease to exist with the disappearance of such conditions. Within a single language, one legal term may refer to many legal concepts and one legal concept may be referred to by many legal terms. It is therefore natural for the same legal term in the same Chinese language to have different signifieds in different jurisdictions, in different fields of law or even in the same code. It is also not uncommon for more than one legal term to refer to one legal concept, although it is a counter-expectation whether for laypersons or for legal professions. The arbitrary aspect of signs also helps to account for the scope for their interpretation in context.

Now that the relationship between a legal term and a legal concept is arbitrary, it makes no difference what legal concept is attached to a legal term initially. But signs are not socially (and spatially) or historically (and temporarily) arbitrary; that is, after a sign has come into existence we cannot arbitrarily change signifiers, for in a specified spatial and temporal context, a signifier does have its normal association with a signified. For example, a criminal suspect accused before 1997, when the Criminal Law of the People's Republic of China was revised, would be assigned with the legal term '*renfan*'('criminal') whether he was under interrogation, prosecution, adjudication or supervision. Afterwards, he would be assigned with a term as '*fanzui xianyiren*' ('criminal suspect') prior to trial and as '*beigaoren*' ('defendant') during trial. Such a change is more than merely terminological revision, but implies that China has undergone a substantial development from presumption of guilt to presumption of innocence. So '*renfan*' is not expected to be used any more after 1997. Legal terms, constitutive elements of law, just as law is, are representations of a state or a jurisdiction, which has its own tradition, history, ideology and ethics. Therefore, when legal transplant is concerned, it is rational to take into account all these factors behind law rather than take law as an autopoetic (Van Hoecke 2002) piece of text independent of time and space.

Conclusion and implications

Law, as language, is the product of a particular culture and society. It is natural to use different signifiers to signify the same signified in different languages. It is, however, not unusual for citizens in different states or regions to use the same signifiers in a different way, signifying different signifiers. As the common law jurisdictions and English-speaking communities – the UK, the US and Australia – may assign different signifieds to the same legal term as a signifier in law and render different interpretation in adjudication, each state may assign different cultural and social connotation to the same legal term. The similar case exists in Mainland China, Hong Kong, Macao and Taiwan, where the Chinese language is commonly used.

From the above discussions, we conclude it as a fact that diversity of legal terms, not to mention law as a whole, exists in the same state among different jurisdictions, or even in the same code. It is therefore natural that diversity of law also exists among different states just because of different social, cultural background and various understandings of law *per se*. In the context of legal pluralism, concepts of tolerance and diversity have been given significant consideration by the European courts within the ambit of the principle of non-discrimination and to respect this European cultural ecumene (Wagner 2008, 20). In the socio-linguistic context, language represents an essential element of the human personality which has a deep effect on identity and dignity (Wagner 2008, 25), and so is the way to use a language. Attitudes as such should also be adopted towards legal terms, a sign system to represent both legal pluralism and linguistic diversity. So it is not very reasonable to promote terminological standardisation and legal unification among different jurisdictions or states and we shall take a more open attitude towards legal diversity, treating it as prosperity rather than chaos, just as enshrined in UNESCO's Declaration of Principles on Tolerance: 'Tolerance is respect, acceptance and appreciation of the rich diversity of our world's cultures, our forms of expression and ways of being human. It is fostered by knowledge, openness, communication, and freedom of thought, conscience and belief. Tolerance is harmony in difference.'

Only when similarities are sought and differences are allowed can law as a discipline have a brighter future, but we shall always bear in mind that legal pluralism is a kind of socially constructed double-edged sword (Wagner 2008, 5).

Chapter 12
Women as Legal Subjects and Objects in Contemporary China

Deborah Cao[1]

'Tolerance' has both a positive and a negative connotation. In a symbolic way, it suggests the ways women are placed in contemporary China: being tolerated but not treated as real equals. In this chapter, I first present a brief overview of the contemporary Chinese legislative regime related to women. This is followed by an examination of gender inequality in the legal, cultural and linguistic contexts through a number of recent cases. It is suggested that Chinese women are describable as both subjects and objects in the legal process with both positive and negative implications for women's rights. Lastly, the changing status of women in China is conceptualised within the legal system as a hierarchical social order in the male-dominated Chinese culture, with the symbolic as well as actual power of law both empowering Chinese women in the legal process and yet placing them in an un-winnable position in the social strata. I argue that Chinese women's rights and genuine liberation will not be achieved unless and until equality at home in family relationships is first obtained. This will require the fundamental change of Chinese thinking regarding men and women, to involve all members of the society and the Chinese culture as a whole, if Chinese women are to play a meaningful role in a civil society that is yet to emerge but needs to emerge in China.[2]

---

1 The author would like to thank Professor Rosemary Hunter of Kent Law School, Professor Margaret Woo of Northeastern University and Professor Randall Peerenboom of the Oxford Foundation for Law, Justice and Society for their invaluable advice and comments. Acknowledgement is also made of the Griffith University Research Development Grant (2005).

2 It is undeniable that major progress has been made in China in the last two decades of economic reform, with significant improvement in the standard of living for the Chinese population, including women. However, the situation for Chinese women is not as optimistic as it is sometimes portrayed, for instance, McLaren (2004), and West et al. (1999), and the Chinese government's portrayal of women's situation in China paints a much more optimistic picture than it is in reality: <http://www.china.org.cn/e-white/chinesewoman/index.htm>.

The Chinese legislative regime regarding women

Under the Chinese Constitution, women enjoy equal rights to men in all spheres of life, in political, economic, cultural, social and family life, and the State protects the rights and interests of women, and applies the principle of equal pay for equal work to men and women alike, and trains and selects cadres from among women.[3] Equality between the sexes has been part of the Chinese Communist Party's (CCP) agenda from its early days.[4] The Marriage Law (1950) was the first legislative instrument of the PRC shortly after the CCP came to power in 1949. It is a significant statute both historically and presently for Chinese women in the recognition of their basic rights, and in contemporary Chinese social and legal development. As officially stated, the Marriage Law represented the socialist values replacing the old feudal Chinese family values and practices, including polygamy, arranged marriages and superiority of males over females, among other things. The 1950 Marriage Law introduced the concept of freedom of marriage and of divorce, gender equality and institutionalised monogamy, representing a sharp break in the continuity of Chinese traditional ideas and practices (see Chen 1999 and Buxbaum 1978), which has since become the guiding principle in Chinese marriage law. A new Marriage Law was adopted in 1980. For discussion of post-Mao Chinese families, see Davis and Harrell (1993), based on a revision of the 1950 Marriage Law, which lays down the basic principles for marriage and family relations; that is, a marriage system based on freedom, monogamy and equality between men and women.[5] The law also stipulates that the lawful rights and interests of women, children and the elderly shall be protected, and birth control shall be practised.[6] It prohibits third party intervention in marriage, mercenary marriage and dowries for marriage, bigamy and domestic violence (see Zhao 2001).[7]

Another important statute is the Law for the Protection of Women's Rights and Interests (1992) and the corresponding local implementing regulations. In late 2005, this law was amended to include a sexual harassment clause, stipulating that women are not to be subjected to sexual harassment and measures need to be taken to prohibit sexual harassment. The legislation encourages women to sue if they feel they are being sexually harassed. Other main points of the amendment were to include equality between men and women into China's basic state policy; to forbid examinations to discover the gender of a foetus through ultrasound technologies; and to include measures to prevent domestic violence. This new provision breaks the traditional thinking that prevented government from meddling in family affairs.

3 Art. 48 of the Constitution.

4 For a brief historical perspective of law related to women in pre-1949 and post-1949 China and the legal development post-1949, see Han (2000).

5 Art. 2 of the Marriage Law (1980, amended in 2001). For discussion of the Marriage Law, see Feng (2001/02)

6 Art. 2 of the Marriage Law.

7 Art. 3 of the Marriage Law.

There are other laws, including The General Principles on Civil Law (1986),[8] the Criminal Code (1979), the Labour Law (1994) and the Inheritance Law (1985) that have general or special provisions related to women and gender equality; also the Law on the Healthcare of Mothers and Infants (1994) and the NPC Standing Committee's Decision Regarding the Severe Punishment of Criminals Involved in the Trafficking and Kidnapping of Women and Children (1991). Besides, China has ratified the UN Convention on the Elimination of All Forms of Discrimination Against Women, and the Convention on Equal Pay for Equal Work for Men and Women through the International Labour Organisation within the UN System.

Of the broad legislative regime described in the foregoing, there are two major areas of social and legal developments that are of particular interest to our discussion here: firstly the increase in 'illegal cohabitation' and bigamy in violation of the monogamy system reconfirmed in the Marriage Law, and the related marital and property complications for the parties concerned, and the laws governing them; and secondly, the increase in violence and other forms of abuse against women, and the governing laws. For the purpose of this chapter, bigamy and marital matters mainly concern Chinese women's rights and equal status in family relationships, and their independence, personal dignity and the freedom of choice in modern society. The latter relates to Chinese women's rights of the person, and the basic human rights as an individual and the freedom from violence and abuse; that is, the physical and other form of violation by their husbands or partners in domestic relationships.[9] The chapter focuses on the laws and Chinese women in such domestic contexts, not at the workplace or other social and public settings.

8 The General Principles of Civil Law (1986) stipulates that Chinese citizens enjoy freedom in marriage, and that buying and selling in marriage and arranged marriage and other interference in the freedom of marriage are prohibited (Art. 103); also that marriage, family, the elderly, mothers and children are protected by law (Art. 104), and that women enjoy equal civil law rights as men (Art. 105).

9 The Chinese government until recently always insisted that women's rights are not part of human rights. Such a position has many fundamental flaws. For instance, violence against women is often viewed primarily as a social problem, and has not resulted in the recognition of this violence as a human rights abuse: Hom (1991/92, 251). However, one positive effect of such a position is that women's groups in China have been able to strongly and legitimately advocate and promote women's rights while the talks of human rights have always been suppressed. This has changed with the recent reversal of the Chinese government's attitude toward human rights, incorporating state protection of human rights into the Constitution in 2004 (Art. 33). For instance, in a recent statement to the UN Commission on Human Rights, entitled 'Women's Human Rights', Mr Liu Zhenhua of the Chinese delegation stated that 'China has always attached a great importance to women's rights and taken gender equality as a basic policy. The Amendment to the Constitution adopted in 2004 has included therein the provision on the respect for and guarantee of human rights. The legal and policy framework for the protection of women's rights and on women's entitlement has been further improved.'

Specifically, in the legislative regime concerning marriage and family relations, the Constitution stipulates that marriage, the family and mother and child are protected by the State, and the violation of the freedom of marriage is prohibited, and maltreatment of the elderly, women and children are prohibited.[10] Regarding marriage based on monogamy, the Marriage Law underwent major amendment in 2001 after 10 years' deliberations. The amended Marriage Law reaffirms the principle of monogamy, and that husband and wife shall be faithful to and respect each other and family members shall help each other so as to maintain an equal, harmonious and civilised matrimonial and family relationship.[11] The Marriage Law prohibits bigamy and cohabitation with a person other than one's legal spouse.[12] The Marriage Law further stipulates that when a party is involved in bigamy or cohabitation with someone other than one's legal spouse, divorce shall be granted after mediation if either side files such an application.[13] Additionally, criminal liabilities will result in bigamy or those who cohabit with another person other than the legal spouse.[14] Under the Criminal Code, committing bigamy may lead to criminal sanction, with a maximum of two years' imprisonment or detention.[15] The Marriage Law also provides that the innocent party in cases of bigamy may be entitled to compensation in divorce.

In the area of law governing domestic violence and other forms of abuse and violence against women, the Marriage Law stipulates that domestic violence and maltreatment of family members are prohibited.[16] The victim has the right to make petition for mediation and for the cessation of such acts. Administrative and criminal liability will be imposed on the perpetrator of domestic violence.[17] Under the Criminal Code, the crimes of disrupting marriage and family may result in sentences of up to two years' imprisonment in cases of physical abuse, and up to seven years' imprisonment if violence results in serious injury or death.[18] Under the Marriage Law, the victim may file a private prosecution in the court,[19] and if domestic violence results in divorce, the innocent party shall be entitled to compensation.[20] The Women Protection Law as recently amended now prohibits domestic violence.

10 Art. 49 of the Constitution.
11 Art. 4 of the Marriage Law.
12 Art. 3 of the Marriage Law.
13 Art. 32 of the Marriage Law.
14 Art. 45 of the Marriage Law.
15 Art. 180 of the Criminal Code.
16 Art. 3 of the Marriage Law.
17 Arts. 43 and 45 of the Marriage Law.
18 Art. 182 of the Criminal Code.
19 Art. 45 of the Marriage Law.
20 Art. 46 of the Marriage Law.

Chinese women as legal objects

Although Chinese law protects women's rights of the person, and specifically prohibits the selling of women as brides or for other purposes as described above, women are still subject to trade, either covertly or overtly. The facts of the following case provide a snapshot of the kind of prevailing male attitude towards women at home regarding the wife as property and a commodity of trade.

Liu is a farmer in the county of Liangdang, Gansu Province, in northwestern China. He was married to Wang and they have two children, one aged eleven and the other six. In early 1997, Liu was struck by a sudden illness, and the left side of his body became paralysed. He was the family breadwinner, and life had been a struggle even before he was sick. Now he was largely bedridden, unable to work, and the family barely managed to survive. One day after the funeral of a villager, according to the local tradition, associated activities were organised in honour of the dead. One activity was a movie show. Liu was there, and the film was about a woman and her life, and how she had to support and care for two husbands due to her family financial difficulties. The film provided some food for thought for Liu. A woman with two husbands might very well solve his family difficulties. The woman he had in mind was his wife. Liu soon found a suitable candidate, a casual labourer working in the village, Feng, 35 years old, from another province, dirt poor. In fact, he was too poor to get married. But Feng had his good points. He was strong and hardworking. Feng even once asked Liu to be his matchmaker and find him a wife.

Soon after the movie show, Liu invited Feng to his house and told him that he had found a possible match for him. At the dinner table, Liu finally revealed that his wife was the person he had in mind for Feng. Feng could not believe what he heard, but after pleading and begging from Liu that he was desperate to find a way to support his family, Feng agreed. After all, Feng was sympathetic to the family misfortune. He could assist the family as a helping hand in return for food and lodging, and he would leave the family when the two children grew up. So, Liu and Feng drew up a written contract for the purpose. The 'wife lease' agreement ('*zu qi hetong*') reads like this:

> Liu, of his own will, leases his wife Wang to Feng for a period of ten years. In return, Feng undertakes to do all the household work for the Liu family, and to support their two children for ten years. During the ten-year period, Feng may cohabit with Wang, and any children born between them shall belong to Feng. We hereby sign this written agreement as proof.

This 'wife lease' agreement was signed by both Liu and Feng on 18 November 1997. Liu later on told his wife, Wang, about this 'lease'. Wang could not believe this had happened, but after repeated begging and pleading by the husband, Wang gave in. Four days later, Feng moved in with the Liu family, and a few months later, Feng and Wife started to live together as a couple under the same roof with Liu.

After a while, Liu, the husband, started to feel uneasy and sorry for himself. About one and a half year later in 1999, a village official got wind of the relationship between Wang and Feng, and came to Liu's house to give the husband a dressing down for his misdeed. Liu and Feng started to have frequent arguments over the wife. In such arguments, Feng would remind Liu of the written agreement and would threaten to take him to court if he went back on the agreement. Liu thought to him that he would surely lose in court. After all, they did sign a contract. One day in April 1999, the wife, Wang, and Feng eloped and left the Liu home for good. They took the son with them too. For the next few days, Liu struggled in his crutches with his teenage daughter all over town, but the pair had disappeared without a trace.

This case did not go to court but was widely reported in the Chinese press.[21] Two issues deserve further elaboration. Firstly, in the 'wife lease agreement', the wife was the property or chattel being traded. It was a violation of Wang's right of the person, contrary to the provisions of the Women Protection Law, thus unenforceable because of its illegality. Secondly, there is the issue of bigamy. As stated earlier, the Chinese Marriage Law prohibits bigamy or illegal cohabitation, and both civil and criminal liabilities may result, with the possibility of two years' imprisonment or detention for the offence. Furthermore, under the Chinese Marriage Law, the state may prosecute people for bigamy. In China, for various reasons, people who are victims of bigamy do not often make a complaint to the police or the relevant authorities. Under the Chinese law, other people apart from the victims themselves, such as social organisations and relevant work units or the marriage registration bureau, may bring a complaint to the authorities for the procurators to decide whether or not to prosecute. In this case, Feng and Wang, the wife, can be said to be in an illegal cohabiting relationship. They could be prosecuted. The wife, as a party to the illegal relationship, even though coerced into it initially, would not be regarded as a victim as she later became a willing participant. Under the circumstances, it seems that the wife who was a victim in the lease agreement would be a guilty party in the resulting illegal relationship. According to some Chinese commentators, the illegal and unenforceable contract aside, she was just as guilty as the other two men, and was also blamed for being ignorant of the law and her rights, and for being a willing participant in the illegal cohabitation.[22]

On another level, I think that this case can also inform us about gender equality, or the lack thereof, in Chinese families, and about Chinese women as non-autonomous and non-persons in family relationships.

In the last twenty years or so, with the economic reform and progress, greater emphasis has been given to market forces and monetary values of commodities in all spheres of life in China. Unfortunately, this seems to have extended to women, with women being considered as part of the monetary and economic equation.

21 *Minzhu yu fazhi* (Democracy and Legal System) 297: 16 (1999), 38.
22 *Minzhu yu fazhi* (Democracy and Legal System) 297: 16 (1999), 40.

Women and sex have become objects of commodification ('*shangpinhua*'),[23] as they were in imperial and pre-949 China when all women were regarded fundamentally as disposable merchandise (Hershatter 1991, 258). Today, Chinese women are once again being regarded as commodities, and being denied of their intellectual, moral and political dimensions. They are not only required to fulfil their traditional roles as wives and mothers or as revolutionary productive workers in the workforce. They must now also in increasing numbers take on the new role as an object of trade and desire. They are not just part of the growing consumers of goods in the vast Chinese market, but constitute some of the goods to be picked and consumed by men. They have to acquire a competitive edge as consumer goods to win men's approval and favour in their commodity status. This relates and corresponds to the resurgence in various forms of prostitution (see Jeffreys 2004; Spahn 1998).

The idea of women as the objects of men's property and as commodities has deep roots in Chinese culture. Women were traditionally regarded by men as property or chattels that could be disposed of or traded with. Leasing or pawning a wife, in fact, was a common customary practice in traditional China. It was called '*dianqi*', ' *diangu qi*', *or* '*zhiqi*' ('leasing wife'). ('*Dian*' or '*zhi*' refers to a type of lien or charge, or pawn, in traditional Chinese customary law; '*gu*' means to hire, or to be hired or rented, and '*qi*' means 'wife').[24] In such practice, the husband rented out the wife to be somebody else's wife in return for a cash payment for an agreed leasing period. At the end of the lease period, the husband could redeem or take the wife back. During the Song dynasty (960–1279 CE), such wife-hiring practices were allowed. However, it was prohibited during the Yuan dynasty (1279–1368 CE) by law. During the Ming (1368–1644 CE) and Qing (1616–1911 CE) dynasties, '*diangu qiqie*' (leasing or hiring a wife or concubine for consideration) would result in caning by bamboo for 80 strokes. But the practice never completely ceased in traditional China.[25]

Linguistically, the Chinese language has two characters for 'to marry', '*qu*' (for a man to marry a woman), and '*jia*' (for a woman to marry a man).[26] *Qu* is formed by the character *qu* (to get, to fetch), and *nü* (woman); that is, for a man to marry a woman, he simply goes and fetches a woman. But for a woman to

23 See Woo (2003) who discusses the increasing use of the formal legal process by Chinese women in recent years, which has altered women's sense of entitlement and equality in Chinese society.

24 In traditional Chinese law, '*dian*' was a kind of property right, using real property as a type of charge, mostly based on customary law. The landowner could transfer, but not alienate, his land in return for a cash loan. The lender of the loan received the full possession and use of the land, but not the ownership, and the borrower (the landowner) reserved the right to redeem the land. For a study of women's rights to property in traditional China, see Bernhardt (1999).

25 Leasing or pawning also extended to women or young girls as prostitutes. See Hershatter (1991, 256–85).

26 For a linguistic analysis of Chinese law, see Cao (2004).

get married, *jia* is formed by the character *jia* (home, family) and *nü* (woman); that is, a woman finally finds a home when she gets married. In the Chinese mind, unmarried women were homeless and were to be despised or pitied. Thus, marriage was regarded as the ultimate destiny for women in China. Furthermore, in the traditional Chinese family, when a woman got married and thus found a home, she became completely subject to her husband and his family (see Baker, 1979). As a Chinese saying goes, 'Married to a chicken, the women follows the chicken; married to a dog, the woman follows the dog.' Not only did she have to behave as her husband required, but her identity and status were totally dependent upon her husband and his family.[27]

However, one must not think that the thinking and practice of regarding women as commodity and accessory was exclusively Chinese. Women were regarded as men's chattels in the West until fairly recently. The practice of wife sale, with the wife regarded as the property of her husband in England, famously depicted in Thomas Hardy's novel, *The Mayor of Casterbridge*, represented a semi-formal means of transferring the property in the wife to a new freeholder.[28] According to Lévi-Strauss (1969, 115),

> the total relationship of exchange which constitutes marriage is not established between a man and a woman, where each owes and receives something, but between two groups of men, and the woman figures only as one of the objects in the exchange, not as one of the partners between whom the exchange takes place.[29]

In China's case, marriage between two people in traditional China was always regarded as a matter between two families in establishing relationships, not at all a matter between the two individuals involved. It was an exchange of commodity and monetary transfer, with symbolic and substantive dowries part of the transfer. Wife leasing or hiring may be seen as a variation of the monetary exchange for men to get further returns for their investment. The idea that marriage was considered primarily as a form of family property belonging to the family lasted well into the twentieth century in China, and marriage was a process that turned women into something that husbands and households would possess (see Ocko 1991).

27 For detailed discussions of the traditional Chinese family and marriage and their historical development, see Watson and Ebrey (1991).

28 See Barnett (1998, 34–5). For the discussion of wife sale in England, see Kenny (1929); Menafee (1981).

29 Claude Lévi-Strauss (1969, 115). Lévi-Strauss also touched upon the kinship and marriage systems in the pre-imperial period in China. For discussions of the theorisation of exchange of women in Lévi-Strauss, see Rubin (1975) and Rifkin (1980). For a critique of Lévi-Strauss and Rubin, see Hartsock (1998). See also Pateman (1988) for discussion of the contract that establishes modern patriarchy and the political rights of men over women in the West.

Wife leasing or hiring is a type of spousal abuse and violation of the basic human rights of women. It degrades women and de-personifies women, treating them as commodities to be exchanged and controlled by men as the latter choose. Although this is different from physical abuse, it is a violation of the woman's right of the person, abuse nevertheless.[30] However, for Chinese men, as in the case described here, the husband and the other man justified themselves and their acts as wanting to help the family in difficulty and, in their minds, an understandable or decent and reasonable act in the circumstances. The logic is not very different from saying that one has to sacrifice a family machine tool to feed the starving kids.[31]

As we have seen, women are regarded as objects of trade and their rights as autonomous individuals are being denied not so much by the law but by family members. Both similarly and dissimilarly, in law, women are also regarded as an object, albeit of protection. As has been pointed out, law is a double-edged sword in that the very laws designed to protect women subject women to discrimination and disadvantage.[32] While the laws appear to protect women on paper, the practice and application of such laws, in China as in other nations, distinctly subordinate women, and have the potential to perpetuate gender segregation in the workplace and discrimination against women.[33]

On another level, if we look at the issue of marriage exchange or treating women as commodities or properties, some implications can be drawn. In Western law and legal tradition, or at least in the last two hundred years or so, there has always been a rejection of and abhorrence at the idea and practice of owning persons as property. However, this did not prevent the slave trade or the treating of women as properties

30 Physical abuse and violence against women in domestic settings is also serious and often shocking. In a recent case from Liaoning Province in 2003, a man forced a divorced female neighbour into living with him, as he threatened to kill and harm her child and other family members. He constantly and violently beat and sexually abused the woman who endured psychological and physical torture. But the woman was too terrified to report him, although her family members and the man's family members all knew about the abuse. In the end, he even sewed up, with needles, the woman's genital area and put a lock between her legs so that when she went to work, she could not supposedly have an affair with other men. She was so badly mutilated and injured that her co-workers noticed her pain and agony that she could not walk properly. They reported him to the police and he was later charged and prosecuted.

31 It is noted that in recent years, Chinese men are also subject to degradation and commodification due to poverty. For instance, there are male prostitutes servicing older Chinese women and some women also 'keep' men. Some Chinese men marry out of economic consideration although doing so is also problematic for men in that Chinese men are supposed to make more money and to be more capable than their wives. I thank Prof. Peerenboom for pointing this out.

32 See Woo (1993) for her discussion of the Chinese emphasis on the female biological differences in women's law. See also Woo (1994).

33 See Ogletree and de Silva-de Alwis (2002); and Woo (1994, 279–98).

by the male members of the family. As in slavery, not only was labour bought and sold, so was autonomy of action, hereby depriving the person of agency (Strathern 2004, 210). The same can be said to a large extent of women being treated as properties in marriage arrangements in traditional China. As discussed earlier, women were deprived of their individuality and autonomous action and thinking. They were used in marriage agreements for functions other than being women as individual persons. They were used as part of the power relationships in Chinese marriage agreements that are actions along multiple axes of power than as a single, one-dimensional trajectory (Riles 1991, 512). As noted, as in many societies, the contracting of marriage in China was a competitive and vitally important game governed by the rules of exchange (Riles 1991, 513). Through exchange, families traded their daughters for wives and again as valuable productive and reproductive labour (Riles 1991, 513). In Marilyn Strathern's studies of Highland New Guinea societies, there are different notions of female personhood: first, women are defined as units of exchange – 'detachable wealth' separate from the heart of male society; second, women are defined as the product of and producers of the group (Strathern 2004, 512). For our purpose, Chinese women are also often defined as separable items of exchange, and Chinese women are defined as marginal members of their husbands' families or as detachable symbols of their natal families, and are objects of exchange. As is rightly put, as 'total social phenomena', marriage exchange and dispute involve the total complexity of human interaction (Riles 1991, 518).

Women as legal subjects

In recent years, the Chinese legislative and judicial systems have allowed and witnessed Chinese women as legal actors and litigants. Firstly, in terms of legislative regime, as discussed earlier, women have certain rights and freedoms under the Chinese law. They have the right to take men to court for violation of their rights in domestic and other situations. Secondly, in terms of the judicial process, in China, the number of lawsuits has increased greatly. In particular, with the jump in the divorce rates, many couples go to court for the petition of divorce. More people including women are using the legal process (Woo 2003). In the 1990s, the use of formal civil litigation in the Chinese courts has increased while the use of informal dispute resolution, such as mediation by neighbourhood committees and work units, has decreased (Woo 2003, 101).[34] With the growing awareness of legal rights among the Chinese population, it is a fact that Chinese as individuals now enjoy more rights and freedoms. More people use private lawsuits to resolve family and other disputes than ever before. This is believed to be part of the general shift or migration from the

34 According to Woo (2003), divorce filings with the court increased by 14.9 per cent from 1997 to 2001; in Shanghai, the divorce rate grew more than fivefold, and in Beijing and Tianjin, more than threefold. The national divorce rate in 1997 was 19.4 per cent; in 1980, there were 389,000 divorces, and in 1996, there were 1.13 million.

collective to the individual in terms of employment and family matters, and the shift from the public to the private (Woo 2003).

The court decisions of the following recent cases from China can illustrate the changing status of women in the Chinese legal process, suing and being sued.

Gan was 61 years old and was married for almost 40 years, with grown-up children. In recent years, he became a very successful businessman with a construction company of a considerable size. In 1998, he got to know a 28 year-old actress, Lu, and they started an affair. A year later, at the request of the mistress, Gan bought her an apartment to continue their affair. The property was registered in her name so that the wife would not find out. However, after another nine months, Lu, the mistress, fell in love with a much younger man and wanted out. She changed the locks to the apartment and refused Gan's entry. Gan wanted the return of his apartment or 50,000 *yuan* cash for the cost of the purchase. Lu refused and insisted that she would not have slept with him for three years in return for nothing. Besides, she said, Gan gave the apartment to her as a gift registered in her name. Around August 2001, Gan went to the police, claiming that he was defrauded. After investigation, the police found that this was a case of an illicit affair, with no fraud involved, and they did not pursue the matter. Gan eventually confessed to his wife about the affair. In September 2001, Mr and Mrs Gan took the mistress to court, requesting the return of the apartment or in lieu the 50,000 *yuan*. This is the first case that went to court in China involving a couple suing a mistress.

In 2001, the Beiliu city court in Guangxi Zhuang Autonomous Region handed down its decision. It found that the apartment was bought with the money saved during the marriage of Gan and his wife, and was the joint property of the couple. However, Gan used the money to purchase the apartment as a gift to Lu in her name. Thus, the apartment could not be regarded as the joint property of Gan and his wife. The claim for the return of the apartment was rejected. The court also found that Gan, without the consent of his wife, used the money that belonged to both him and his wife, violating his wife's legitimate rights and interests. Further, the illicit affair between Gan and Lu violated the monogamy principle in marriage as stipulated in law, and such an affair seriously affected the stability of the married family, and also social stability and morality. The court found that the apartment was bought for the purpose of conducting the illicit affairs on a long-term basis, an illicit activity. Although the apartment was in the mistress's name and she was the legitimate owner in law, the gift was given for an illegal purpose, violating the law and rendering the title null and void. The apartment was an illegal gain. Gan and his mistress would face legal sanction. Thus, the court rejected the claim by Gan and his wife for the return of the property, and the apartment was to be confiscated by the state as a property used for an illegal purpose. Thus, in this case, the wife was not financially compensated at all for her husband cheating on or defrauding her.[35]

35 According to reports, the Women's Law Research and Aid Centre of Peking University receives over 100 complaints related to women's rights every month in recent

In another case involving a mistress, the court in another city decided very differently.

Xue was a successful salesman, living in Yixing city, Jiangsu province. He was married with a daughter. In 1996, Xue met Zhang, aged 21. They maintained a sexual relationship from 1996 to 2002. During this time, Xue bought an apartment costing 120,000 *yuan* in Zhang's name, and gave her money to start a shop, a car, and further 120,000 *yuan* in cash for her to buy a new car. Zhang later ended the affair. In October 2002, Xue and his wife took Zhang to the Yixing city court, accusing Zhang of interfering with their marriage and family life, demanding the return of the 162,000 *yuan* that Xue had given Zhang, and claiming that the money was the married couple's joint property.

According to various reports and commentaries about the case, the judges, in deciding the case, thought that on the one hand, if the gift was deemed void, the defendant, Zhang, would have to return all the property to the plaintiffs (the husband and wife). However, they reasoned that such a decision would have a negative social impact and would encourage Chinese men to have mistresses. On the other hand, the judges also believed that, if the gift was deemed valid, and the defendant mistress were allowed to keep the properties obtained during the illegal relationship, such a decision would also have the negative social impact in that it would send the message that the 'returns' of the 'physical investment' by mistresses are legitimate. The judges felt that they needed to find a balance between law and morality in deciding such cases.

The court found that Xue, the husband, was married in the duration of the illegal cohabitation and he should be held wholly responsible for conducting the illicit affair. Zhang, as the mistress, was culpable but not as culpable as Xue, and she was also a victim in this matter. Accordingly, the court held that the gift was partially void; that is, the part of the property that belonged to Xue was transferred legally when he gave it to the mistress, but the money that had belonged to Xue's wife was given to the mistress by Xue was not validly transferred. The court held that, of the property given to the mistress as gift, half of it belongs to the mistress and half to the wife. The judges also pointed out that, although being a mistress is

years, and about half of them concern marriage, with most divorce cases caused by unfaithful husbands. However, the wife usually cannot get compensation due to the lack of sufficient evidence in such divorce cases, despite the law that holds the unfaithful party responsible for marriage breakdown, thus liable to pay compensation. The Chinese government also claims that the Chinese Women's Federations in various parts of the country have set up about 9,000 legal aid centres to provide legal services to women. See Statement to the United Nations Commission on Human Rights by China. However, legal aid may yet to reach the grassroots. In a personal experience in early 2005, I was in a major bookshop in Beijing. A middle-aged woman approached me as she saw I was going through law books on women and women's rights. She asked me for legal advice for her upcoming divorce. She was from a rural area from northwest China and was desperate to find out what would happen to her and her child upon divorce.

immoral, nevertheless mistresses' legitimate rights should be protected, and their rights should not denied because of their special status.

In considering and contrasting the facts and decisions of the two cases, a number of issues are worth our attention in terms of Chinese women's status.

The cases show that Chinese women are indeed resorting to and utilising the legal process more than before, as other studies have found. They are taking their private family matters into the public arena in the court. Husbands having affairs and mistresses is something that many in China would regard as not just private but also that it is face-losing, bringing shame to the wronged wife and to the children. However, increasingly Chinese women are using law to settle such private family matters. They are becoming active legal actors, as litigants being the wronged wives or former mistresses, the roles and positions that men put the women into in the first place. The new positions and status are new to Chinese law directly resulted from the changed roles of women in their family relationships.

However, it seems that, in bigamy and illegal cohabitation cases, women are suing other women – the wife suing the mistress, not to reconfirm her legal status as the wife, but to recover property and money that is either hers or her husband's. In this sense, both the wife and the mistress are being used by the husband in the different stages of the man's life to suit his convenience. Moreover, there is the also the issue of morality and law, and moral behaviour of both men and women. The Chinese court and the law as discussed earlier consider illegal cohabitation and bigamy and both the men and women involved as immoral and unacceptable. The court passes moral as well as legal judgments accordingly. Besides, socially, '*ernai*', the second wife or the long-term living-in mistresses, are considered by most Chinese as just one type of prostitute as described in Jefferies' study. Many Chinese people view them in such a low light, as gold-diggers, ruining marriages and family life, as if they were the sole perpetrators. In recent years, they have become a distinctive group or class in Chinese society. There are villages and towns in southern China with the nickname '*ernai cun*' ('second wife village') as the resident population or most of it consists of such women. Now the law and the courts are giving their verdicts, formally and legally describing and classifying them as a class of persons. Legal rulings from the court can have a major impact on how society views such litigants and their moral worth and status.

Related to this is the fact that the Chinese court does not follow a system of precedent. As we have seen, different courts and judges use different moral and other standards to interpret the law and decide cases; particularly, how they view and decide on the morality and legality of such cases may vary greatly given the vast differences in the facts of such cases. The resulting uncertainty and unpredictability, although this is not the focus of this chapter, also affect the rights and the interests of the parties, in particular the women involved on both sides.

The rights and wrongs for women in Chinese law

We may draw a number of implications from the cases discussed in this chapter for the consideration of rights and gender equality for Chinese women. Both the facts and decisions of these cases can reveal a great deal about the status of Chinese women today, their position in relation to law, and how their rights are being affected.

I propose that the law in China both empowers women and perpetuates the low and unequal status of women. I believe that Chinese culture and law are mutually constitutive in maintaining its discriminatory treatment of women, and that China's developing and emerging law and legal system, while empowering women, continues and contributes to the male dominance that has always been part of Chinese culture.

In this regard, law is powerful both as a symbol and vehicle of male authority. This power is based on an ideology of law and an ideology of women which is supported by law (Rifkin 1980, 84–5). Moreover, law, in relation to women, 'is seen as a measured and rational set of beliefs which at the same time asserts a mythological vision which is believed by many to present an accurate statement of the world' (Rifkin 1980, 84–5). The historical image of males – objective, rational and public – is the dominant image of law. As Rifkin points out, law emerged as a form of rationality, retained the pre-existing hierarchy of masculine authority and made more explicit the subordination of women to men by increasingly excluding women from working in trades and relegating them to the private world of the home (Rifkin 1980, 92). Law plays a primary and significant role in social order, and 'legal change does not lead to social reordering' (Rifkin 1980, 92). Litigation and other forms of formal legal relief cannot lead to social change or challenge the fundamental patriarchal social order, because in upholding and relying on the paradigm of law, the paradigm of patriarchy is upheld and reinforced (Rifkin 1980, 88).

If we consider this in the Chinese context, China has always been a male-dominated patriarchal society.[36] In particular, Confucianism, as the state orthodox ideology for over two thousand years, advocated the idea of male superiority over the female ('*nanzun nübei*'), and the differentiation of people, especially between men and women.[37] These were reflected in Chinese traditional laws.[38] Women, as

36 For discussions of women in Chinese culture, see Gilmartin et al. (1994). For a different view on patriarchy and Chinese culture, Diamant (2000) in his recent study challenges the view that there is an all-pervasive Chinese cultural and political reality oppressive to all women. The word 'patriarchy' derives from the Greek, meaning 'the rule of the father'. I use the term in the sense as described by Hom (1991/92, 255) – 'the fundamental and universal status of male dominance, authority and control exercised by men over women, embodied in social institutions of power such as the family, law and government and their legitimating ideology.'

37 For a different view of Confucianism and women in pre-modern East Asia, see Ko et al. (2003).

38 For instance, in the successive Chinese imperial codes, women were generally denied rights in inheritance. Women would be criminally sanctioned for bringing a lawsuit

taught and advocated in Confucianism, must follow certain rules of behaviour, the famous Confucian code of conduct prescribed to Chinese women, '*san cong si de*' ('three obediences and four virtues': that is, obedience to the father before marriage, obedience to the husband after marriage, and obedience to the son after the husband's death; and the four virtues of morality: proper manner and speech, housemaking skills and appearance. Wives must stay at home, '*neiren*', the 'inside person', as she was called until recently. There were specific domains that men dictated and prescribed for women. Chinese women's roles and entire job or life descriptions were within the family under the control of men. Naturally, in Chinese society, political power and public matters were exclusively men's business. The traditional denial of women's participation in public life perpetuated women's low status as a whole person throughout Chinese history. The conceptual separation of the public and private spheres of life was allied to the Chinese patriarchal attitude which accords male superiority over women.[39] It is naïve to think that such deeply entrenched traditional cultural values and Confucian teachings and the centuries-old prejudices against women have disappeared or were eliminated with the social and political transformation and modernity over the last two hundred years. As Riles notes, an analysis of the Chinese judicial sphere reveals that, at its core, it rests upon a thinly transformed construction of traditional Chinese identity. Maoist theoreticians adopted only those aspects of Communist identity which conformed in essence with traditional Chinese notions of identity. The Chinese marriage law reflects Confucian ideals about the proper relationship of the person to the state which are in turn founded on the notion of the person as subsumed within the lineage and as the product of the relationships that surround him/her (Riles 1991, 516). In fact, the current new marketisation policy has served to rekindle some of those old traditions and prejudices (Han 2000, 403). Thus, today in China, the male-dominated paradigm of family and political power continues and it extends to the paradigm of law.

If one regards law as a powerful symbol and vehicle of male authority, and as a paradigm of maleness, then the Chinese family can equally be said to be a symbol and vehicle of male authority, a miniature of the male-dominated state power structure and hierarchy. Chinese law, in particular, its courts, may also very well be described as a big male-dominated Chinese family. The judge is the domineering husband/father, with the image of being rational and authoritative, who decides who can speak, when to speak and what one may speak of.[40] He is surrounded by

---

against the husband or other elder family members.

39 For discussion of women in public and private spheres in relation to law and legal theory, see Barnett (1998). See also Thornton (1995).

40 The majority of judges in China are men. According to the latest Chinese official figure from 2005, there are 43,384 female judicial officers out of a total of 194,000 judges in China, or 22.3 per cent. See China Xinhua News Agency report: <newsxinhuanet.com>, 8 March 2005. This figure compares favourably to other countries. We need to remember that the percentage of females on the bench is generally low in most countries.

other males, the sons who come way ahead of the wife/mother. The wife/mother is, in contrast, emotional, weak and irrational. She is in a slightly higher position than the other females, the daughters or daughter-in-laws. She is surely part of the family, and there may even be turns for her to speak, but when she is allowed to speak and what she says, interrupted by her intermittent sobbing and tears, are often of little or no consequence. The husband/father offers the solution and makes the final decision. I am describing the Chinese family not just in the 1890s, but also the 1990s and of the more recent past. With the reduction of the number of children in Chinese families in the last two decades, such typical large Chinese families have started to change, although the position of the wife has not altered much, with her being forever subordinate to the husband, in a position often lower even than the children or child in importance and priority.

Of course, there are many differences between the past and today. The recent legal reform and the emphasis on individual rights and market-oriented economic era have led to the increasing awareness of individual rights, against each other and against the state, and to the reliance on the law and the formal legal process in dispute resolution. According to Woo's study which focuses on divorce but has wider implications, the individualisation and privatisation of family and personal relations is exemplified by female litigants turning to the courts, in particular in divorce petitions (Woo 2003). When in court, female litigants are asked to act less like members of collectivist groups and more like individuals, with all the attendant benefits and pitfalls of asserting individual rights. Woo argues that while the litigation process may be heightening women's sense of individual entitlement, at the same time it lowers women's sense of collective well-being.[41] Women are at a disadvantage as they have always been. The state structures that once militated against discrimination have been dismantled, and women are left hostage to the prevailing gender bias (Woo 2003).[42] As Woo points out, the court process treats women and men as autonomous individuals, but since women on average face unequal economic powers and have fewer resources to make their stories heard, the movement towards a more adversarial system and the placement of burdens of proof on individual parties may not have worked to the advantage of most

41 According to Woo (2003, 101–2, 131–2), in the public sphere of courts, where the private matter of divorce is litigated, the culture of transition breeds a confluence of tensions.

42 Another example of bias of Chinese judicial officers against female litigants was the Hu Haiying divorce case from Harbin in 2001. The case concerned the Marriage Law and its newly amended provisions on property division in divorce, and was a high-profile divorce case involving property division after the amended Marriage Law came into effect in 2001. According to the study by Guo Li (2003), the court decided that the wife, upon divorce, was not to be given any of her husband's assets. Some of the judges were reported as saying that they believed that the wife, a woman with no particular status or financial means, had married the powerful and rich husband for his easy money.

women (Woo 2003, 131–2), and formal law and legal procedures by themselves are insufficient (Woo 2003, 133).[43]

Chinese law is still developing and emerging, against the backdrop of nascent capitalism or market economy with badly regulated or unregulated market forces at play. Law is being used by increasing number of Chinese citizens, including women, to solve disputes, and law is being promoted as the rational, objective, authoritative and public arbiter and adjudicator in China's quest for modernity and rule of law. Law is being increasingly seen as the answer that offers rationality and justice for people who otherwise have no power or status in society. In this sense, it is not just a case of women being victims of the law and society. However, despite or because of this, how the law categorises and sees Chinese women and how it deals with women and provides answers to their problems, has a major impact on how the Chinese society views women as a social group and how Chinese women view themselves, in both private and public life. In China, law is starting to replace, to some limited extent, the government and the Communist Party as an adjudicator. Not just the government and the Party say so, which, now many people have realised, is arbitrary, unsympathetic, increasingly irrelevant and often ineffectual. But now the law, being promoted and perceived as the higher, rational, objective and authoritative institution, says and decides that this or that is the case. It has to be said that, in China, against the omnipresent and all-powerful government and CCP, if law is to replace them as a new objective and rationale authority, it is in fact a progress. However, one wonders to what extent the law is the embodiment of male power that has dominated the Chinese culture and controlled Chinese women since the dawn of the Chinese civilisation. Symbolically, it is progress in that the wife is now given a seat at the dinner table, traditionally denied in the Chinese family, and she is allowed to speak, as women now are in the legal process. However, the position they speak from and the contents of their speech are yet to make an impact on the mind and deed of the major actor (the husband or the judge) in the final decision-making.

Lastly, in terms of law and social order, I propose that the current emphasis on law and rule of law which is necessary and encouraging, and the focus on judicial pronouncement and litigation, will not, however, result in the fundamental lifting of Chinese women's status, or any radical improvement in Chinese women's low position. China has always been a male-dominated society, manifested long in its history, culture and language, not the least of which is its the traditional laws on marriage, inheritance and family relationships in the discriminatory treatment of women. Women's liberation in China started around the turn of the twentieth century. That liberation and revolution, despite all the problems and flaws,

---

43 Woo (2003) also argues that China must determine what priority it will give to equality, women's rights protection and other redistributive goals, even when these goals conflict with other state goals, such as economic development and nation-building. She believes that greater institutional support is also needed for the enforcement of existing enacted equality rights.

succeeded in some of the fundamental changes in women's status and perception of women in modern society. Gender equality was proclaimed and advocated, more in rhetoric but also to some extent in practice. The power of rhetoric should not be easily dismissed. Language and words hold powerful influence over people, over people's thought and behaviour. In Mao's China, women were told that they had equal rights and freedom at home and work. I believe that gender equality then was more widely accepted or effective in public life than in the family. The basic male-dominated Chinese family structure or hierarchy was superficially or hardly touched. At the workplace, gender equality went to the extreme where women were regarded the same as men without any regard for their differences. The slogan was that 'men and women are the same', the sameness in the way people lived and worked, and the way they spoke, behaved and dressed.[44] However, at least women were not regarded as commodities to be disposed of or promoted as sexual objects to be purchased by men. Girls at school were encouraged to think that they were just as capable as boys. As someone grew up in China in the 1970s and went to university in the 1980s, the ideas of being inferior to my male counterparts and a goal in life in making myself useful to men were rather alien to me. Unfortunately, such thinking is alive today and has a growing audience and converts in China, even among young educated Chinese. As Han (2000, 399) noted, if the gains for women under Communism were more theoretical than real, under current marketisation those gains are anomalous at best, and the movement from Communism to privatisation has given rise once again to the subordination of women.

Two relevant points need to be made at this juncture. Generally speaking, there seems to be a view in legal studies regarding China that gender is irrelevant or not particularly significant in the context of a developing legal system like China's (Hom 1991/92, 252), and that to single out gender issues and treating women as a class of disadvantaged persons in the legal spheres masks or obscures real and supposedly bigger issues. I believe that women's issues are the larger issues that concern the whole society and they are also a major reflection of the directions a society is going and a reflection of the well-being of the society. In addition, in this chapter, I am not arguing that men and women are the same, biologically or otherwise, or that men are to become child-bearers and home-makers in order for women to achieve equality. What I am arguing is that it is the dominant patriarchal ideology and male cultural orientations that are deeply entrenched in the Chinese society and thinking that need to be changed. As is noted,

> Even though women do not yet kill in wars, do not shape government policy equally with men, they, along with male ruling groups and most men, believe

---

44 China seems to go from one extreme to another. As Woo (1994) points out, the more recent women-related legislation in China seems to give excessive focus on the biological differences between women and men, thus (in many instances) further reinforcing discriminatory practices against women.

> in the dominant ideology of the culture. Were they to rule, society would not be organized that differently from the way it is currently organized. They would organize it differently only if they had a different value system (Hooks 1984, cited in Hom 1991/92, 309).

Today, law plays a much greater role in Chinese people's lives than it has ever done before, and for the better. Law offers the prospect and reality of having one's rights asserted and recognised in public. It empowers women to take legal actions and make legal demands against their husbands, the only public domain where a wife can challenge and take on the husband. It is a fact that law has a significant role to play in changing the attitudes and conduct of the people it regulates. However, we also need to recognise that deeply entrenched cultural mores such as sexism and patriarchy are much harder to change through law. As pointed out, law has limited utility and effectiveness as a mechanism for social change, and an overemphasis on law as opposed to social change distorts the significance of law which is but one form of social relations (Barnett 1998, 38). I argue that law will not change the social ordering of the Chinese patriarchal society and male dominance, in particular at home. The complex and unsympathetic nature of law towards women and also men, stereotyping of women in their various roles, the massive and often incompetent bureaucracy, lawyers' reluctance to take on women's cases, and judges' bias towards women litigants as shown in both anecdotal evidence and documented studies, are just symptoms of the inherent prejudice against women in the Chinese law and society, starting from the family at home. To the outcry sometimes heard in China today, 'I want a second liberation!', there is no easy solution. Political agitation and collective demanding of rights and powers, together with the fundamental change of perspectives for both men and women and in Chinese thinking and cultural values regarding women and their place at home and in society, may go a long way. And Chinese women's equality at home is both a good starting and finishing point. Symbolically, it is time that the phrase 'father and mother' as it is used in the Chinese language was changed to 'mum and dad' in terms of priority.

Conclusion
Researching "Exploration" in the Semiotics of the Law

Christopher N. Candlin

In this Conclusion I would like to focus on a remarkable and original gathering of commissioned papers and case studies on the theme of '*exploration*' signalled in the title of the volume. What could we mean by *exploration* in the contexts of language and the law, especially in the sites characterised by diversity and tolerance as we have here? We might, firstly, align ourselves with the stance taken by researchers into discourse analysis along the lines set out by Hall, Slembrouck and Sarangi in their recent study in the discourses of social work, when they say:

> Our approach is discourse analytic. This means that we wish to foreground how professional processes are constructed in everyday activity and how they depend on communicative processes. It is suggested that any claims to truth by social workers, clients or other professionals have to be acted out in professional settings for them to matter. Facts, opinions and assessments have to be worked on and worked up in talk or in writing (2006, 15).

Here *exploration* would be at once *legal* in the sense that the matters under study are so institutionally and professionally located, but at the same time they are imbricated in language as *discourse*. Note that we are immediately talking here about an *exploration* not of law *and* language but rather law *in and through* language, language *in and through* law. This is an important distinction to make, and quite generally so. This is not a simple comparative or matching enterprise. We need to resist the idea that exploring 'communication' within professions can be isolated, studied, practised and even taught without having to take account of the nature of the given profession itself – how it is constituted, what governs its membership, what implications and requirements such membership imposes, not least upon the (im)permissibles of professional actions and their associated discourses. At the same time, we need also to note that even if professional discourse is recognised as being 'professional' in some way, we need to ask questions about how such a discourse is constituted – what is implied by discourse in such a discussion. Is it only profession-specific linguistic choices that are salient? Is professional communication only a matter of terminology? Thirdly, and perhaps not even much canvassed at all, other questions arise such as the transferability across professionals in different disciplines (professions/organisations) of such practices and such discourses, however constituted. To what extent is being a professional a signal of some generalisable set of attributes and actions, with transferable discourses? How important is the particular site in relation to other sites?

In making such a statement it is clear, then, that we are not, nor should we be, talking about language *per se*; rather we are talking about exploring discourses through language, focusing both on the interactive, contextualised and located, often co-constructed, frequently semiotically multimodal processes and products of communication and not just on matters of, say, their particular terminology. We are committed accordingly to exploring text as realised evidence but also to exploring the discourses, namely the institutionalised systems of knowledge, belief and ideology that in a sense underpin those texts, much in the manner of Foucault's *ordres du discours*.

Exploration will thus require us as researchers to draw on our text analytical skills as well as our socio-philosophical and certainly disciplinary and professionally relevant understandings of the systems and functions of the discipline in question, and the attributed roles of co-participants in these systems. Not that either orientation, to text or to discourse, is any simple matter: principally because there are no simple texts any more than there are simple discourses. All texts are *intertextual*, requiring close analytical exploration of their contributing texts, but they are at the same time, and much more demandingly of the researcher, always *interdiscursive*, requiring the closest, but also the most critically understanding appraisal of their contributing discourses, which, we may find, will not necessarily be congruent, indeed more often than not, as we see in this volume, they are, or may be, in contestation.

Although we have distinguished this textual exploration from its discursive counterpart (and their mutual relation) we have still not satisfactorily charted the exploratory territory. What of history? What of the biographies of individuals and their identities? What of the conditions of production and reception of these texts/discourses?

In his book *New Strategies of Social Research* (1993) Derek Layder sets out what he calls a *Resource Map for Research* in which he attempts what I think our explorer needs, namely, what we might term a 'textured' analysis of social reality, in which the various 'elements' or 'levels' of exploratory analysis he identifies are best seen not as separated entities but as interwoven

> Although I have presented the resource map as a series of separable elements with their own properties, I have also continually stressed their interconnected nature in relation to the analysis of specific research problems. In this regard, macro phenomena make no sense unless they are related to the social activities of individuals who reproduce them over time. Conversely, micro phenomena cannot be fully understood by exclusive reference to their internal dynamics so to speak; they have to be seen to be conditioned by circumstances inherited from the past. In other words, micro phenomena have to be understood in relation to the influence of the institutions that provide their wider social context. In this

> respect, macro and micro phenomena are inextricably bound together through the medium of social activity and thus to assert the priority of the one over the other amounts to a 'phoney war' (Layder 1993, 17).

In our discussion here of explorations into the semiotics of the law in the contexts of tolerance and diversity it may be that this position of Layder's is one that will commend itself and which will allow us to interrelate and interconnect the various papers in this volume, in both its Parts. How so? Particularly because such a position, such a Map, accommodates not only the historical and the individual perspective we refer to earlier, but also because it allows us to relate practice to theory, thus enabling generalisability of the results of our exploration while firmly anchoring them in the sites of engagement with which we are concerned.

In this cartography, Layder sets out four *research elements*, each of which is interconnected with the others, and each of which has a particular, and equally connectable, *research focus*. Layder argues that none of the elements is prime, and research may begin with any, providing that all are severally and differentially addressed. From the interplay of the data arising from each element, theory 'emerges'. We take it this is the basis of his construct of 'adaptive theory' (Layder 1993, 132ff).

What are these elements? Firstly, *Context*: Layder combines micro and macro contexts, arguing that the 'micro phenomena have to be understood in relation to the influence of the institutions that provide their wider social context. In this respect macro and micro phenomena are inextricably bound tighter through the medium of social activity' (Layder 1993, 102–3). More specifically, context focuses on the distribution of power in society; what values and ideologies determine normative behaviour in a social setting; and the nature of the political, religious and economic setting related to the subject of analysis. *Context* is that element which implicates the macro social organisation, the values, traditions, forms of social and economic organisation and power relations within the social formation, and illustrates these in terms of what he terms 'legally sanctioned forms of ownership, control and distribution: interlocking directorships, state intervention' (Layder 1993, 71). Secondly, *Setting*: here the focus is on the nature of the setting, 'the typical forms of attachment and commitment that individuals have in these types of setting ... the characteristic forms of power and authority in the setting' and the extent to which the broader social context impinges on the setting. This element focuses then on the intermediate social organisation, categorised as *work-related* and *non-work-related*. Important to *Setting* is what Layder identifies as its already established character; that is, the social and institutional structure and practices within which a particular *situated activity* occurs. Thirdly, *Situated Activity*: if settings are in Layder's terms *established* – although we should be cautious here not to equate establishment with stability, as such stability will be highly relative across and within social formations, and certainly relative to sectors of the population – then Layder's third element of *situated activity* involves a focus on that face-to-face or mediated social activity involving what he calls 'symbolic communication by skilled, intentional participants implicated in the contexts and settings' (Layder 1993, 71). We may note here how Layder explicitly draws on the discursive turn in sociological research, characteristic by the way of the legal studies of this volume, referring to 'emergent meanings, understandings and definitions of the situation as these affect and are affected by contexts and settings, and the subjective dispositions of individuals' (Layder 1993, 71). This aspect of social reality focuses on symbolic communication by skilled participants. What is the underlying meaning of the patterns of interaction taking place and to what extent are these intended by the participants? What forms of communication are being used to achieve these meanings? And, what aspects of setting are pertinent to the analysis of particular episodes of activity? How do they influence the action? Penultimately, Layder identifies a fourth aspect he terms *Self*, focusing here on the individual's sense of identity and his or her conception of the world. How does a person function within and respond to his/her social environment? Do the perceptions of such individuals change over time? And, he asks, what is 'the interplay between social and psychological factors involved in the formation of these subjective feelings and experiences'. If we see *Self*, with Layder, as invoking identity within the context of social experience, what he refers to as the 'unique psychobiography of the individual' (Layder 1993, 71) located within the time-space of a life career, then the struggle between the individuality and the collectivity of the self as at once body, mind and person is revealed.

These four 'elements' do not exist separately but each, as he and we have argued, implicates the other. What is significant for our exploratory map is that the four research elements (*Context, Setting, Situated Activity, Self*) are *all* set within a frame of *History* (more particularly the time-space of History), even though we need to note that in Layder's conception, all elements, as social processes, have their own time-space frames. Interactions among persons, for example, operate within a different time-space perspective from changes in social institutions, as Candlin and Candlin (2007) note in a study of nursing practices, although both may influence the conduct and practices of the other, and these differences will be significant.

The message is plain: the appraisal of discourse in action requires a clearly defined programme of sociolinguistic and discourse analytical study of a range of differentiated encounters, and one which goes beyond what may otherwise be a reductionist reliance on uttered (spoken/written visualised) text. But *description* is not enough. As we have announced earlier, and now supported by Layder's Research Map, our description of the territory needs to be accompanied by interpretive, ethnomethodological accounts of the meaning-making of individuals in interaction in particular situated activities, emphasising the members' resources that can be brought to bear, or, as we see in this volume, are often *prevented* from being brought to bear, on the communicative challenges of the moment. However, even such a focus on interpretation will not adequately include and bring to bear in and of itself Layder's elements of *Context* and *Setting*, and certainly not the overarching construct of *History*. The significance of context and setting only emerges from the talk, writings and visualisations of the participants, from their narratives when set against socio-historical accounts and studies of organisational change, shifts in national or local policies, whether governmental or institutional, and analyses of decision-making processes over time. Including this more encompassing and more dynamic dimension, as Layder argues, requires us to shift the exploration from description and interpretation to a view of research we may call *critical explanation.*

What themes would such a critically explanatory research agenda focus upon, and draw upon, and what would be the candidate methodologies for its toolbox? We may draw our responses in part from the admirably apt chapters in this collection by Anne Wagner and Vijay Bhatia. What they display is the need in such research to bring together what Roberts and Sarangi (2005) refer to as *focal themes* and *analytical themes*. As their overview states:

> A theme-oriented approach links analytic themes from linguistics and sociology to focal themes relevant to a professional domain, such as shared decision making or intercultural misunderstanding. Both the detail of moment by moment inferencing and larger rhetorical patterns are analysed to shed light on how meaning is negotiated and judgements made in interaction (p. 633).

Their *focal themes* (from the discourse world of medicine) may not be immediately, or even typically, seen as those of the law, although there is no reason why they might not be, or in fact, are. Indeed, within the chapters in this volume they find resonance along those others especially focused on issues of tolerance within diversity which are its mainspring. We may note in this context the chapters by Strauber, Lewis, Szilágyi and Pencak, with their particular focus on specific sites, or Hobbs' paper on the macro theme of 'tolerance' (but again viewed through a particular prism and time-space), or Cao's emblematic call on history for her study of women as legal subjects and objects in contemporary China. It is then not at all difficult, drawing on Layder (1993), to map such *focal themes* onto *discourse analytical themes*, familiar to those concerned with professional communication research. Once again the chapters in this volume afford us many and valuable examples. We may note here the methodologically highly innovative chapter by Summerfield, and those by Brigham, Le Cheng, van Schooten and Petrinic, each of which affords distinctive descriptive perspectives on the focal themes. For example, we find resonances with conversational analysis focusing on charting interaction, interactional sociolinguistics focusing on participant interpretation and inferencing, together with studies of narratives of experience, all of which can be, and are, readily married to, say, textual and grammatical and prosodic/kinesic analyses of textualisations, whether they be drawn from spoken, written or otherwise semiotically realised modalities, and whether or not assisted by corpus-based analyses. There is, however, yet another perspective on such a critical explanatory research, namely that of the study of *discursive practices*, much foregrounded in this volume. By discursive practices we mean here foci such as topic introduction and control, speaker/writer participation rights more generally (as they are either promoted or proscribed), management and transformation of discourses from the professional to the lay and vice versa, relationships between the pragmatics of information, advice, warning and vice versa. All of which, as we see in these chapters, can in turn be located in the contexts of a range of social and institutional/professional constructs such as:

- *agency* (in the micro and/or the macro context)
- *identity* (gender, class, age, ethnicity, culture)
- *role* (role shifts, negotiation, (dis)enfranchisement
- *knowledge management* (control, differential expertise, risk and outcome assessment)
- *interpretive repertoires/perspectives* ((mis)framings, lay versus expert, researchers and participants)
- *reasoning* (explanations and conceptualisation)
- *ethics* (moral behaviours and expectations)

and, then be further grounded within broader social themes of age, gender, rights and obligations, personhood, ethnicity, race and class.

In putting forward here what perhaps amounts to a research agenda we are at the same time reflecting, as we have noted, the individual affordances of the chapters contained in this volume; indeed, such an agenda is stimulated by reading them. Not to say that the authors would necessarily subscribe to the agenda; certainly the breadth of what is being proposed here cannot easily be accommodated within a particular study or paper, even if the author(s) wished. Nonetheless, there is a common ground, and one which, at very least, might serve to inform further similar studies in the semiotics of the law. What would be the chief characteristics of such an agenda?

1. That the perspectives of such research are not prioritised: entry is possible in a variety of ways and drawing on different but complementary discourses of research. What is central is maintaining the mutuality and the integrity of the perspectives. In this way, distinct research discourses evoke each other and permit an inbuilt corroborating and warranting of the data produced by the workings of the research discourses associated with each perspective.

2. That the research reinforces the central orientations of professional discourse studies: towards authenticated and evidence-based analyses drawing on a multiple and multimodal perspective on research methodology which sees the integration of social interactional analyses, narrative and ethnographic analyses, textual analyses, and social institutional analyses as needing to be harmonised in accounts which are at once descriptively, interpretively and explanatorily adequate. This is of course the goal of the 'thick' description advocated by Clifford Geertz (1973), now augmented by analytical techniques of discourse and text analysis.

3. That there is a need to match that 'thick' description with the necessary 'thick' participation of the researcher collaborating with the participants in the research project. As Sarangi puts it:

> A 'thick description' of professional practice, in Geertz's (1973) sense, can only be premised upon what I would call 'thick participation'. The notion of participation has to be taken broadly to include continuity of involvement in a research setting, including the maintenance of relationships with participants in temporal and spatial terms. … 'Thick participation' for me, extends beyond data gathering and data interpretation – it also includes the provision of feedback and the facilitation of conditions for potential uptake of discourse analytical findings (Sarangi 2005).

4. That there is a need to emphasise not only the outcomes but also the impacts of research. Thus, in addressing the 'so what?' question, central to critical explanation, we necessarily must have the local and involved communities of practice in mind while at the same time recognising the ever-present challenge of generalisation beyond the 'case'. As Smart sets out (2006, 195 and 197) quoting Goetz and LeCompte (1984):

> The implications of [an ethnographic] study indicate how the research is useful beyond an intriguing analysis of a unique case … It is difficult to respond to the question, 'So what?'. However any study is weakened if the researcher cannot answer that question …

> Interpretive ethnography, with its capacity for showing how a social group uses a particular configuration of symbol systems to construct a distinctive conceptual world, can serve well for researchers wishing to study a professional organization's use of technology-supported, symbol-based analytic practices and representations in producing and applying specialised knowledge.

5. That there is a need to reflect upon the challenges researchers face, and the various and differing roles they inhabit in such an enterprise is well-evidenced in the 'Editorial' by Sarangi and Candlin (2003):

> A precise example of such challenges facing applied researchers positioned as outsiders to the professional practice and knowledge under study is the need to remain *au courant* with the discoursal shifts within a given workplace context … However, recognizing and describing such shifts in discourse is not just a matter of making a link to shifting workplace practices, but, more fundamentally and problematically, that of the non-transparence of the significance of these shifts to the outside researcher to whom such professional practices based on tacit

knowledge will always remain inaccessible unless collaborative interpretation is taken seriously.

Concerning researcher roles, the distinctive stance we have taken vis-à-vis data in this exploratory research calls up at least the following, some of which at least find their resonance in the papers in this volume:

Very crudely, the applied linguist can be profiled along the following lines:

- applied linguist as mediator (linguistics applied in a post hoc mode)
- applied linguist as problem-solver (in a responsive consultancy mode)'
- applied linguist as educator (in a proactive, futurist mode)
- applied linguist as joint collaborator and co-researcher (in a consultative, reflexive mode) (Sarangi 2005).

And finally,

6. That such research privileges, more than other modes of practice, two key constructs:

(a) The one to do with the nature of the site and its communities of practice, regarding the *categorisation* of its concepts, addressing questions such as:

- What are some of the categories and classifications that are being worked with in that site (in relation to events, persons, cases)?
- How are such categorisations arrived at? How do people 'do' categorising? What kinds of actions, interactions, verbal behaviours are associated with 'establishing, defending, defining, refuting' such categorisations?

(b) The second (that is, *accountability*), which has more to do with the researcher's integrity vis-à-vis his or her participants, matters of professional membership, themes and foci of action, and the communities of practice with which such a researcher is engaged, addressing such questions as:

- How is *accountability* realised and defined in context?
- What instruments, procedures, artefacts does accountability call up in contexts of practice? How is accountability worked on and worked up in talk, writing, visualising?

So, as a conclusion to what I count to be a remarkable volume, the issues of impact and generalisability come clearly to the fore. Exploration of course has its goals; it is quite generally directed at Goffman's famous question: '*what is it that's going on here?*'. But not all goals are so specifiable in advance; goals emerge in transit as it were, and are seen differently by explorers (and the communities they 'explore'). Furthermore, explorations, like journeys, need accounts. But they need generalisable accounts if they are to have impact and significance beyond the personal and biographical. Here, inquiries into professional role, the potential and cautions surrounding participation, the dubieties surrounding the relevance of data, all contribute to the central question of interpretability and understanding, but they also contribute to the issue of generalisability from the explored case.

Here again the two Parts of this volume not only afford significant interplays within each other, they do so across the volume. But to see them as more than parts of a whole is the challenge of achieving relevance. Cases are not just generalisable in relation to other, potentially 'similar', cases; cases engender generalisability through the challenges they pose, both philosophical and methodological. At the same time, 'thick participation' and the achievement of 'thick descriptions' remains the goal which will underwrite such generalisability. Apart from everything else of value, what such exploratory research focused on critical explanation does do is to enhance the evidential warrants for any claims we jointly make. That objective is the *most* important of all.

Bibliography

Aissaoui, M. (2005), 'Pavloff: une passerelle entre deux rêves', *Le Figaro*, 1 September, 2.

Ament, J. (2005), Report 10: American Jewish Religious Denominations, in *United Jewish Communities Report Series on the National Jewish Population Survey 2000–01*.

Anderson, B. (1991), *Imagined Communities: Reflections on the Origin and Spread of Nationalism*, rev. edn (London and New York: Verso).

Anderson, C. (2005), 'Real and Ideal Space of Disability in American Stadiums and Arenas', in Shelly Tremain (ed.), *Foucault and the Government of Disability* (Ann Arbor MI: University of Michigan Press).

Anker, K. (2005), 'The Truth in Painting: Cultural Artefacts as Proof of Native Title', *Law Text Culture* 9, 91–124.

'Annual ADL Audit: Anti-Semitic Incidents Decline in 2005 But Levels Still of Concern in US.' 2006 Advance Press Release.

Anon. (2003), 'Building Effective Indigenous Governance: The Way Forward for Northern Territory Regions and Communities' – background issues paper prepared for the NT Indigenous Governance Conference, Jabiru, 4–7 November 2003.

Anon. (1971), 'The Texas Decision', *New York Times*, 16 January, F.14.

Archbold, B. (2005), Solicitor, Marsdens Law Group, Parramatta, NSW. Personal communication, 26 May.

Augoustinos, M., Tuffin, K. and Rapley, M. (1999), 'Genocide or Failure to Gel? Racism, History and Nationalism in Australian Talk', *Discourse & Society* 10, 351–78.

Australian Law Reform Commission (2005), *Review of the Uniform Evidence Acts*, Discussion Paper 69 (Sydney: ALRC).

Baile, D. (1998), 'The Melting Pot and Beyond', in David Baile, Michael Galchinsky and Susannah Heschel (eds), *American Jews: Insider/Outsider and Multiculturalism* (Berkeley CA, Los Angeles and London).

Baker, H.D.R. (1979), *Chinese Family and Kinship* (London and Basingstoke: Macmillan).

Balkin, J.M. (1998), *Cultural Software: a Theory of Ideology* (New Haven CT: Yale University Press).

Bamforth, N. (1997), *Sexuality, Morals and Justice: a Theory of Lesbian and Gay Rights Law* (London and Washington DC: Cassell).

Barcelona in Progress, Center for Architecture, 536 LaGuardia Place, New York, NY 10012.

Barkat, A. (2007), 'Marked Rise in Attacks on Jews in Europe over the Past Year', *Haaretz*, 29 January.

Barnett, H. (1998), *Introduction to Feminist Jurisprudence* (London: Cavendish Publishing).

Bass, G.J. (2006), 'What Really Causes Civil War?', *New York Times Magazine*, 13 August.

Batty, D. (dir.) (1998), *Jila: Painted Waters of the Great Sandy Desert Mangkaja* [Video] Arts Resource Agency Aboriginal Corporation and the Kimberley Land Council in association with SBS Independent and Desert Pictures (Fitzroy Crossing).

Bergalli, R. (1997), 'Talk on Imprisonment', Okupa Can Cadena, Barcelona.

Bernhardt, K. (1999), *Women and Property in China: 960–1949* (Stanford CA: Stanford University Press).

Bernstein, R.A. and Dyer, J.A. (1992), *An Introduction to Political Science Methods*, 3rd edn (Englewood Cliffs NJ: Prentice Hall).

Bhatia, V., Engberg, J., Gotti, M. and Heller, D. (eds) (2005), *Vagueness in Normative Texts* (Bern: Peter Lang).

Billinghurst, M. and Kato, H. (2002), 'Out and About – Real World Teleconferencing', *BT Technology Journal* 18/1, 80–82.

Birdwhistell, R. (1970), 'Kinesics and Context: Essays on Body Motion Communication', in Burgoon, J.K., Buller, D.B. and Woodall, W.G. (eds), *Nonverbal Communication: the Unspoken Dialogue*, 2nd edn (New York: McGraw-Hill).

Bishop, H. and Jaworski, A. (2003), '"We Beat 'Em": Nationalism and the Hegemony of Homogeneity in the British Press Reportage of Germany versus England during Euro 2000', *Discourse & Society* 14, 243–71.

Bittker, B.I. (1973), *The Case for Black Reparations* (New York: Random House).

Blanck, P.D., and Rosenthal, R. (1992), 'Nonverbal Behaviour in the Courtroom', in Knapp, M.L., and Hall, J.A. (eds), *Nonverbal Communication in Human Interaction*, 5th edn (Victoria, Australia: Nelson Thomson Learning).

Blinder, A.S. (1973), 'Wage Discrimination: Reduced Form and Structural Estimates', *Journal of Human Resources* 8, 436–55.

Blommaert, J. (2005), *Discourse: a Critical Introduction* (Cambridge: Cambridge University Press).

Bollinger, L. (1986), *The Tolerant Society* (New York: Oxford University Press).

Braman, D. (1999), 'Of Race and Immutability', *UCLA Law Review* 46, 1375–1462.

Brigham, J. (1996), 'The Other Countries of American Law', *Social Identities: Journal for the Study of Race, Nation and Culture* 2/2, 237–254.

Brigham, J. (1997), *Constitution of Interests* (New York: New York University Press).

Brigham, J. and Moore, K. (1997), 'Symposium on Domestic Colonialism', *The Legal Studies Forum*, vol. 21.

Bromage, M.C. (1956), *De Valera and the March of a Nation* (New York: Noonday Press).
Bruner, M.L. (2002), *Strategies of Remembrance: the Rhetorical Dimensions of National Identity Construction* (Columbia SC: University of South Carolina Press).
Buchanan, R. and Pahuja, S. (2004), 'Law, Nation and (Imagined) International Communities', *Law, Text, Culture* 8, 137–66.
Burgoon, J.K., Buller, D.B. and Woodall, W.G. (1996), *Nonverbal Communication: the Unspoken Dialogue*, 2nd edn (New York: McGraw-Hill).
Burke, T. (2004), 'The Judicial Implementation of Statutes: Three Stories About the Courts and the Americans with Disabilities Act', in Mark C. Miller and Jeb Barnes (eds), *Making Policy, Making Law* (Georgetown: Georgetown Press).
Buxbaum, D.C. (ed.) (1978), *Chinese Family Law and Social Change: In Historical and Comparative Perspective* (Seattle WA: University of Washington Press).
Campbell, D. (1992), *Writing Security: United States Foreign Policy and the Politics of Identity* (Minneapolis MN: University of Minnesota Press).
Candlin, S. and Candlin, C.N. (2007), 'Nursing over Time and Space: Some Issues for the Construct "Community of Practice"', in R. Iedema (ed.), *The Discourse of Hospital Communication: Tracing Complexities in Contemporary Health Care Organizations* (London: Palgrave), 244–67.
Cao, D. (2004), *Chinese Law: a Language Perspective* (Aldershot: Ashgate).
Carbado, D.W. and Mitu, G. (2003), 'Book Review: *The Law and Economics of Critical Race Theory: Crossroads, Directions, and a New Critical Race Theory*, Francisco Valdes, Jerome McCristal Culp, and Angela P. Harris (eds)', *Yale Law Journal* 112, 1757–1828.
Carroll, L. (1865), *Alice's Adventures in Wonderland* (London: Macmillan & Co).
Celis, W. (1994), 3d, 'San Antonio,' *New York Times*, 10 April, EDUC30.
Chakravarty, D. (2001), *Provincializing Europe: Post-Colonial Thought and Historical Difference* (Princeton NJ: Princeton University Press).
Chandler, D. (2002), *Semiotics – the Basics* (New York: Routledge). Reprinted with text corrections 2006 (twice).
Chayette, S. (2002), '"Un 11 septembre politique", suggère la presse de province', *Le Monde*, 23 April.
Chen, J. (1999), *Chinese Law: Towards an Understanding of Chinese Law, Its Nature and Developments* (The Hague: Kluwer Law International).
Chen, J. and He, Y. (2005), 'On the Standardization of Legal Terms and the Development of Legal System', *Standardization of Legal Terms and Information Technology* 2, 33–5.
Cohen, A. (2004). 'The Supreme Struggle', *New York Times*, 18 January, 22–27.
Cohen, N.W. (1988), '*Shaare Tefila Congregation v. Cobb:* A New Departure in American Jewish Defense?', *Jewish History* 3, 95–108.
Colombani, J.M. (2002), 'Editorial: La Blessure', *Le Monde*, 23 April.

Condor, S. (2000), 'Pride and Prejudice: Identity Management in English People's Talk about "This Country"', *Discourse & Society* 11, 175–205.
Conley, J.M. and O'Barr, W.M. (1990), *Rules versus Relationships: the Ethnography of Legal Discourse* (Chicago: University of Chicago Press).
Conley, V.A. (ed.) (1993), on behalf of the Miami Theory Collective, *Rethinking Technologies* (Minneapolis MN: University of Minnesota Press).
Cotton, J. (1988), 'On The Disposition of Wage Differentials', *Review of Economics and Statistics* 70, 236–43.
Coulthard, M. (2004), 'Whose voice is it? Invented and Concealed Dialogue in Written Records of Verbal Evidence Produced by the Police', in Cotterill, J. (ed.) *Language in the Legal Process*, 2nd edn (New York: Palgrave Macmillan), 19–34.
Courtright, N. (2005), 'Medici Florence and the Invention of Queenly Authority in France', *Queens, Queens, Queens and Empresses*, symposium, 29 October, Amherst College, Mass. (unpublished).
Cover, R. (1992), 'Violence and the Word', in Martha Minow, Michael Ryan and Austin Sarat (eds), *Narrative, Violence, and the Law: the Essays of Robert Cover* (Ann Arbor MI: University of Michigan Press).
Coward, R. and Ellis, J. (1977), *Language and Materialism* (London: Routledge & Kegan Paul).
Csajbók A., Kelemen, E., Szilágyi István, H. and Baksa, A. (2002), *Among Roma* (Miskolc).
Csepeli, Gy., Örkény, A. and Székely, M. (1997), 'Rendőrök és romák. Szertelen módszerek. A megkülönböztetésmentes viselkedés lehetőségei és akadályai' ['Policemen and Romas. Excentric Methods. The Possibilities and Limits of Non-Discriminative Behavior'], in Csányi, K. (ed.), *Szöveggyűjtemény a kisebbségi ügyek rendőrségi kezelésének tanulmányozásához* [*A Reader for the Study of Cases of Minority Handling by the Police*] (Budapest: COLPI), 130–172.
Dahl, R.A. (1989), *Democracy and Its Critics* (New Haven CT: Yale University Press).
Daily Telegraph, The (2004), 'Courting Violence: 67 Prison Officers Hurt by Criminals', 25 September.
Davila, A. (2000), 'Mapping Latinidad: Language and Culture in the Spanish TV Battleground', *Television and New Media* 1, 75–94.
Davis, D. and Harrell, S. (eds) (1993), *Chinese Families in the Post-Mao Era* (Berkeley CA: University of California Press).
De Cillia, R., Reisigl, M. and Wodak, R. (1999), 'The Discursive Construction of National Identities', *Discourse & Society* 10, 149–73.
de Gaulle, C. (1954), *Mémoires de guerre*, vol. I: *L'Appel* (Paris: Librairie Plon).
De Jong, H.G. (1990), *De oorlogsverklaring in het internationale en het nationale recht* [*The Declaration of War in International and National Law*], in *RM Themis* 3, 102.

Delgado, R. and Stefancic J. (1994), *Failed Revolutions: Social Reform and the Limits of Legal Imagination* (Boulder CO, San Francisco and Oxford (UK): Westview Press).

Dewitte, P. (2003), *Deux siècles d'immigration en France* (Paris: La Documentation Française). [Publication of the Agence pour le Développement des Relations Interculturelles].

Diamant, N.J. (2000), *Revolutionizing the Family: Politics, Love, and Divorce in Urban and Rural China, 1949–1968* (Berkeley CA: University of California Press).

Dianina, K. (2005), 'The Russian Minerva: Catherine the Great and Her Hermitage Museum', *Queens, Queens, Queens and Empresses*, symposium, 29 October, Amherst College, Mass. (unpublished).

Di Lisi, R.A. (1989), 'Note: Justice White Mixes More Than Just Color To Create a New Shade of Racial Protection', *Case Western Reserve University* 39, 1343–1370.

Dowley K.M. and Silver, B.D. (2000), 'Subnational and National Loyalty: Cross-National Comparisons', *World Association for Public Opinion Research* 12, 357–71.

Drucker, P.F. (1989), *The New Realities* (New York: Harper & Row).

Dumm, T. (1999), *A Politics of the Ordinary* (New York: New York University Press).

Duncan, W. (2005), representing the Community Relations Commission, a division of the Attorney General's Department, NSW, personal communication, 6 May.

Dunmire, P. (2005), 'Preempting the Future: Rhetoric and Ideology of the Future in Political Discourse', *Discourse & Society* 16, 481–513.

Durand, J. and Tourancheau, P. (2004), 'Violentée devant des passagers passifs', *Libération*, 12 July, 2.

Eastwood, C. and Patton, W. (2002), *The Experiences of Child Complainants of Sexual Abuse in the Criminal Justice System* (Queensland: University of Technology).

Eco, U. (1976), *A Theory of Semiotics* (Bloomington IN: Indiana University Press).

Egyed, M. (1996), 'Cigányok az igazságszolgáltatásban' ['Gypsies in the Administration of Justice'], *Esély* 5, 78–88.

Ekman, P. (1965), 'Differential Communication of Affect by Head and Body Cues', *Journal of Personality and Social Psychology* 2, 726–35.

Ekman, P. and Freisen, W.V. (1967), 'Head and Body Cues in the Judgement of Emotions: a Reformulation', *Perceptual and Motor Skills* 24, 711–24.

Ekman, P., and Friesen, W.V. (1971), 'Constants across Cultures in the Face and Emotion', *Journal of Personality and Social Psychology* 17/2, 124–9.

Ekman, P., O'Sullivan, M. and Frank, M.G. (1999), 'A Few can Catch a Liar', *Psychological Science* 10/3, May, 263–6.

Elysée (2004), 'Chirac en visite au Chambon-sur-Lignon', *Le Figaro*, 2 July, 6.

Fairclough, N. (1989), *Language and Power* (London: Longman).
Fairclough, N. (1995), *Critical Discourse Analysis: the Critical Study of Language* (London and New York: Longman).
Fauroux, R. and Chérifi, H. (2003), *Nous sommes tous les immigrés* (Paris: Robert Laffont).
Feigenson, N. and Dunn, M.A. (2003), 'New Visual Technologies in Court: Directions for Research', *Law and Human Behavior* 27/1, February, 109–126.
Fellows, L. (1974), 'Connecticut School Taxing Is Ruled Unconstitutional; Special to The New York Times Connecticut School Taxing Overturned', *New York Times*, 28 December, 1.
Fellows, L. (1977), 'Only Money', *New York Times*, 1 May, CN26.
Feng, X. (2001/2002), 'A Review of the Development of Marriage Law in the People's Republic of China', *University of Detroit Mercy Law Review* 79, 331–68.
Fischer, D.H. (1989), *Albion's Seed: Four British Folkways in America* (New York: Oxford University Press).
Fish, S. (1980), *Is There A Text In This Class?* (Cambridge MA: Harvard University Press).
Fish, S. (1994), *There's No Such Thing as Free Speech ... and It's a Good Thing, Too* (New York and Oxford: Oxford University Press).
Fish, S. (1999), *The Trouble with Principle* (Cambridge MA and London: Harvard University Press).
Fishman, J.A. (1972), *Language and Nationalism: Two Integrative Essays* (Rowley MA: Newbury House).
Fiske, E.B. (1977), 'The Growing Dilemma of Inequities in School Financing Based on Property Taxes', *New York Times*, 17 February, 16.
Fiske, E.B. (1982), 'A Setback for the Move to Alter School Financing', *New York Times*, 24 June, B7.
Fiske, J. (1987), *Television Culture* (New York: Routledge).
Fitzgerald, F.S. (1926). 'The Rich Boy', *The Red Book Magazine*, January–February 1926.
Formoso, B. (1986), *Tsiganes et sédentaires* (Paris: L'Harmattan).
Freeman, S. (1986), 'Defaced Synagogue Raises Civil Rights Issue – Statute Should Protect Jews', *Legal Times*, 20 October.
Friedman, B.P. (2005), *The Moral Consequences of Economic Growth* (New York: Random House).
Gattegno, H. and Ridet, P. (2002), 'Le duel Chirac-Le Pen provoque un séisme politique', *Le Monde*, 4 April.
Gaze, B. (2002), 'Context and Interpretation in Anti-Discrimination Law', *Melbourne University Law Review* 26, 325–54.
Geertz, C. (1973), *The Interpretation of Cultures* (New York: Basic Books).
Gibson, B. (2006), Prison guard, Silverwater Correctional Centre, Silverwater, NSW; personal communication, 2 June.

Gilmartin, C.K., Hershatter, G., Rofel, L. and White, T. (eds) (1994), *Engendering China: Women, Culture, and the State* (Cambridge MA: Harvard University Press).

Giscard d'Estaing, V. (2000), *Les Français: réflexions sur le destin d'un peuple* (Paris: Plon/Compagnie 12).

Gluckman, M. (1965), *Politics, Law and Ritual in Tribal Society* (Chicago: Aldine).

Goetz, J. and LeCompte, M. (1984), *Ethnography and Qualitative Design in Educational Research* (Orlando FA: Academic Press).

Goffman, E. (1981), 'Footing', in E. Goffman, *Forms of Talk* (Oxford: Blackwell), 124–59.

Goodrich, P. (1986), *Reading the Law: a Critical Introduction to Legal Method and Techniques* (Oxford: Blackwell).

Graham, E.L. (2002), *Representations of the Posthuman: Monsters, Aliens and Others in Popular Culture* (Manchester: Manchester University Press).

Griffiths, J. (1986), 'What is Legal Pluralism?', *Journal of Legal Pluralism* 24, 1–50.

Griffiths, J. (2003), 'The Social Working of Legal Rules', *Journal of Legal Pluralism* 48, 1–84.

Grönfors, M. (1997), 'Institutional Non-Marriage in the Finnish Roma Community and its Relationship to the Roma Traditional Law', *The American Journal of Comparative Law* 2, 305–29.

Grossfeld, B. (1990), *The Strength and Weakness of Comparative Law*, trans. T. Weir (Oxford: Clarendon Press).

Grotius, H. (1993), *De Jure Belli ac Pacem, Libri Tres* (Aalen: Scientia Verlag) (first publ. 1625).

Guattari, F. (1993), 'Machinic Heterogenesis', in Conley, V.A. (ed.), on behalf of the Miami Theory Collective, *Rethinking Technologies* (Minneapolis MN: University of Minnesota Press), 13–27.

Guo, L. (2003), 'Xin hunyinfa yu lihun funu de caichanquan: Hu Haiying lihunan ge'an yanjiu' ['The New Marriage Law and Property Rights of Divorced Women: a Case Study of Hu Haiying Divorce Case'], seminar paper at the Chinese University of Hong Kong, <www.iolaw.org.cn/paper/paper76.asp>.

Hacker, A. (1970), *The End of the American Era* (New York: Atherton).

Halbwachs, M. (1980), *The Collective Memory*, trans. F.J. Ditter (Jr.) and V.Y. Ditter (New York: Harper & Row).

Hall, C., Slembrouck, S. and Sarangi, S. (2006), *Language Practices in Social Work: Categorisation and Accountability in Child Welfare* (London. Routledge).

Hall, S. (1996), 'The Question of Cultural Identity', in Stuart Hall, David Held, Don Hubert and Kenneth Thompson (eds), *Modernity: an Introduction to Modern Societies* (Oxford and Cambridge MA: Blackwell), 595–634.

Han, A.M. (2000), 'Holding Up More than Half the Sky: Marketization and the Status of Women in China', in Adrien Katherine Wing (ed.), *Global Critical*

Race Feminism: an International Reader (New York: New York University Press).

Hare, R.M. (1952), *The Language of Morals* (Oxford: Clarendon Press).

Harrington, C. (1985), *Shadow Justice: the Ideology and Institutionalization of Alternatives to Court* (Westport CT: Greenwood Press).

Hart, H.L.A. (1983), 'Self-Referring Laws', in his *Essays in Jurisprudence and Philosophy* (Oxford: Oxford University Press).

Hartsock, N.C.M. (1998), 'The Kinship Abstraction in Feminist Theory', in Nancy C.M. Hartsock (ed.), *The Feminist Standpoint Revisited and Other Essays* (Boulder CO: Westview Press), 171–91.

Havas, G. (1999), *Gazdálkodó cigányok* [*Managing Gypsies*] (Budapest: Autonómia Alapitvány).

Havas, G.. and Kemény, I. (1995), 'A magyarországi romákról' ['On the Hungarian Romas'], *Szociológiai Szemle* 3, 3–20.

Hawkes, T. (1977), *Structuralism and Semiotics* (London: Routledge).

Hellman, S.C. (1995), *Portrait of American Jews: the Last Half of the 20th Century* (Seattle WA and London: University of Washington Press).

Hershatter, G. (1991), 'Prostitution and Market in Women in Early Twentieth-Century Shanghai', in Rubie S. Watson and Patricia Buckley Ebrey (eds), *Marriage and Inequality in Chinese Society* (Berkeley CA: University of California Press), 256–85.

Hickson, M., Stacks, D.W. and Moore, N. (2004), 4th edn, *Nonverbal Communication: Studies and Applications* (Los Angeles CA: Roxbury).

Hodge, R. and Kress, G. (1988), *Social Semiotics* (Cambridge: Polity Press).

Hoffman, S. (2004), 'Is There a Place for "Race" as a Legal Concept?', *Arizona State Law Journal* 36, 1093–1159.

Holland, J.A. and Webb, J.S. (2003), *Learning Legal Rules*, 5th edn (Oxford: Oxford University Press).

Hom, S.K. (1991/92), 'Female Infanticide in China: the Human Rights Spectre and Thoughts Towards (An)other Vision', *Columbia Human Rights Law Review* 23, 249–314.

Hoover, K. and Todd, D. (1995), *The Elements of Social Scientific Thinking*, 6th edn (New York: St. Martin's Press).

Horn, R. (1956), *Groups and the Constitution* (Palo Alto CA: Stanford University Press).

Howell, A.J. and Buxton, H. (2002), 'Active Vision Techniques for Visually Mediated Interaction', papers of the 16th International Conference on Pattern Recognition (ICPR), August 2002, Quebec (Canada), IEEE Computer Society.

Hunter, J.D. (1991), *Culture Wars: the Struggle to Define America* (New York: Basic Books).

Huszár, L. (1998), *És bűnhődés ... A magyar fogvatartottak szociológiai vizsgálata* [*And Punishment ... A Sociological Examination of the Hungarian Detainees*] (Budapest: 1998) (candidate thesis).

Hutchinson, D.L. (2002), 'Critical Race Studies: Progressive Race Blindness?: Individual Identity, Group Politics, and Reform', *UCLA Law Review* 49, 1455–1480.

Ihde, D. (1979), *Technics and Praxis: a Philosophy of Technology* (Dordrecht: Reidel).

Ihde, D. (1990), *Technology and the Lifeworld* (Bloomington IN: Indiana University Press), Chapter 5 at 72–115.

Ihde, D. (1993), *Philosophy of Technology: an Introduction* (New York: Paragon House).

Innis, E.R. (ed.) (1985), *Semiotics – an Introductory Anthology* (Bloomington IN: Indiana University Press).

Jackson, B.S. (1985), *Semiotics and Legal Theory* (London: Routledge & Kegan Paul).

Jackson, B.S. (1992), 'The Wisdom of the Inessential (Review Article on Douzinas, Warrington and McVeigh, *Postmodern Jurisprudence*)', *Legal Studies*, 12/1, 103–117.

Jackson, B.S. (1995), *Making Sense in Law* (Liverpool: Deborah Charles).

Jackson, B.S. (1999), 'Legislation in the Semiotics of Law', in H. van Schooten (ed.), *Semiotics and Legislation. Jurisprudential, Institutional and Sociological Perspectives* (Liverpool: Deborah Charles).

Jackson, K.T. (1985), *Crabgrass Frontier: the Suburbanization of the United States* (New York: Oxford University Press).

Jacobs, J. (1961), *The Death and Life of Great American Cities* (New York: Random House).

Jeffreys, E. (2004), 'Feminist Prostitution Debates: Are There Any Sex Workers in China?', in Anne McLaren (ed.), *Chinese Women: Living and Working* (London: Routledge), 83–106.

Jenkins, E. (1973a), 'School Funding Viewed as Chaotic and Unjust', *New York Times*, 11 March, 1.

Jenkins, E. (1973b), 'Court's School Ruling Gives States Breathing Spell on Taxes and Reformers a Setback', *New York Times*, 22 March, 33.

Jenkins, E. (1973c), 'Oregon to Vote on School Taxes', *New York Times*, 29 April, 31.

Jennings, J. (2000), 'Citizenship, Republicanism and Multiculturalism in Contemporary France', *British Journal of Political Science* 30, 575–98.

Johnson, R. (2005), 'Blurred Boundaries: a Double-Voiced Dialogue on Regulatory Regimes and Embodied Space', *Law, Text, Culture* 9, 157–77.

Karst, K.L. (1995), 'Myths of Identity: Individual and Group Portraits Of Race and Sexual Orientation', *UCLA Law Review* 43, 263–323.

Katyal, S.K. (2006), 'Semiotic Disobedience', *Washington University Law Review* 84, 489–572.

Kellman, M. (1987), *A Guide to Critical Legal Studies* (Cambridge MA and London: Harvard University Press).

Kennedy, D. (1997), *A Critique of Adjudication: Fin de Siècle* (Cambridge MA and London: Harvard University Press).

Kenny, C. (1929), 'Wife Selling in England', *Law Quarterly Review* 45, 494.

Ketcham, H. (1958), *Civilization and Climate* (New Haven CT: Yale University Press).

Ketley, H. and Ozich, C. (2003), '"Snapshots of Adventitious Content": the Assessment of Oral and Historical Evidence in Native Title Claims', *Studies in Western Australian History* 23, 83–94.

Kevelson, R. (1988a), 'Perspectives on the Legal Systems', in *The Law as a System of Signs* (New York and London: Plenum Press), 23–31.

Kevelson, R. (1988b), 'A Comparatist View', in *The Law as a System of Signs* (New York and London: Plenum Press), 33–47.

Kevelson, R. (1988c), 'Legal Semiotics: the Peircean Framework', in *The Law as a System of Signs* (New York and London: Plenum Press), 3–21.

Kevelson, R. (1988d), *The Law as a System of Signs* (New York and London: Plenum Press).

Kiefer, C.S. (2006), 'Introduction', *Queens, Queens, Queens and Empresses*, symposium, 29 October, Amherst College, Mass. (unpublished)

Knapp, M.L., and Hall, J.A (eds) (2002), *Nonverbal Communication in Human Interaction* (Victoria, Australia: Nelson Thomson Learning).

Ko, D., JaHyun, K.H. and Piggott J.P. (eds) (2003), *Women and Confucian Cultures in Premodern China, Korea and Japan* (Berkeley CA: University of California Press).

Kotler-Berkowitz, L. (2004), 'Report 5: Economic Vulnerability in the American Jewish Population', in *United Jewish Communities Report Series on the National Jewish Population Survey 2000–01*.

Krampen, M. (1997), 'Semiosis of the Mass Media: Modeling a Complex Process', in Noth, W. (ed.), *Semiotics of the Media: State of Art, Projects and Perspectives* (Berlin: Mouton de Gruyter), 87–98.

Landowski, E. (1988), 'Towards a Semiotic and Narrative Approach to Law', *International Journal for the Semiotics of Law* I/1, 79–105.

Laurence, J. and Vaisse, J. (2005), 'Understanding Urban Riots in France', *New Europe Review*, 1 December. Posted on <www.brookings.org> (last accessed 1 April 2006).

Layder, D. (1993), *New Strategies of Social Research* (Cambridge: Polity Press).

Lerman, C.L. (1983), 'Dominant Discourse: the Institutional Voice and Control of Topic', in Howard Davis and Paul Walton (eds), *Language, Image, Media* (Oxford: Blackwell), 75–103.

Lessig, L. (2004), *Free Culture* (New York: Penguin).

Lévi-Strauss, C. (1969) *The Elementary Structures of Kinship*, ed. by R. Needham, trans. by J. Harle Bell and J.R. von Sturmer (Boston MA: Beacon Press).

Lewis, F.P. (1988), Book Review, *American Political Science Review* 82, 2, June, 622–23.

Liu, H. (2002), 'Legal Effects on de Facto Marriage', *The Journal of Zhenzhou Communist Party Committee* 59/5, 44–5.
Lipsky, M. (1980), *Street-Level Bureaucracy: Dilemmas of the Individual in Public Services* (New York: Russell Sage Foundation).
Lopez, Ian F. Haney (1994), 'The Social Construction of Race: Some Observations On Illusion, Fabrication, and Choice', *Harvard Civil Rights-Civil Liberties Law Review* 29, 1–62.
Loss, S. and H. Szilágyi, I. (2001), 'A "cigány per"' [The 'Gypsy Trial'], *Beszélő* VI, 41, 94–101.
Lyotard, J.-F. (1984), 'The *Différend*, the Referent, and the Proper Name', *Diacritics* 14/3, 4–14.
McCann, M. (1999), 'How the Supreme Court Matters in American Politics: New Institutionalist Perspectives', in H. Gillman and C. Clayton (eds), *The Supreme Court in American Politics: New Institutionalist Interpretations* (Lawrence KS: University Press of Kansas), 63–97.
McLaren, A. (ed.) (2004), *Chinese Women: Living and Working* (London: Routledge).
Maine, H. (1861), *Ancient Law: Its Connection With the Early History of Society, and Its Relation to Modern Ideas* (London: John Murray).
Marcus, Kenneth L. (2007), 'Anti-Zionism as Racism: Campus Anti-Semitism and the Civil Rights Act of 1964', *William and Mary Bill of Rights Journal* 15, 837.
Marusek, S. (2005), 'Wheelchair as Semiotic: Space Governance of the American Handicapped Parking Space', *Law, Text, Culture* 9, 177–88.
Mehrabian, A. (1976), *Public Places and Private Spaces* (New York: Basic Books).
Mehrabian, A. and Ferris, S. (1967), 'Inferences of Attitudes from Nonverbal Communication in Two Channels', *Journal of Consulting Psychology* 31, 248–52.
Menafee, S. (1981), *Wives for Sale* (Oxford: Oxford University Press).
Michelet, J. (1946), *Le Peuple* (Paris: Librairie Marcel Didier).
Minow, M. (1987), 'The Supreme Court, 1986 Term: Forward: Justice Engendered', *Harvard Law Review* 101, 10–95.
Minow, M. (1996), 'Speech: Not Only for Myself: Identity, Politics, And Law', *Oregon Law Review* 75, 647–98.
Minow, M. (1997), *Not Only for Myself: Identity, Politics, and the Law* (New York: The New Press).
Minsker, N.L. (1998), '"I Have a Dream – Never Forget": When Rhetoric Becomes Law, A Comparison of the Jurisprudence of Race In Germany and the United States', *Harvard BlackLetter Law Journal* 14, 113–169.
Moore, S.F. (1973), 'Law and Social Change: the Semi-Autonomous Social Field as an Appropriate Subject of Study', *Law and Society Review*, 719–46.
Moore, S.F. and Myerhoff, B.G. (eds) (1977), *Secular Ritual* (Assen: Van Gorkum).

Morphy, H. (1998), *Aboriginal Art* (London: Phaidon Press).

Nancy, J. (1993), 'War, Law, Sovereignty – Techne', in Conley, V.A. (ed.), on behalf of the Miami Theory Collective, *Rethinking Technologies* (Minneapolis MN: University of Minnesota Press), 28–58.

Native Title Newsletter 2002, no. 3, May–June.

Neate, G. (1997/98), 'Dispensing with the Rules of Evidence – s82(3) of the Native Title Act – Welcome the Rules of Rafferty?', *Native Title News* 3/4, 54–6.

Neate, G. (2004), '"Speaking for Country" and Speaking about Country: Some Issues in the Resolution of Indigenous Land Claims in Australia', paper delivered to the Joint Study Institute Sydney, Australia, 21 February.

New York State Supreme Court (1982), 'Excerpts From Ruling On Financing Schools', with commentary, *New York, Times*, 24 June, B6–B7.

Nietzsche, F. (1909), 'The Use and Abuse of History', in Frederick Nietzsche, *Complete Works*, vol. 1, part 2, ed. O. Levy, trans. A. Collins (Edinburgh and London: T.N. Foulis), 1–100.

Nursanlo, C. (2004), Former prison inmate of Cessnock Prison, Newcastle, NSW; personal communication, 14 October.

Ocko, J. (1991), 'Women, Property and Law in the People's Republic of China', in Watson, Rubie S. and Ebrey, Patricia Buckley (eds), *Marriage and Inequality in Chinese Society* (Berkeley CA: University of California Press), 313–46.

O'Connell, L. and Birdsall, N. (2001), 'Race, Human Capital Inequality, and Income Distribution,' in C.V. Hamilton (ed.), *Beyond Racism: Race and Inequality in Brazil, South Africa, and the United States* (Boulder CO: Lynne Rienner), 275–322.

Ogletree, C.J. (2004), *All Deliberate Speed: Reflections on the First Half-Century of Brown vs. The Board of Education* (New York: Norton).

Ogletree, C.J, and de Silva-de Alwis, R. (2002), 'When Gender Differences Become a Trap: The Impact of China's Labo[u]r Law on Women', *Yale Journal of Law and Feminism* 14, 69–96.

Oliver, M.C. (2001), 'The Social Cost of Racial Privilege in the United States: an Asset Perspective', in C.V. Hamilton (ed.) *Beyond Racism: Race and Inequality in Brazil, South Africa, and the United States* (Boulder CO: Lynne Rienner), 251–74.

Pancho, M. (2004), 'Racisme: l'appel de Chirac au "sursaut" des Français', *Le Monde*, 9 July.

Parliament of New South Wales Legislation Review Committee (2007), *Legislation Review Digest No. 7 of 2007* (New South Wales, Australia: Parliament of New South Wales), 23 November.

Pateman, C. (1988), *The Sexual Contract* (Stanford CA: Stanford University Press).

Pearce, C.S. (1931–58), *Collected Papers of C.S. Pearce* (8 vols, Cambridge MA: Harvard University Press).

Pearson, M. (2004), *The Journalist's Guide to Media Law: Dealing with Legal and Ethical Issues*, 2nd edn (Crows Nest, NSW: Allen & Unwin).

Pederson, I. (2005), ‘A Semiotics of Human Action for Wearable Augmented Reality Interfaces’, *Semiotica*, 155, 1/4, 183–200.

Phillips, K. (2006), *American Theocracy* (New York: Viking).

Pinkerton, S. (1998), ‘Poll Analysis: American Jews Express Diverse Opinions on Jewish Life in the U.S.’, *L.A. Times*, 19 April.

Póczik, Sz. (1997), ‘Etnikai hátrányok és a roma kisebbség kriminológiai nézőpontból’ [‘Ethnic Disadvantage and the Gypsy Minority from a Criminological Perspective’], *Belügyi Szemle* 7–8, 15–40.

Prochaska, P.A. (1987), Civil Rights Protection for Caucasian Ethnic Groups: *Saint Francis College v. Al-Khazraji* and *Shaare Tefila Congregation v. Cobb* (Washington DC: Congressional Research Service, Library of Congress).

Prónai, Cs. (1995), *Cigánykutatás és kulturális antropológia* [*Gypsy Lore and Cultural Anthropology*] (Budapest, Kaposvar: ELTE Btk., Csokonai V. M. Főiskola).

Putnam, R. (2007), ‘*E Pluribus Unum*: Diversity and Community in the Twenty-First Century,’ *Scandinavian Political Studies* 30, 2, 137–74.

Redmond, J.G. (1989), ‘Note: Redefining Race in *Saint Francis College v. Al-Khazraji* and *Shaare Tefila Congregation v. Cobb*: Using Dictionaries Instead of the Thirteenth Amendment’, *Vanderbilt Law Review* 42, 209–31.

Reilly, A. (1998), ‘Entering a Dream: Two Days of a Native Title Trial in the Northeast Kimberley’, *Law/Text/Culture* 4/1, 196–211.

Reilly, A. (2003), ‘Cartography and Native Title’, *Journal of Australian Studies* 79, 3, 3–14.

Reinhold, R. (1972), ‘John Serrano Jr. et al., and School Tax Equality’, *New York Times,* 10 January, E1.

Renan, E. (1947), ‘Qu’est-ce-qu’une nation?’, in E. Renan, *Oeuvres Complètes*, ed. H. Psichari (Paris: Clamann-Lévy), vol. 1: 887–906. (Orig. publ. 1884.)

Ricento, T. (2003), ‘The Discursive Construction of Americanism’, *Discourse & Society* 14, 611–37.

Richmond, V.P., and McCroskey, J.C. (1995), *Nonverbal Behaviour in Interpersonal Relations*, 3rd edn (Boston MA: Allyn & Bacon).

Rifkin, J. (1980), ‘Toward a Theory of Law and Patriarchy’, *Harvard Women’s Law Journal* 3, 83–96.

Riles, A. (1991), ‘Spheres of Exchange and Spheres of Law: Identity and Power in Chinese Marriage Agreements’, *International Journal for the Sociology of Law* 19, 501–523.

Riley, T. (2006), *On-Site: New Architecture in Spain* (New York: MOMA).

Ringmar, E. (1998), ‘Nationalism: the Idiocy of Intimacy’, *British Journal of Sociology* 49, 534–49.

Roberts, C. and Sarangi, S. (2005), ‘Theme-Oriented Discourse Analysis of Medical Encounters’, *Medical Education* 39, 632–40.

Roche, J. (1963), *The Quest for the Dream* (New York: Macmillan).

Roche, J. (1964), ‘We’ve Never Had More Freedom’ and ‘American Liberty’, in *Shadow and Substance* (New York: Collier Books).

Roithmayr, D. (2001), 'Left over Rights', *Cardozo Law Review* 22, 1113–34.
Rosenthal, R. et al. (1978), in Knapp, M.L. and Hall, J.A. (eds) (2002), *Nonverbal Communication in Human Interaction* (US: Thomson Learning).
Rousseau, J.J. (1916), *Lettre à M. d'Alambert sur les Spectacles* (Paris: Librairie Hachette et Cie).
Rubin, G. (1975), 'The Traffic in Women: Notes on the Political Economy of Sex', in R. Reiter (ed.), *Toward An Anthropology of Women* (New York: Monthly Review Press).
Rush, P. (1990), 'Semiotics in the Trial of Jurisprudence', *The Modern Law Review* 53, 1, 121–29.
Sahlins, M.D. (1965), 'On the Sociology of Primitive Exchange', in Banton, M. (ed.), *The Relevance of Models for Social Anthropology* (London, New York: Tavistock, Praeger), 139–236.
Samuel, G. (2001), 'Methodology and Sources of Law: English Report', in J.-L. Bergel (ed.), *La Methodologie de l'étude des sources du droit* (Aix-en-Provence: Presses Universitaires d'Aix-Marseille), 29–81.
Santos, Boaventura de Sousa (1995), *Toward a New Common Sense – Law, Science and Politics in the Paradigmatic Transition* (New York: Routledge).
Sarangi, S. (2005), 'The Conditions and Consequences of Professional Discourse Studies', *Journal of Applied Linguistics* 2, 3.
Sarangi, S. and Candlin, C.N. (2003), 'Trading between Reflexivity and Relevance: New Challenges for Applied Linguistics', *Applied Linguistics* 24, 3, 271–85.
Sarat, A. (1990), '"The Law Is All Over ...": Power, Resistance and the Legal Consciousness of the Welfare Poor,' *Yale Journal of Law and the Humanities* 2, 343.
Saussure, F. de (1983), *Course in General Linguistics* (London: Duckworth).
Schappes, M.U. (ed.) (1971), *A Documentary History of the Jews of the United States, 1654–1875*, 3rd edn (New York: Schocken).
Schnapper, D. (1991), *La France de l'integration* (Paris: Gallimard).
Schreiner, A.T.M. (1996), 'Ritual and Law', International Congress of Law and Society, Glasgow, 10–13.
Schuchter, A. (1970), *The Black Manifesto and Its Challenge to White America* (Philadelphia PA: Lippincott).
Service France (2002), 'La France mobilisée pour un 1er Mai anti-Le Pen', *Le Monde*, 2 May.
Sharp, P. (2004), Coordinator Video Conferencing, Officer of the Commissioner, New South Wales Government Department of Corrective Services; personal communication, 19 October.
Silbey, S. and Cavicchi, A. (2005), 'The Common Place of Law: Transforming Matters of Concern into the Objects of Everyday Life', in B. Latour (ed.) *Making Things Public: Atmospheres of Democracy* (Cambridge MA: MIT Press), 556–65.
Silbey, S. and Ewick, P. (1998). *The Common Place of Law: Stories from Everyday Life* (Chicago: University of Chicago Press).

Smart, G. (2006), *Writing the Economy: Activity, Genre and Technology in the World of Banking* (London: Equinox).

Smith, D.A. (1998), *Tax Crusaders and the Politics of Direct Democracy* (New York: Routledge).

Smith, T.V. (1941), *The Democratic Tradition in America* (New York: Farrar & Rinehart).

Snyder, L.L. (1954), *The Meaning of Nationalism* (New Brunswick NJ: Rutgers University Press).

Snyder, L.L. (1976), *Varieties of Nationalism: a Comparative Study* (New York: Holt, Rinehart & Winston).

Spahn, E. (1998), 'Shattered Jade, Broken Shoe: Foreign Economic Development and the Sexual Exploitation of Women in China', *Maine Law Review* 50, 255–82.

Staiano-Ross, K. (2005), 'Losing Myself: Body as Icon/Body as Object(s)', *Semiotica* 154, 1/4, 57–94.

Stanner, W.E.H. (1979), 'After the Dreaming', in W.E.H. Stanner, *White Man Got No Dreaming: Essays 1938–1973* (Canberra: ANU Press), 198–248.

Stevens, W.K. (1971), 'U.S. Court Upsets Texas School Tax Tied to Property', *New York Times*, 25 December, 1.

Stevenson, C.L. (1944), *Ethics and Language* (New Haven CT: Yale University Press).

Stewart, M.S. (1987), 'Song Brothers. The Persistence of (Vlach) Gypsy Identity and Community in Socialist Hungary', Ph.D. thesis (London: LSE).

Strathern, M. (2004), 'Losing (Out on) Intellectual Resources', in A. Pottage and M. Mundy (eds), *Law, Anthropology and the Construction of the Social* (Cambridge: Cambridge University Press), 201–33.

Strauber, I.L. (1997), 'Book Review: *Failed Revolutions: Social Reform and the Limits of Legal Imagination* by Richard Delgado and Jean Stefancic', *Law and Politics Book Review* 7, 6, 284–7.

Strauber, I.L. (2002), *Neglected Policies: Constitutional Law and Legal Commentary as Civic Education* (Durham NC and London: Duke University Press).

Strauber, I.L. (2003), 'Framing Pragmatic Aspirations', *Polity* 35, 491–512.

Strelein L (2006), *Compromised Jurisprudence: Native Title Cases Since Mabo* (Canberra: Aboriginal Studies Press).

Szilágyi, István, H. (2005), 'The Roma Way – Comparative Legal Studies: Comparative Law, Sociology and Anthropology', in H. Szilágyi, I. and Paksy, M. (eds), *Ius Unum, Lex Multiplex: Studies in Comparative Law, Theory of State and Legal Philosophy* (Budapest: Szent István Társulat), 129–48.

Szilágyi István, H. and Loss S. (2002), 'Opening Scissors. The Legal Status of the Gypsy Minority in Nowadays Hungary', *Rechtstheorie* 33, 2–4, 483–94.

Tamanaha, B.Z. (2003), 'A Pragmatic Response to the Embarrassing Problems of Ideology Critique in Socio-Legal Studies', in Alfonso Morales (ed.), *Renascent Pragmatism* (Burlington VT: Ashgate).

Tauber, I. (1986), *A hátrányos helyzet és a bűnözés összefüggései, különös tekintettel egyes kisebbségi csoportokra* [*The Relations between Social Disadvantage and Criminality, with Special Regard to Certain Minority Groups*] (Budapest: Tankönyvkiadó).

Tauber, I., Vigh, J. and Madácsi, I. (1988), *A hátrányos helyzet és a bűnözés kapcsolata. Kriminálstatisztika és kriminológiai értékelés* [*The Relationship between Social Disadvantage and Criminality. A Criminal-Statistical and Criminological Evaluation*] (Budapest: BM Könyvkiadó).

Tehranian, J. (2000), 'Note: Performing Whiteness: Naturalization Litigation and the Construction of Racial Identity in America', *Yale Law Journal* 109, 817–48.

Teubner, G. (1986), *Reflexive Law: Autonomy and Regulation* (Berlin: Walter de Gruyter).

Thornton, M. (ed.) (1995), *Public and Private: Feminist Legal Debates* (Melbourne: Oxford University Press).

Tierney, S. (2006), *Constitutional Law and National Pluralism* (Oxford: Oxford University Press).

Tolstoy, L. (1905), *Christianity and Patriotism* (Chicago: Open Court Publishing). (Orig. publ. 1894.)

Tönnies, F. (1887), *Gemeinschaft und Gesellschaft* (Leipzig: Fues's Verlag).

Toulmin, S.E. (1958), *The Uses of Argument* (Cambridge: Cambridge University Press).

Toussaint, S., Sullivan, P. and Yu, S. (2005), 'Water Ways in Aboriginal Australia: an Interconnected Analysis', *Anthropological Forum* 15, 1, 61–74.

Unger, R.M. (1986), *The Critical Legal Studies Movement* (Cambridge MA and London: Harvard University Press).

United States Supreme Court (1972), 'Summary of Actions Taken by the Supreme Court'. *New York Times*, 8 June, 34.

United States Supreme Court (1974), 'Excerpts from Supreme Court Decision Barring Detroit-Suburban School Merger', *New York Times*, 26 July, 17.

Urla, J. (2003), 'Kafe Antzokia: the Global Meets the Local in Basque Cultural Politics', *Papeles del CEIC* 10, 6.

Vanderlinden, J. (1987), 'D'une bonne lecture des sources du droit: essai d'histoire comparée', *Journal of African Law* 31, 1/2, 29–36.

Van der Valk, I. (2003), 'Right-Wing Parliamentary Discourse on Immigration in France', *Discourse & Society* 14, 309–348.

van Dijk, Teun A. (1993), 'Principles of Critical Discourse Analysis', *Discourse & Society* 4, 249–83.

Van Hoecke, M. (2002), *Law as Communication* (Oxford: Hart).

van Leewen, T. (2007), 'Legitimation in Discourse and Communication', *Discourse & Communication* 1, 91–121.

van Schooten, H. (2001), 'The Declaration of War in the Dutch Constitution and Models of Legal Communication', *International Journal for the Semiotics of Law* 14, 329–44.

van Schooten, H. (2004), 'On War, Peace and Armed Conflict', *International Journal for the Semiotics of Law* 17, 169–83.
van Schooten, H. (2005), 'Oorlog en vrede' ['War and Peace'], in *Getuigend Staatsrecht* [*Testifying Constitutional Law*], *Liber Amicorum A.K. Koekkoek* (Nijmegen: Wolf Legal Publishers), 83–99.
van Schooten, H. (2007), 'A Peacekeeping Mission as a New Category of War? An Institutional Analysis', in Luc Wintgens (ed.), *Legislation in Context: Essays in Legisprudence* (Aldershot: Ashgate).
Vertigan, N. (2005), Senior Advocate, Legal Aid New South Wales, Parramatta, NSW; personal communication, 1 June.
Virilio, P. (1993), 'The Third Interval: a Critical Transition', in Conley, V.A. (ed.), on behalf of the Miami Theory Collective, *Rethinking Technologies* (Minneapolis MN: University of Minnesota Press), 3–12.
Viroli, M. (1995), *For Love of Country: an Essay on Patriotism and Nationalism* (Oxford: Clarendon Press).
Voloshinov, V.N. (1973), *Marxism and the Philosophy of Language* (London: Seminar Press).
Voltaire, F.-M.A. (1961), *Philosophical Letters* (New York: Macmillan). (Orig. publ. 1734.)
Vrij, A. and Semin, G.R. (1996), 'Lie Experts' Beliefs about Nonverbal Indicators of Deception', *Journal of Nonverbal Behavior* 20, 65–80.
Wagner, A. (2005), 'Semiotic Analysis of the Multistage Dynamic at the Core of Indeterminacy in Legal Language', in V.J. Bhatia, J. Engberg, M. Gotti and D. Heller (eds), *Vagueness in Normative Texts* (London: Peter Lang – Linguistic Insights), 173–200.
Wagner, A. (2008), 'The European Cultural Ecumene, Legal Pluralism', in Marek Zirk-Sadowski, Bartosz Wojciechowski and Mariusz J. Golecki (eds), *Multicentrism as an Emerging Paradigm in Legal Theory* (London: Peter Lang) (forthcoming).
Wagner, A. and Cacciaguidi-Fahy, S. (2005), *Legal Language and the Search for Clarity: Practice and Tools* (Bern: Peter Lang).
Watson, A. (1985), *Sources of Law, Legal Change and Ambiguity* (London: T&T Clark).
Watson, R.S. and Ebrey, P. Buckley (eds) (1991), *Marriage and Inequality in Chinese Society* (Berkeley CA: University of California Press).
Weil, S. (1949), *L'enracinement* (Paris: Gallimard).
Werner, W. and van Schooten, H. (2002), 'Democratic Control on the Use of Force under the Dutch Constitution', in *Tilburg Foreign Law Review* 10, 1, 43–62.
West, J., Zhao, Minghua, Chang, Xiangqun, and Chen, Yuan (eds) (1999), *Women of China: Economic and Social Transformation* (London: Macmillan).
Weyrauch, W.O. and Bell, M.A. (1993), 'Autonomous Lawmaking. The Case of the Gypsies', *Yale Law Journal* 103, 2, 323–401.
White Booklet, 2000 (2001) (Budapest: NEKI).

Williams, P.J. (1987), 'Alchemical Notes: Reconstructing Ideals from Deconstructed Rights', in Richard Delgado and Jean Stefancic (eds), *Critical Race Theory: the Cutting Edge* (Philadelphia PA: Temple University Press).

Winn, P. (1991), 'Legal Ritual', *Law & Critique* 2, 2, 207–31.

Wodak, R. (1995), 'Critical Linguistics and Critical Discourse Analysis', in Jef Verschueren, Jan-Ola Östman and Jan Bliimaert (eds), *Handbook of Pragmatics* (Amsterdam and Philadelphia: J. Benjamins), 204–10.

Wodak, R. (2001), 'The Discourse-Historical Approach', in Ruth Wodak and Michael Meyer (eds), *Methods of Critical Discourse Analysis* (London: Sage), 63–94.

Wodak, R, de Cillia, R., Reisigl, M. and Liebhart, K. (1999), *The Discursive Construction of National Identity*, trans. Angela Hirsche and Richard Mitten (Edinburgh: Edinburgh University Press).

Wolfe, A. (1990), 'The Return of the Melting Pot,' *The New Republic*, 31 December, 27–30.

Woo, M.Y.K. (1993), 'Biology and Equality: Challenge for Feminism in the Socialist and Liberal State', *Emory Law Journal* 42, 143–69.

Woo, M.Y.K. (1994), 'Chinese Women Workers: the Delicate Balance Between Protection and Equality', in Christina K. Gilmartin, Gail Hershatter, Lisa Rofel and Tyrene White (eds), *Engendering China: Women, Culture, and the State* (Cambridge MA: Harvard University Press), 279–98.

Woo, M.Y.K. (2003), 'Shaping Citizenship: Chinese Family Law and Women', *Yale Journal of Law and Feminism* 15, 1, 99–134.

Wright, S. (1999), *Language, Democracy and Devolution in Catalonia* (London: Clevedon).

Yamaguchi, M. (2005), 'Discursive Representation and Enactment of National Identities: the Case of Generation 1.5 Japanese', *Discourse & Society* 16, 269–99.

Yngvesson, B. (1993), *Virtuous Citizens, Disruptive Subjects: Order and Complaint in a New England Court Citation* (New York: Routledge).

Zhao, Y. (2001), 'Domestic Violence in China: In Search of Legal and Social Responses', *UCLA Pacific Basin Law Journal* 18, 211–51.

Online sources

ABC (Kimberley WA) (2004), 'Aboriginal Artwork on Wheels', broadcast 5 March 2004, <http://www.abc.net.au/kimberley/stories/s1059054.htm>. Accessed 14 July 2005.

'ADL Audit: Anti-Semitic Incidents At Highest Level in Nine Years' (2005), Anti-Defamation Press Release, <http://www.adl.org/PresRele/ASUS>. Accessed 2 June 2006.

Anon. (2004), 'Native Title Business', <http://www.rgaq.org.au/exhibitions/exhibitition.asp>. Accessed 4 March 2004.

Australian Bureau of Statistics website (2008), <www.abs.gov.au/>. Accessed 7 January 2008.

Bronitt, S. (2002), *The Law in Undercover Policing: a Comparative Study of Entrapment and Covert Interviewing in Australia, Canada and Europe* [online], as part of research for the International Council for Canadian Studies, Canada Asian-Pacific Award 2002, <www.anu.edu.au/NEC/simon_bronitt.pdf.>. Accessed 6 June 2005.

Chandler, D., *Semiotics for Beginners*, Chapter 1, Introduction, at <http://www.aber.ac.uk/media/Documents/S4B/sem01.html>.

Chief Magistrate's Practice Note 5 of 2007, <www.mauricebyers.com/sueklusspaper.pdf>. Accessed 7 January 2008.

Commonwealth of Australia webpage (n.d.), 'Founding Documents', at <http://www.foundingdocs.gov.au/item.asp?dID=104>. Accessed 7 January 2008.

Debus, B. (2004), NSW Legislative Assembly Hansard, 6 May 2004, p. 8600 [online], <www.parliament.nsw.gov.au/prod/PARLMENT/hansArt.nsf/V3Key/LA20040506013>. Accessed 8 November 2007.

Hatzistergos J, The Hon. M.L.C. (2005), NSW Legislative Council Hansard, 2 March 2005, p. 21 (article 22) [online], <www.parliament.nsw.gov.au/cgi-bin/isys/isyswebext.exe?op=get&uri=/isysquery/irl90bc/1/doc/#hit1>. Accessed 24 June 2005.

HeraldSun Weekly, 14 July 2004, 'NSW Jail Escapes Hit Record Low' [online], <www.heraldsun.news.com.au/common/story_page/0,5478,10133991%255E1702,00.html>. Accessed 12 September 2004.

Huns, E. (2003), UCLS: 'When Actions Speak Louder than Words' [online], <www.careers.lon.ac.uk>. Accessed 7 November 2004.

Kennedy, L. (2005), 'On the Stand, now on the Box' [online], 21 June, <www.smh.com.au/news/national/on-the-stand-now-on-the-box/2005/06/20/1119250928022.html>. Accessed 30 June 2005.

Kinnaird, K. (2004), 'Motorist Dies in Highway 57 Crash' [online], 7 April, <www.bonnercountydailybee.com/articles/2006/07/04/news/news01.prt>. Accessed 15 August 2006.

LawLink NSW website, <www.lawlink.nsw.gov.au/>. Accessed 28 December 2007 and 12 March 2008.

Legal Aid NSW (2007), Annual Report 2007 [online], at <www.legalaid.nsw.gov.au/data/portal/00000005/public/27047001195449641062.pdf>. Accessed 31 December 2007.

Lienert, G. (1992), *Churchill Fellows Report: the Study of Audio/Video Techniques and the Equipment used for Gathering of Evidence, and the Use of Video Conferencing Facilities in Courts – Canada, U.S.A. and the United Kingdom*, The Winston Churchill Memorial Trust [online], at <www.churchilltrust.com.au/Fellows%20Reports/Lienert%20Graeme%201992.pdf>. Accessed 19 April 2004.

McGee, T. (2003), 'Emerging Technology brings New Dimension to Videoconferencing', [online], <www.governmentvideo.com/articles/publish/printer_6.shtml>. Accessed 5 November 2004.

Meares, A. (2005), *Law Text Culture* 9. Available at <http://search.informit.com.au/documentSummary;dn=099219979163080;res=E-LIBRARY>.

Mudie,E.(2007),'AMother'sToughAssignment',*TheSydneyMorningHerald*[online], 22 November, at <www.smh.com.au/articles/2007/11/20/1195321783116.html>. Accessed 28 December 2007.

National Native Title Tribunal (2003), 'Geospatial Technical Guidelines for the Preparation of Maps and Area Description' (June), at <http://www.nntt.gov.au>.

New South Wales Department of Corrective Services website (2005), <www.dcs.nsw.gov.au>. Accessed 19 April 2005.

Northern Land Council Land and Sea Rights (2005), <http://www.nld.org.au/html/land_hist.html>. Accessed 17 June 2005.

Parliament of NSW website (2007), <www.parliament.nsw.gov.au/>. Accessed 28 December 2007.

Pompidou, G. (1972), 'Discours prononcé le dimanche 18 juin 1972 lors de l'inauguration du Mémorial' ('Speech delivered Sunday, June 18, 1972 at the Opening of the de Gaulle Memorial'). Posted on <www.charles-de-gaulle. org/article.php3?id_article=604>. Accessed 16 March 2006.

Price, Judge D. (2003*)*, 'NSW Strategy to Reduce Violence against Women: Launch of 'Stop Domestic Violence Day 2003', 28 April, speech by Chief Magistrate of the Local Court of NSW [online], <www.lawlink.nsw.gov.au/lawlink/vaw/ll_vaw.nsf/pages/vaw_bulletin_mar03>. Accessed 30 June 2005.

Quock, R., Q.C. (1998), *Evidentiary Rules and Aids in the Presentation of Evidence* [online], <www.ajia.org.au/ctr/COCK.Papers3and6>. Accessed 20 September 2004.

Report 101 (2003), *Questioning of Complaints by Unrepresented Accused in Sexual Offence Trials, Section 3*. In NSW Law Reform Commission website (2005), <www.lawlink.nsw.gov.au/_4a2565b5001b20d1.nsf/0/d7cfd8a44cd6088ca256d64007ed683?OpenDocument&Highlight=2,McKinney,Level2,Level3>. Accessed 18 April 2005.

Rose, A. (1998), 'ALRC Urges Rethink on the Use of Technology', in Media. Australian Government Australian Law Reform Commission [online], <www.alrc.gov.au>. Accessed 25 October 2004.

Rosenberg, S. (2003), 'Semi Snooties,' 8 July, on Terry Fisher and semiotics, at <http://blogs.salon.com/0000014/2003/07/08.html>.

Samuel, H. (2005), 'Deaths Spark Riots in Paris Suburbs', *News Telegraph*, 1 November. Posted on <www.telegraph.co.uk/news/main.jhtml :jsessio nid=0X2ZAPQYYYKJFQFIQ MFCFF4>. Accessed 5 April 2006.

Sheff v. O'Neill Agreement (2003), approved by Connecticut Supreme Court, <http://www.cga.ct.gov/2003/olrdata/ed/rpt/2003-R-0112.htm>.

Skipper, P., Nunjun, C., Snell, S. and May, T. (2002), 'Ngajukura Ngurrara', at <http://www.ntrb.net/Default.asp?p=6&photo=58>. Accessed 14 July 2005.

Tasmania Department of Justice website (2007), <www.justice.tas.gov.au/prisonservice/information_for_legal_advisers/video_linkcourt_attendance>. Accessed 31 December 2007.

Toutant, C. (2005), 'Beaming in the Defendant (problems occur during videoconferencing hearings)', 2 May, *New Jersey Law Journal*, Academic OneFile. Thomson Gale: University of Sydney Demo, 24 August 2006.

Wallace, A. (2001), 'Technology and the Judiciary – the Use of Technology in the Criminal Trial Process', paper presented at the 4th National Outlook Symposium on Crime in Australia, 'New Crimes or New Responses', convened by the Australian Institute of Criminology, 21–22 June. See <www.aic.gov.au/conferences/outlook4/Wallace.html>. Accessed 8 April 2008.

Westlaw Australia website (2006), <www.westlaw.com.au/aboutwla.htm>. Accessed 25 August 2006.

Yilli Rreung Regional Council (2003), *Submission to the Senate Legal and Constitutional Reference Committee Inquiry into Legal Aid and Access to Justice*, <www.aph.gov.au/SENATE/committee/legcon_ctte/completed_inquiries/2002-04/legalaidjustice/submissions/sub95.doc>. Accessed 8 April 2008.

'Yirrkala Print Space Yirrkala Print Space – About Yolngu Art' (2005), <http://www.yirrkalaprints.com/about.html>. Accessed 17 June 2005.

Yunupingu, G. (1998), 'We Know These Things to be True: The Third Vincent Lingiari Memorial Lecture', 20 August, at <http://beta.austlii.edu.au/au/special/rsjproject/rsjlibrary/car/lingiari/3yunupingu.html>. Accessed 17 June 2005.

ZDNet Australia (2008), '1Gbps "Superbroadband" Helps Unis Research' [online], 16 January, <www.zdnet.com.au/news/communications/soa/1Gbps-superbroadband-helps-unis-research/0,339285193,00.htm>. Accessed 27 January 2008.

Index

For Product Safety Concerns and Information please contact our EU
representative GPSR@taylorandfrancis.com
Taylor & Francis Verlag GmbH, Kaufingerstraße 24, 80331 München, Germany

www.ingramcontent.com/pod-product-compliance
Ingram Content Group UK Ltd.
Pitfield, Milton Keynes, MK11 3LW, UK
UKHW020011200926
475702UK00014B/1833

* 9 7 8 1 1 3 8 2 6 7 6 7 1 *